Henry and Katharine Jenner

A Celebration of Cornwall's Culture, Language and Identity

Edited by Derek R. Williams

Francis
Boutle
Publishers

First published by Francis Boutle Publishers
272 Alexandra Park Road
London N22 7BG
Tel/Fax: (020) 8889 7744
Email: jenner@francisboutle.demon.co.uk
www.francisboutle.demon.co.uk

ISBN 1 903427 19 3

Henry and Katharine Jenner

A Celebration of Cornwall's Culture, Language and Identity

Henry Jenner

A'n Dasserghyans Kernewek ef o tas,
Mur y gerensa dhe Gernow y wlas,
Py fen-ny, na-ve ef ha'y weres bras?

Down o y skyans, cuf y golon hel,
Rak les Kernowyon mar a-ve y whel,
Gony pan ve tremeneys a'gan gwel.

Gwas Myghal a-wruk gonys has a-sef
Genen-ny, ow tevy yn gwedhen gref,
Hy gwrydhyow war an bys, hy fen yn nef.

To the Cornish Revival he was a father,
great his love for Cornwall his country;
where would we be, were it not for him and his great help?

Deep was his knowledge, kind his generous heart,
great was his work for the good of the Cornish people,
woe to us when he passed from our sight.

Servant of Michael planted seed which rises with
us, growing into a strong tree,
its roots on the world, its head in heaven.

A. S. D. Smith (*Caradar*) 1883–1950

From *The Wheel: An Anthology of Modern Poetry in Cornish 1850–1980*, translation by Tim Saunders

This book is dedicated to Richard Jenkin, E.G.R. Hooper
and all those who have led
Gorseth Kernow and the Cornish Movement
forward through the twentieth century and into the twenty-first

Contents

List of illustrations

Acknowledgements

Ever since the idea of a Jenner Anthology was first mooted by the Gorseth Kernow Archive Committee, under Ann Trevenen Jenkin, back in the summer of 2001, many people have worked assiduously to ensure the appearance of the present volume.

In the first instance, thanks are due, of course, to my fellow contributors who, though scattered throughout Cornwall, England and Wales, have ensured that their essays reached me. Secondly, special thanks must go to Mrs J. Beazley, Katharine Lee Jenner's step-niece, for allowing access to and for lending manuscripts, paintings and photographs, and for her hospitality to at least three of the book's contributors; to Audrey Randle Pool for her willingness both to explore any and every avenue in search of Harry and Kitty Lee and to share the results of those explorations; and to Julie Byngham for allowing us to print the extract from her mother's book *A Grain of Sand*.

I wish also to acknowledge the services rendered by the following in providing information or advice or both: Cressida Annesley, Senior Research Archivist, Canterbury Cathedral Archives; Jad Bienek, Shropshire Libraries; Eira Bowen, Eisteddfod Genedlaethol Cymru/National Eisteddfod of Wales; Geraint Bowen; Angela Broome, Librarian, Courtney Library – Royal Institution of Cornwall, Truro; Kim Cooper and colleagues at the Cornish Studies Library, Cornwall Centre, Redruth; Rob Ebbutt, Arts, Languages & Literature Dept., Birmingham Central Library; Heather Eva; Brian Harrison, Editor, Oxford Dictionary of National Biography; John Hopson, Archivist, British Library; Michael Howarth; Ann Trevenen Jenkin; Catherine Rachel John; Angharad Jones, Archives Officer, Gwynedd Archives Service; Annwen Jones, Archives Assistant, Gwynedd Archives Service; Terry Knight; Rod Lyon,

Grand Bard, Gorseth Kernow; Sue Owen, Shropshire Libraries; Margaret Perry; Annabelle Read, Librarian, Morrab Library, Penzance; Shan Robinson, Senior Assistant, Welsh Library & Special Collections, University of Wales, Bangor; John Simmonds, Morrab Library, Penzance; Charlotte Tucker, Local Studies & History Department, Birmingham Central Library; Dr James Whetter; Dr Christopher Wright, Dept. of Manuscripts, British Library.

Finally, I must mention the assistance I have received from Trystan and Jethan who are far more computer-literate than their father will ever be.

Foreword by the Grand Bard

Henry Jenner a'n jevyth hanow a vry a bes vynytha yn-mysk Kernowyon, mar pens y trygys yn Kernow po scullyes dres an norvys. Heb y ober ha'y dan colon, agan gonesygeth – ha kens oll agan tavas – a vya an moy boghosek. Avel Barth Mur an Orseth Kernow, y carsen vy synsy an chons ma dhe veneges ow grassyans dhe dhen a wruk kemmys rag y vamvro.

Tewennow

Henry Jenner will have an everlasting and respected name amongst Cornish-men, whether they live in Cornwall or are scattered across the world. Without his work and his enthusiasm, our culture – and above all our language – would be the poorer. As Grand Bard of the Cornish Gorsedd, I would like to take this opportunity to express my gratitude to a man who did so much for his home-land.

R.T. Lyon

Preface

Welcome to this first wide-ranging collection of writings on the life and work of Henry Jenner and his wife, Kitty Lee Jenner. Henry Jenner was an important initiator and the first Grand Bard of Gorseth Kernow. He was a fascinating and multi-faceted character, occasionally idiosyncratic, who nevertheless helped to put Cornwall on the map, linguistically, culturally and topographically.

In 2004, we are celebrating two centenaries, first of all the publication of his *Handbook of the Cornish Language*, which started scholars on a renewed quest for knowledge of Cornish. Originally an academic exercise, it gradually became a pilgrimage to establish Cornish as a spoken language, alive and well. Robert Morton Nance's comment, just before he died in 1959, sums up this mood: 'One generation has set Cornish on its feet. It is now for another to make it walk.'

Also important was the increase in the development of a Celtic conscious-ness in Cornwall, with the struggle culminating in Cornwall being recognised at the Celtic Congress in Caernarfon in 1904 as one of the six Celtic countries. Jenner again had an essential part to play in this.

His wife Kitty was just as important as a fine painter, an excellent poet and novelist, and above all a Cornish woman who helped to flesh out emotionally the bare bones of Henry Jenner's original academic interest in Cornish. Together, they made a powerful pair.

This book is a compendium of different views. Both Henry and Kitty are complex characters, as are their ideas and opinions on Cornwall and many other subjects. They were of their time, and one should not judge their reactions to various matters solely from today's perspective, which is on the whole much more favourable to minority interests. There is still further research to be done. For example, how much imaginative creativity was engendered by Kitty's writings and paintings, and how much is owed to her support of her husband's work. Her gentle encouragement of the arts has been one of the strands helping to shape a vibrant Anglo-Cornish Literature, with its detailed observation, its concern for Cornish people and the emotional 'hwl' so much a part of all Celtic writing.

Likewise, without Henry Jenner we might not have had Gorseth Kernow established in 1928, or the Cornish Branch of the Celtic Congress as early as 1904. We might not have been able to acclaim the great progress in the revival of the Cornish language and its present success; for now there are numerous groups working for the language, as well as a huge development in the publication of Cornish language books, cassettes, CDs, videos and films.

This book has been partly sponsored by Gorseth Kernow with funds from the Talek Legacy (E. G. R. Hooper, third Grand Bard 1959–64) and also from a substantial donation from the Richard Garfield Jenkin Memorial Fund. Map Dyvroeth, Barth Mur, 1976–82 and 1985–1988, died in 2002, when work on the publication had already started. He would have been delighted to know that material about the great contribution of Henry Jenner and his wife was now available to the general public to help us understand the importance of Cornwall, its language and its people, in the wider world.

A great debt of gratitude is owed to two people: Derek Williams/*Map Jethan*, who as editor and compiler, has followed a difficult but rewarding odyssey. He has shown dedication and persistence over nearly three years, with long distances to travel between his work in Shropshire and Cornwall. Thanks also to Clive Boutle for his support of the project. Without him, it would have been more difficult to proceed with its publication.

Ann Trevenen Jenkin (Bryallen, Kens Barth Mur)
Chair Gorseth Kernow Archives and Publications Committee.
Mys Genver 2004.

Introduction

Although the names of Henry and Katharine Lee Jenner were put forward too late for inclusion in the printed edition of the *Oxford Dictionary of National Biography*, scheduled for publication in 2004, they will feature in the on-line version, the editorial team being keen to strengthen the dictionary's 'non-metropolitan dimension' in the planned quarterly supplements.[1] Even in their native Cornwall, where their reputations are secure, the pair have hitherto generated little in the way of original research, although Henry Jenner's groundbreaking work for revived Cornish is covered in the standard works on the subject.[2] Both were well-known figures in London society before their retirement to Cornwall in 1909. Indeed, it can be argued, as Alan Kent does in his contribution to this volume, that Katharine Lee Jenner was, as a novelist, poet and writer on art, more famous than her librarian husband. Her work was, after all, sufficiently well known for her to be listed in *Who Was Who* after her death in 1936, a mark of recognition denied him two years earlier. Even so, Jenner himself spent thirty years in the Printed Books Department of the British Museum where he placed what 'John Bull' described as his 'vast stores of knowledge'[3] at the disposal of the great and the good of Victorian and Edwardian London. Henry Irving would consult him about costumes, Tennyson sought his advice and Ruskin and Whistler were visitors to the Museum.[4] Invitations to dine were issued and what 'John Bull' called Jenner's 'urbanity of manner'[5] ensured that, though occasionally outshone, he could always hold his own. Indeed, as late as 1955, James Palmer could write that the name of Henry Jenner was 'still magic at the British Museum'.[6]

On the surface, retirement would appear to have altered all this. In reality, though, the Jenners would henceforth hold court in Cornwall instead of in

Henry Jenner and Katharine Lee Jenner in 1881. By permission of Mary Beazley

London. As Peter Pool once pointed out, his polymathic knowledge, vast capacity for work and dominant personality meant that from 1909 onwards Jenner came to dominate the resurgent cultural life of Cornwall.[7] For the British Museum, read the Penzance Library, for the Society of Antiquaries read the Royal Institution of Cornwall and the Royal Cornwall Polytechnic Society, and for 'The Old House', Bushey Heath read 'Bospowes', Hayle. Of course, this is too simplistic and further research would surely reveal the extent to which the Jenners retained their London links. Writing to Edward Garnett in March 1920 with a bibliographical query, W.H. Hudson makes it clear that he can always ask 'old Jenner … to write to one of his Brit. Museum friends to find out'.[8] What is certain is that from 1909 onwards he threw his weight behind a huge number of Cornish causes and embarked on an ambitious programme of research, the fruits of which would be published in the pages of the leading Cornish journals of the day. Visitors would beat a path to his door just as they had to his desk at the British Museum, and the queries that his numerous correspondents put to him on Cornish matters would be answered with exhaustive replies.

Indeed, it could be – and has been – argued that the very quality that earned him his reputation as the complete librarian – the breadth of his knowledge – resulted in a dissipation of his energies. This is just the line that 'Cornubia' took in an article marking Jenner's 81st birthday. '[I]t has been often remarked,' he wrote, 'that excellent scholars who become librarians lose their taste for specialised work and as a result produce nothing original of their own.' While this charge could not be levelled at Jenner, it was nevertheless regrettable that his penchant for contributing to the correspondence columns of 'certain westcountry newspapers' might well have diverted his attention from greater work. 'One feels,' continued 'Cornubia', '…that work of this sort is too ephemeral for him. It has prevented him from producing those monumental books which his learning would have entitled him to write. His excellent "Cornish Grammar" … should have been the first and not the last of a shelfful of books on Cornwall from his pen.'[9] The production of a shelfful of books is a rather crude yardstick with which to measure a scholar's output. After all, the results of Jenner's research are there for all to savour, albeit in the form of hundreds of papers and articles contributed to journals as diverse as *The Journal of the Royal Institution of Cornwall*, *The Royalist* and *Cennad Catholig Cymru* [*The Catholic Messenger of*

Wales]. And many of these papers, of course, were initially delivered to the societies in which he was so active. In his later years Jenner was a visiting lecturer at the then University College of the South West in Exeter – a symbolic halfway house between the country in which he lived and worked for so many years and his own Celtic nation whose cause he promoted with dedication and vigour. That he was valued here, too, is clear from a letter that Principal John Murray wrote to Kitty Lee Jenner on her husband's death in May, 1934, in which he described Jenner as 'a much admired man, wide in knowledge, large-minded and large-hearted'. 'His physique,' he continued, 'bespoke the character and the intelligence. He had variety: he was gracious and exciting, conscientious about the small things and penetrating and luminous about the big, dignified and friendly, gentle and stern. As age advanced he aspired the more…'[10]

That Henry Jenner's death caused a void in the life of Cornwall is undeniable. Fortunately, though, others were well placed to continue the work that he had helped instigate. What was irreplaceable was the originality of both his scholarship and his mind, the latter, as the *Royal Cornwall Gazette* put it, 'so well stored that he could always add some apt and interesting comments to any discussion, whatever the subject might be'.[11] His legacy was substantial and various suggestions as to how his memory might be perpetuated were put forward almost immediately, including a sculpture-cum-bust and a portrait by a St Ives or Newlyn artist.[12] In the event the Jenner Memorial Fund was set up in order that the work for Cornwall to which he devoted so much of his life should continue and that his name should continue to be associated with it. Originally made in recognition of research into the 'history, language and traditional lore of Cornwall, and the popularising of these as a means of fostering local patriotism',[13] the Jenner County Memorial Awards were later enlarged in scope to cover other aspects of research into the history and culture of Cornwall. Simultaneously, the Royal Institution of Cornwall proposed that a medal should be given to those who rendered service to Cornwall by conducting research into subjects in which Jenner had been particularly interested. The first recipient, in 1936, was A.S.D. Smith (*Caradar*) for his outstanding work for the Cornish language.[14]

On Tuesday 8 May 1984, the fiftieth anniversary of his death, a small gathering of people, including representatives of the Royal Institution of Cornwall and St Ives Old Cornwall Society, joined the then Grand Bard, Hugh Miners as he placed a cross of flowers on Jenner's grave in Lelant churchyard. Later that same day, his life and work were commemorated in the Market Square, St Columb by the unveiling of a simple slate memorial plaque. The previous year, E.G. Retallack Hooper – himself a former Grand Bard and recipient of the Jenner Memorial Award – concluded his personal recollections of his predecessor with a statement to the effect that the time was ripe to raise a subscription to erect a statue to him.[15] Although Jenner is still waiting for his statue, his achievements and legacy, together with those of Kitty Lee Jenner, were given a ringing endorsement on Saturday 12 October, 1996 when a slate plaque in their memory was unveiled at 'Bospowes' their Hayle home. 'Henry Jenner is famed for his work for the Cornish language and as first Grand Bard,' said the then Grand Bard, Brian Coombes, 'but his work was for all parts of our culture. He gave great example and encouragement to others. He and his wife represent much of that wide range of expression that must be included in our Cornishness.'[16]

In the year that marks both the centenary of the publication of *A Handbook of the Cornish Language* and the seventieth anniversary of Henry Jenner's death, I hope that a similar 'wide range of expression' will be seen as a feature of this volume, with Cornwall's distinct culture, language and identity very much to the fore. I hope, too, that *Henry and Katharine Jenner* will bring an awareness of the couple's achievements to a wider public and help foster in the Cornish people 'the sentiment of local patriotism' that both felt so strongly throughout their long and influential lives.

Given the wealth of manuscript material and correspondence that survives – true to form for a dedicated librarian, Jenner threw little away – there is ample scope for a definitive biography of Henry and Katharine Lee Jenner. This volume does not pretend to be that. Instead, six original essays by contributors from varied backgrounds who share a knowledge and appreciation of Cornwall's unique place in the British Isles, explore particular aspects of the couple's lives and work. These essays are interspersed with examples of the Jenners' prose and poetic output.

The publication of Jenner's *Handbook of the Cornish Language* in July 1904 came at a crucial time for Cornwall. Three years earlier, despite L.C.

Duncombe Jewell's eloquent and spirited presentation to delegates attending the second Pan-Celtic Congress in Dublin, the resolution 'That Cornwall be recognised as a Celtic Nation' was provisionally rejected by them, with a final decision being deferred until the next Congress. The official objections centred on the view that Cornish as a spoken tongue was dead, and over the next three years those within the newly-formed *Cowethas Kelto-Kernuak* (Celtic Cornish Society) did their utmost to refute this argument. The appearance of a book which, just a month before the third Pan-Celtic Congress was due once again to debate the issue of Cornwall's place within 'the Communion of Celts', ostensibly made the language a cornerstone of Cornish nationality, was a master stroke. And despite subsequent fissures in the Cornish Language revival, Jenner's *Handbook* is rightly still seen as its starting point. In 'The Answer is Simple: Henry Jenner and the Cornish Language', Tim Saunders considers the extent to which Jenner's view of nationhood and race was tied up with the language, as well as exploring how he devised a standard form for it and made that standard form accessible to a general public. In examining the book's preface and contents, Saunders draws on his own extensive knowledge of the Cornish situation to argue that Jenner was the first to offer a coherent theory of Cornish nationality.

If the publication of the *Handbook of the Cornish Language* and Cornwall's acceptance as a Celtic nation and their aftermath are the raison d'être for this volume, then the early lives of those at the centre of these events – Henry and Katharine Jenner – are crucial to an understanding of them. As much of the work of my fellow contributors focuses on the Cornish components in the story, I have, in 'Henry Jenner F.S.A.: City Scholar and Local Patriot', explored his childhood and upbringing before turning my attention to Jenner the librarian, antiquarian, royalist, socialite and traveller. The writer Alan Bennett rather unkindly said of librarians: 'I've always found them close relatives of the walking dead.' More positively, a junior colleague described Jenner himself as being 'the last, or all but the last, survivor of the mid-nineteenth century B.M. Library Assistants, that strange assortment of the brilliant and the odd, offering the same contrast to modern librarians that Dickens' characters do to those of the twentieth-century novel.'[17] He was certainly not a career librarian and, as Heather Eva has pointed out in her study of the man, in a sense he marked time

Jenner Medal, Royal Institution of Cornwall.
Reproduced from An Baner Kernewek.

at the British Museum from 1900 onwards, or even earlier, waiting for the opportunity to retire to Cornwall.[18] Jenner chose not to define himself exclusively by what he did at the British Museum and, crucially, his many interests outside work were as important – if not more so – as work itself. Exile, as opposed to fame, was the spur and reinforced his sense of his own worth. Coming home in 1909 clearly gave him a new lease of life. What had gone before was purely a dress rehearsal; exit the city scholar, enter the local patriot.

In 'Song of our Motherland: Making Meaning of the Life and Work of Katharine Lee Jenner 1853–1936', which takes its title from her poem 'Can Gwlasol Agan Mam-vro (Patriotic Song of our Motherland), Alan Kent argues that Jenner's wife was a strong and determined woman who, within the social circumstances of her time, contributed much, not only to the Cornish Revival, but in many other areas of literary, cultural and religious life. Her vision, he maintains, was equal to that of her husband's or his successor as Grand Bard, Robert Morton Nance. Building on preliminary studies that he made for a chapter of his *Wives, Mothers and Sisters: Feminism, Literature and Women Writers of Cornwall* (1998), he uses the opportunity presented by this volume to take 'a much-needed multi-disciplinary approach to her life and work'. For Kent, she was a woman ahead of her time whose *Songs of the Stars and the Seas* was the first book in which a Cornish woman expressed her commitment to the Cornish identity and language. She was, too, one of the first two women to be made Bards of the Cornish Gorsedd and attended the early meetings of its Council. Kent has also used the collection of several hundred letters in the British Library from Jenner to Rawlings to explore their courtship during the years leading up to their marriage in 1877.

The fact that only a handful of representatives of the Old Cornwall Movement were present at Henry Jenner's funeral on Saturday 12 May 1934 understandably aroused some comment in certain sections of the Cornish press.[19] Were uncertainty as to the order of the proceedings and the lack of definite arrangements to blame? Did Jenner's late conversion to Roman Catholicism, which meant that there was a Requiem Mass prior to the actual interment, cause offence to some of his friends and add to the general uncertainty? It was anticipated, too, that Bards would attend in their robes, but this proposal was dropped in the face of strong opposition from one leading member of the Gorsedd. Jenner himself had been wary of being seen as 'a sort of Pope of Old Cornwall'[20] because of his linguistic, cultural and academic credentials and his championing of all things Cornish. Quite possibly, then, the very close link between the two organisations – the Federation of Old Cornwall Societies and Gorseth Kernow – meant that their respective members were unclear as to whether they were paying their respects first and foremost to the Federation President or to the Grand Bard. That link and the stages in its development are examined in 'Gathering the fragments…', where Brian Coombes draws on his own personal knowledge and on interviews with fellow Bards and Old Cornwall members to supplement contemporary newspaper accounts.

In 1903 or 1904, the position that Jenner would come to fill as the prime mover behind the Old Cornwall societies and Gorseth Kernow was some years away, and he was still the exiled Cornishman putting his feelings into lines such as 'Re wrellen bos en Kernow!' (Oh that I were in Cornwall!). The sonnet from which this is taken, 'Gwaynten yn Kernow' (Spring in Cornwall), is part of Jenner's not insubstantial poetic output which playwright and poet Donald Rawe puts under the microscope in 'The Poetry of Henry Jenner'. The importance that Jenner attached to prosody, or the theory and practice of writing verse, is evident from the fact that he devotes a chapter of his *Handbook* to it, examining briefly the rules of Welsh and Breton literature before turning his attention to Cornish verse and providing an analysis of some of the surviving examples. That he was himself regarded as being more than competent as a poet is clear from an article in *The Royalist* in July 1898, in which the anonymous author suggests that Jenner, with his 'poetic faculty', would be ideally placed to provide an accessible edition of the poetical and musical Jacobitism of the Highlands. Much of Jenner's work is to be found in such hard to come by publications as *Celtia* and *The Royalist*, while quite a number of poems remain unpublished. Donald Rawe has, therefore, done both his literary achievement and his memory a great service by bringing much of his output to our attention.

In his introduction to *Seeking a See: A Journal of The Right Reverend Henry Lascelles Jenner D.D. of his visit to Dunedin*, John Pearce quotes from some notes that Bishop Jenner's son made in his 84th year about 'a number of harmless and sometimes pleasing affectations of pronunciation, phraseology and practice' that those who were brought up in the principles of the combined Oxford and

Cambridge Movement were carefully taught. These included always saying *ahmen* not *aymen*, even if the word occurred in ordinary conversation, always prefixing *Blessed* to Virgin and saying *Epiphany* rather than *Twelfth Day*, *St Michael's Day* rather than *Michaelmas* and the *Purification* rather than *Candlemas*. As for the use, from the 1850s onwards, of the sign of the cross, Jenner remembered 'the pretty practice of crossing oneself the last thing before getting into bed'. 'Such is the force of association habits,' he continued, 'that to this day it is a slight and almost unconscious effort to avoid doing that when I blow out a candle, even when lighted to seal a letter in broad daylight.'[21] As David Everett demonstrates in his essay 'Henry Jenner and the Anglo-Catholic Movement', Jenner's knowledge of the Bible, church history, ritual and liturgy, and Christian art and architecture is outward evidence of what Pearce called 'his deeply mystical spiritual life'.[22] It is clear, too, that wherever they travelled, the Jenners would often visit a place specifically to see some sacred relic and their fascination with liturgy and Christian art is evident in both their published and unpublished writings, and more particularly, of course, in those of Kitty Lee.

On his deathbed in May 1934 Jenner granted an interview to 'Castle-an-Dinas' of *The Cornishman* and confided in him at some length. The whole object of his life, he acknowledged, had been to inculcate in the people of Cornwall a consciousness of their Cornishness. Whether he had been right or wrong, he did not know; whether he had failed or succeeded, he was uncertain.[23] This book is surely the proof that the path that he and Kitty Lee chose was both right and successful.

Notes

1. E-mail from the *Oxford Dictionary of National Biography* editor, Brian Harrison, 9 May 2003.
2. See Derek Williams (1996a) 'Henry Jenner: The Early Years' in *An Baner Kernewek/The Cornish Banner*, no. 84, pp. 17–20; Derek Williams (1996b) 'Henry Jenner: The Years of Fulfilment' in *An Baner Kernewek/The Cornish Banner*, no. 85, pp. 15–18; Heather Eva (1970) [*Henry Jenner, librarian and Cornishman*]? A.L.A. dissertation submitted to the College of Librarianship Wales; Peter Berresford Ellis (1974) *The Cornish Language and its Literature*, London: Routledge & Kegan Paul; Martyn F. Wakelin (1975) *Language and History in Cornwall*, Leicester: Leicester University Press.
3. Unidentified newspaper cutting in Mary Beazley's Jenner archive.
4. Henry Jenner, 'Some Reminiscences of Notable People', unpublished lecture, Nance Collection Box 3: Jenner Essays and Lectures, Courtney Library, Truro.
5. Unidentified newspaper cutting.

6. Jas. L. Palmer (1955), 'Was George Borrow a Cornishman?' A lecture delivered before Penzance Library, Morrab Gardens, Penzance, on 19 January 1955, p. 8.
7. Peter Pool (1988), 'Henry Jenner 1848–1934' in *Celebration Essays*, Penzance: Morrab Library, p. 26.
8. *Letters from W.H. Hudson to Edward Garnett*, London: Dent, 1925, p. 199.
9. 'Cornubia', 'Mr Henry Jenner: the spirit of youth in age', *West Briton*, 22 August 1929.
10. Cited by John Pearce in his preface to *Seeking a See: A Journal of The Right Reverend Lascelles Jenner D. D. of his visit to Dunedin, New Zealand in 1868–1869*, Dunedin: Standing Committee of the Diocese of Dunedin, 1984, p. 15.
11. *Royal Cornwall Gazette* 9 May 1934.
12. The Gorsedd Kernow Archive Survey [n.d.], *A Summary of the Minutes of the Cornish Gorsedd (August 1928–September 1939)*, pp. 17 and 24.
13. R. Morton Nance (1935), 'The Jenner Memorial Fund' in *Old Cornwall* vol. ii, no. 9, Summer 1935, p. 40.
14. E.G.R. Hooper (1985), 'The Jenner Medal' in *An Baner Kernewek* 40, May 1985, p. 13.
15. E.G.R. Hooper (1983), 'Recollections of Henry Jenner' in *An Baner Kernewek* 34, November 1983, p. 14.
16. Douglas Williams (1996), 'The first Grand Bard honoured at Hayle' in *West Briton* 17 October 1996.
17. Arundell Esdaile, Obituary in *The Library Association Record*, June 1934, p. 184.
18. Eva (1970), p. 28.
19. 'Late Mr Henry Jenner', unidentified newspaper cutting [week beginning 13 May 1934].
20. Henry Jenner, 'Projects and suggestions for a Cornish Dictionary', Presidential address to the St Ives Old Cornwall Society [n.d.], Nance Collection Box 3: Jenner Essays & Lectures, Courtney Library, Truro.
21. Pearce (ed.) (1984), pp.26–30.
22. Ibid. p. 15.
23. *Cornishman* 9 May 1934.

Henry and Katharine Jenner:
A Chronology

1848	*8 August*	Birth of Henry Jenner at St Columb Major
1849	*May*	Revd. Henry Lascelles Jenner becomes curate at Maryfield, Antony
1851	*mid*	Revd. Jenner resigns the curacy of Maryfield and moves his family to Leigh, near Southend where he becomes curate-in-charge
1852	*early*	Revd. Jenner becomes curate of St Martin's, Brasted, near Sevenoaks, Kent
	Autumn	Becomes a minor canon at Canterbury
1853	*12 September*	Birth of Katharine Lee Rawlings at 'The Downes' Trelissick Downs, Hayle, Cornwall
1854		Revd. Jenner is appointed vicar of Preston-next-Wingham, Kent
	9 January	Christening of Katharine Lee Rawlings at St Erth Church
1857	*May*	Jenner has his first taste of foreign travel on a two-day visit to France
1858–1865		Attends St Mary's College, Harlow
1860		Erection of monument to Dolly Pentreath at Paul, Cornwall

1860–1861		Jenner's first contact with the Cornish language in Latham's *Smaller English Grammar*
1866	*24 August*	Revd. Jenner is consecrated the first Bishop of Dunedin, New Zealand at Canterbury Cathedral
1867		Jenner visits Dolly Pentreath's monument in Paul churchyard on his first visit to Cornwall for 16 years
	November	Holidays in Belgium
1868	*late June*	Jenner takes a break from teaching duties in Rhyl to undertake a short walking tour of Snowdonia
	August	Has a week in Paris
	18 November	Travels to Liverpool to see his father embark for New Zealand
1869	*January*	Jenner abandons teaching and takes up a clerical post in the Principal Registry of the Court of Probate in London
1870	*5 July*	Jenner takes up the post of Junior Assistant in the British Museum's Department of Manuscripts. Gives his address as 15, Beaumont Street, Portland Place on his job application
1871	*16 June*	Revd. Jenner resigns any claims to the see of Dunedin
1872		Jenner provides Tennyson with background material for his poem 'One Last Tournament'
1873		Katharine Lee Rawlings living at 30, Richmond Terrace, West Brompton
	21 March	Jenner reads 'The Cornish Language' before the Philological Society
	27 August	Start of correspondence between Rawlings and Jenner
1874		Jenner sends questionnaires about the Manx language to clergymen on the Isle of Man
	Summer	Katharine Lee resident at 14, Euston Square

1875	*18 June*	Jenner reads 'The Manx Language...' before the Philological Society, having spent a week on the Isle of Man
	July	Jenner tours West Cornwall with the Revd. W.S. Lach-Szyrma searching for survivals of the Cornish language
	November	Katharine Lee living at 41, Westbourne Park Crescent, Bayswater
1876	*4 February*	Jenner reads 'Traditional Relics of the Cornish Language in Mount's Bay in 1875' before the Philological Society
	19 August	Jenner reads 'The History and Literature of the Ancient Cornish Language' before the British Archaeological Association at Penzance
	2 October	A prospectus compiled by Jenner and William Copeland Borlase for the proposed Cornish Manuscripts Society is issued
1877		Jenner discovers the 'Charter Fragment' at the British Museum
	12 July	Marriage of Katharine Lee Rawlings and Henry Jenner at St Erth Parish Church. They honeymoon in France, Switzerland, northern Italy, Austria and Germany
	27 December	Commemoration of the centenary of Dolly Pentreath's death at Paul, Cornwall
1878	*21 June*	Birth of Cecily Katharine Ysolt, the Jenners' only child
1879		Publication of *Early Drawings and Illuminations* by Walter de Gray Birch and Henry Jenner. Jenner moves to the Department of Printed Books
1880	*June*	Continued ill health forces Jenner to take extended sick leave and he and Kitty Lee holiday in the Swiss Alps
1881		The Jenners are resident at 18, St John's Street, Hampstead

1882   Publication of Kitty Lee Jenner's *A Western Wildflower*.
              The Jenners take a walking holiday in the Vosges
              Mountains

1883   Publication of Kitty Lee's *In the Alsatian Mountains: a
              narrative of a tour in the Vosges*. The Jenners take a walk-
              ing tour through the Eifel range

1 March   Jenner is elected a fellow of the Society of Antiquaries

1884   Publication of Kitty Lee's *In London Town*. The Jenners
              holiday in Switzerland. Jenner becomes 'Placer' in the
              Department of Printed Books

1886   Publication of Kitty Lee's *Katherine Blythe*. The Jenners
              holiday in Germany

1888   Publication of Kitty Lee's *An Imperfect Gentleman*

1889   The Jenners holiday in Switzerland. Jenner meets
              Gladstone and helps organise the Stuart Exhibition at
              the New Gallery, Regent Street. He serves on the Council
              of the Society of Antiquaries

1890   Jenner helps organise the Tudor Exhibition at the New
              Gallery and begins a long association with *The Royalist*
              Serves on the Council of the Society of Antiquaries and
              is promoted to the first class of Assistants in the
              Department of Printed Books

1891   Publication of Kitty Lee's *Love or Money*. The Jenners'
              'great Italian tour' includes an audience with Pope Leo
              XIII. Jenner helps organise the Guelph Exhibition at the
              New Gallery

1892   The Jenners' first Scottish holiday

              Jenner helps organise the Victorian Exhibition at the
              New Gallery

1893   The Jenners again holiday in Scotland

1894		They holiday in Dalmatia, Montenegro, Herzegovina and Bosnia
1895	*January*	Publication of Kitty Lee's *When Fortune Frowns*. The Jenners again holiday in Scotland, chiefly in the Outer Hebrides
	Autumn	They spend a week in Paris in order to take their daughter to school at the Sacré Coeur convent at Conflans
1896		The Jenners spend a month at Sobernheim, south west of Bingen
1898		Jenner again serves on the Council of the Society of Antiquaries. He and Kitty Lee holiday in France and Germany
	18 September	Death of the Revd. Henry Lascelles Jenner
1899		Jenner serves on the Council of the Society of Antiquaries
1900		He is appointed Assistant Keeper in the Department of Printed Books. The Jenners holiday in Rome, visiting Florence and Venice on the way back
	June	Their address is The Old House, Bushey Heath, which remains their home until 1909
1901		They visit Bertrick in the Eifel 'to try unsuccessfully to get rid of rheumatism'
	15 August	Formation of the *Cowethas Kelto-Kernuak*, with Jenner as Vice-President
1901–1902		Jenner organises the Monarchy of Great Britain and Ireland Winter Exhibition at the New Gallery
1903		Jenner joins the Celtic Association
	September	He is made a Bard of the Gorsedd of Brittany and addresses the *Union Régionaliste Bretonne* in Cornish at Lesneven, Finistère

1904		Kitty Lee is made a Bard of the Welsh Gorsedd at Rhyl. Jenner is elected a Vice-President of the Celtic Association.
	July	Publication of Jenner's *A Handbook of the Cornish Language*
	August	He reads his seminal 'Cornwall: a Celtic Nation' before the Pan-Celtic Congress at Caernarfon and Cornwall is accorded membership
1906		The Jenners holiday in the Tyrol. Publication of Kitty Lee's *Christ in Art*
1907		Publication of Kitty Lee's *Our Lady in Art*. Jenner attends Celtic Congress in Edinburgh In collaboration with G.F. Barwick, he completely revises and reorganises the Reference Library in the British Library Reading Room
1909	*May*	Jenner retires from the British Museum and he and Kitty Lee return to Cornwall.
	June	Jenner attends the London Eisteddfod as a representative of the Royal Institution of Cornwall
	9 December	Jenner's reading of 'Cornish Place-names' before the annual meeting of the Royal Institution of Cornwall marks the start of a long and distinguished association
1910		Publication of Kitty Lee's *Christian Symbolism*
1911		Jenner is elected a Council member of the Royal Institution of Cornwall. The Jenners spend a few weeks in the Swiss Alps
	14 February	Jenner is elected a member of the Royal Cornwall Polytechnic Society
1912		Jenner is elected Vice-President of the R.C.P.S.
1912–1920		Serves as Secretary of the R.I.C.

1913		Jenner is elected honorary librarian of the R.C.P.S. and editor of its journal, a post he holds until his death
	23 July	He is elected Chairman of Cornwall County Council's committee for the preservation of ancient monuments
1914		The Jenners enjoy 'a nice little Italian tour'
1916	*15 February*	Jenner is elected President of the R.C.P.S.
	September	Jenner is elected President for 1917 of the Cornwall Music Competition
1917		Jenner is made Vice-president of the Celtic Congress
	22 November	Awarded the Henwood Gold Medal by the R.I.C.
	19 December	Presented with the Henwood Medal
1918		Jenner attends Welsh Eisteddfod at Neath
1919		Publication of Kitty Lee's *Christmas Verses.* Jenner becomes editor of the *Journal of the Royal Institution of Cornwall*
	11 February	Re-elected President of the R.C.P.S.
	5 December	Admitted to the degree of honorary M.A. by the University of Wales
1920		The Jenners return to the Swiss Alps for their holiday
	Spring	Jenner and Robert Morton Nance form the first Old Cornwall Society at St Ives, with Jenner as President
	15 July	Jenner receives his honorary M.A. at Bangor
1922–1923		Is elected President of the R.I.C.
c. 1923		Is elected to represent the Royal Institution of Cornwall on the Court of Governors of the University College of the South West at Exeter
1923	*10 February*	Becomes founder-President of Hayle Old Cornwall Society
1924		Formation of the Federation of Old Cornwall Societies with Jenner as permanent President. On holiday with

		Kitty Lee in the Pyrenees, Jenner views Cornish ms. at Bilbao in the Basque country
1925	*April*	Jenner contributes 'The Preservation of Ancient Monuments in Cornwall' to the first issue of *Old Cornwall*
1926		Publication of Kitty Lee's *Songs of the Stars and the Sea*. G. K. Chesterton takes tea at 'Bospowes'
1927	*Spring*	Jenner is appointed Honorary St Petrock Lecturer in Celtic Studies at the University of the South West
	25 June	He reads 'The Gorsedd of Boscawen-Un' to a gathering of the Federation of Old Cornwall Societies at Boscawen-Un
1928		Publication of Jenner's *Who are the Celts and what has Cornwall to do with them?*
	7 August	Initiation of eight Cornish men and women as bards of Wales at Treorchy. This nucleus of a Cornish Gorsedd decide that they and Jenner shall constitute the Council of the Cornish Gorsedd, with Jenner as Grand Bard
	21 September	Installation of Jenner as Cornwall's first Grand Bard at Boscawen-Un
1930		Jenner presides over the International Arthurian Congress in Truro
1932		Jenner presides over the first meeting of the Celtic Congress in Cornwall, at Truro
1933	*27 August*	Jenner attends the first church service in Cornish for 250 years, at Towednack, and Gorseth Kernow at Roche Rock
1934	*8 May*	Death of Henry Jenner
	12 May	Requiem mass at St Michael's Roman Catholic Church, Hayle, followed by interment in Lelant Cemetery
1936	*21 October*	Death of Katharine Lee Jenner

'The Answer is Simple': Henry Jenner and the Cornish Language

Tim Saunders

Introduction: Questions and Answers

A century after Henry Jenner published his *Handbook of the Cornish Language*, Cornish people still give his answer when asked why they are learning Cornish: 'The question is a fair one, the answer is simple. Because they are Cornishmen'.[1] The Cornwall in which Jenner grew up has been transformed into a land that would have alarmed him even more than the steam-driven, chapel-going, Radical-voting Cornwall of his time. Jenner made up for being born in 1848 by opposing every radical cause from Italian unity onwards. It is no wonder that his ideas had little immediate effect among people ready to shelter Garibaldi on the run. Yet we now have a small community of Cornish speakers. Jenner's *Handbook of the Cornish Language* was the double helix through which that community received crucial messages from its linguistic forebears. It still informs the consciousness of the community, although few nowadays have read it.

Henry Jenner's encounter with the Cornish language was emotional, erudite and esoteric. This encounter, incorporated in the *Handbook*, underlies our experience of the language, even though both language and society have been transformed. It was highly emotional because Cornish represented an ideal of the lost homeland to which Jenner yearned to return. It was erudite, because he approached all issues of description, analysis and standardisation with impressive resources of judgement and scholarship. Finally, it was esoteric because it belonged primarily to his inner life, the realm of aspirations whose fulfilment might not be for this world. In all its aspects, Jenner's encounter with Cornish was fully compatible with the popular racial ideology to which he adhered.

The Ideology of Jenner's Cornish

The book begins, even before the table of contents and the preface, with a poem to his wife – in Cornish. In this poem he thanks God for guiding him to research oral traditions of the language in the very area where she lived. He is persuaded that the Archangel Michael, guardian of Cornwall, was protecting them personally. He remembers the years of happiness that they have enjoyed, a happiness of which the Cornish language has been a part:

> Dheso mî re levar dha davas teg,
> Flogh ow empinyon vî, dhô 'm kerra Gwrêg.
>
> [*To you I speak your beautiful language,*
> *my brainchild, to my dearest wife.*][2]

The language matters because it brought him and his Katharine together. It also matters because, as Alan M. Kent has now shown, it played an important part in their life together over the years. But Cornish involves wider emotions. To begin with, Cornish is associated with the land of Cornwall, and has thus been moulded by the experience and thought of generations of Cornish people. As Jenner notes:

> It is highly probable, from the number of places still retaining undoubtedly Celtic names, and retaining them in an undoubtedly Cornish form, that until the fifteenth century the Tamar was the general boundary of English and Cornish; though there is said to be some evidence that even as late as the reign of Elizabeth, Cornish was spoken in a few places to the east of the Tamar, notably in the South Hams.[3]

As usual, when dealing with questions of fact, Jenner is careful about evidence and the nuances of its interpretation. He does not claim that Cornish is a central element of daily life in modern Cornwall:

Most Cornishmen habitually speak English, and few, very few, could hold five minutes' conversation in the old Celtic speech. Yet the memory of it lingers on, and no one can talk about the country itself, and mention the places in it, without using a wealth of true Cornish words.[4]

Although no longer a medium of instrumental communication, Cornish remains the linguistic manifestation of an historic identity, but what identity is this, and how is it defined? The Celtic nationality of Cornwall is not a concept that Jenner formulated. Hawker, Polwhele, Pryce, the Borlases and the Bosons were only a few of the thinkers who had postulated it, and Williams, Zeuss and Lhuyd were not the only linguists to have analysed the relationships of the Celtic languages and placed them within the Indo-European family.[5] Jenner's achievement is to take all this as read and to formulate a theory that, with one important qualification, is the basis of Cornish nationalism today. That qualification is the doctrine of race, which has now been marginalised, unlike, say, in the context of British nationality law. For Jenner, it is axiomatic that language is a function of race, with individual languages being carried by their specific races and dividing as groups from a race separate from one another.

It is typical of Jenner that he is cautious as to the exact geographical source of the Indo-European languages. Nonetheless, he accepts unquestioningly the doctrine that the first speakers of this tongue were members of a superior race:

The Celtic languages belong to the type known as Aryan or Indo-European, the language of the higher or white races whose original habitat was once taken to have been near or among the Himalayas, but is now located with much less exactness than heretofore.[6]

Jenner does not discuss the relationship between the Celtic languages and the Italic languages, including Latin and Oscan, much less attempt to place Celtic within the Indo-European group as a whole. He rather proceeds directly to the conventional binary division within Celtic, between Goidelic and Brythonic. His characterisation of the relationship between the Celtic languages of Scotland, Man and Ireland is succinct and acute:

Henry Jenner at the Celtic Congress, Caernarfon 1904. Gwynedd Archives Service

It has been said, with some truth, that these three are as far apart as three dialects of the same language can well be, but are not sufficiently far apart to be counted as three distinct languages.[7]

In describing the Brythonic group, Jenner freely admits that the relationships are more complicated:

The Brythonic (or British), consisting of Welsh, Cornish and Breton. These may be said to be as near together as three separate languages can well be, but to have drifted too far apart to be accounted three dialects of the same language.[8]

He incidentally refers to apparent affinities between Brythonic and Gaulish. However, while he has made nothing of the closer affinity between Manx and Scottish Gaelic, he draws particular attention to the close relationship between Cornish and Breton:

Cornish is very much nearer to Breton than Welsh is.[9]

The affinity with Breton bears more than linguistic significance for Jenner. He finds in the milieu inhabited by the Breton autonomist Right a set of political and religious tenets with which he sympathises deeply. In a note to the above passage, Jenner relates that he experienced the high degree of intercomprehensibility between Cornish and Breton at a gathering of Breton autonomists:

In September 1903, at the end of the Congress of the Union Régionaliste Bretonne at Lesneven in Finistère, the present writer made a speech in Cornish, perhaps the first that had been made for two hundred years, and rather to his astonishment he was fairly well understood by the Bretons. It is true that all were educated men, but only one of them had studied Cornish.[10]

This statement is entirely consistent with his estimation of the degree of congruence between the Brythonic languages:

> In grammatical forms Cornish almost invariably in cases where Welsh and Breton differ follows the latter, but, as in vocabulary, it sometimes has also ways of its own.[11]

However, his search for affinities with Brittany encompasses more than morphology and syntax. Cornish is a manifestation of Cornwall's nationality: most place-names are in their Cornish form, as are many family names. Cornish literature expresses some admirable principles, especially since the surviving texts largely antedate the Reformation. Jenner makes it plain that he would prefer Cornwall, like Brittany, to have remained loyal to the Papacy – reminiscent of that Breton maxim that *Ar Brezoneg hag ar Feiz/A zo breur ha c'hwoar e Breiz* [The Breton language and the Faith/Are brother and sister in Brittany]. The Reformation made both Papal loyalty and Cornish speech unviable:

> The Reformation did much to kill Cornish. Had the Book of Common Prayer been translated into Cornish and used in that tongue, two things might have happened which did not – the whole language might have been preserved to us, and the Cornish as a body might have been of the Church of England, instead of remaining (more or less) of the old religion until the perhaps unavoidable neglect of its authorities caused them to drift into the outward irreligion from which John Wesley rescued them.[12]

In politics, Jenner could wish Cornwall to have persisted in the Legitimism ascribed to it in the Wars of the Five Peoples[13] (1642–1654). Once again, this would parallel the monarchist allegiances attributed to the Breton Right during most of Jenner's lifetime. At the same time, it would remove any premise which might forward an argument whose conclusion would be separatism:

> The Bretons of to-day habitually speak of Brittany as "notre petite patrie", and France as "notre grande patrie", and none have fought and died for France more bravely than these. As soldiers (and still more as sailors) they are to France what the Highlanders are to Britain, and avenge the atrocities of 1793 in the same noble fashion as that in which the Gaels have avenged the horrors of Culloden and its sequel.[14]

Attachment to Faith and Throne, as well as to Fatherland (however defined), is inherent to the character of Jenner's Cornish: loyalty is in the blood of the Celts, whether to clan or to great or little Fatherland. Immutable human attributes are essential to Jenner's worldview, albeit with an interesting qualification.

In effect, Jenner is proposing a modified Unionism, leaving the structure of the imperial polity unquestioned:

> But every Cornishman knows well enough, proud as he may be of belonging to the British Empire, that he is no more an Englishman than a Caithness man is, that he has as much right to a separate local patriotism to his little Motherland, which rightly understood is no bar, but rather an advantage to the greater British patriotism, as has a Scotsman, an Irishman, a Welshman, or even a Colonial; and that he is as much a Celt and as little of an "Anglo-Saxon" as any Gael, Cymro, Manxman or Breton.[15]

The quotation marks around 'Anglo-Saxon' are deliberate and significant, for Jenner holds much of the population of England to be of other than Anglo-Saxon descent. Some are, in fact, Celtic by race, while others by contrast are not even Aryan. While Celtic blood is common closer to the borders of Wales and Cornwall, over much of England the population consists largely of a naturally servile pre-Aryan race:

> [T]he labouring classes of Devon, Cornwall, Somerset, Wales and the Welsh border are of a type infinitely superior in manners, morals and physique to the same class in the Midlands, because they now consist almost entirely of the descendants of the free Britons who were driven westward rather than submit to the overwhelming invasion of the Teutonic tribes.[16]

For Jenner, the incompatibility of the working classes of most of England with both their Celtic neighbours and their own compatriots was the result of a subtly modified form of social Darwinism:

> [W]hen there was any fighting to be done, the aboriginal hid in the woods until it was all over, and only then came out to share in the spoil

Henry Jenner (centre) *at a Breton gathering, early twentieth century.*
By Permission of Mary Beazley

and the glory and the drinks; while the white man, whether Briton, Saxon, or Norman, went out to fight, and not infrequently to be killed. A survival, perhaps, of the unfittest was the result...[17]

From this, it follows that populations must sometimes change their languages, regardless of their own ancestry: 'Language is less than ever a final test of race.' Jenner goes into some detail to describe how the Cornish had changed from their own language to English. English was the language of power and wealth, and knowing it became a matter of survival. Between 1700 and 1735 it ceased to be a community language, even in Penwith and Kerrier.[18] Nevertheless the oral tradition persisted until Jenner's time

Cornish as Sacrament

In effect, Cornish is to have a sacramental role. A sacrament is defined as the outward and visible sign of an inward and spiritual grace. Race, for Jenner, is of the essence. It is race that separates the Cornish from the working class of England's big cities. That racial essence, like grace, is freely offered. In order to accede to this essence, it will be necessary to undertake the sacramental act of acknowledging the Cornish language as one's own. One advantage of sacraments is that they do not necessarily have to be repeated often, if at all. Depending on denominational understandings the Christian is obliged to take part in the Sacrament of the Lord's Supper at prescribed intervals during the year. The Sacrament of Baptism, on the other hand, may only be undertaken once. There is a nice juxtaposition here. Sacramental acts, undertaken on special occasions, are peculiarly suited for expression through classical languages. Learning the classical Cornish that Jenner is codifying, and making appropriate use of it, will itself constitute a sacramental act.

Jenner's cautious account of the language and its literature are not in themselves incompatible with a minority ideology view. Indeed, by concealing the contingency of any relationship between race and language, he frees himself to add whatever ideological content he pleases to the form of Cornish. What is harder to account for is his apparent ignorance of matters which would amply reinforce his overall cause. He appears quite unaware, for instance, of the contemporary renewal of Hebrew. Leaving aside the common academic prejudice which refused to admit the existence of vernacular Hebrew, and which still cannot cope with vernacular Cornish, Jenner's ignorance of the century-old flowering of Hebrew letters is surprising for a man working in any major library. What is astounding for a man working in the British Museum Library where a scholar from Graubünden had been Librarian and demonstrated to the Royal Society that his Romantsch language was a branch of Gallo-Romance, is the assertion that Romantsch is a local dialect of Italian in German spelling.[19]

His failure to take up several points about Basque nationalism points to some interesting defects in his view of Cornwall. While he was aware of the Basque language and institutions, and even visited the country later in life, he did not consider that the Basques constituted a nation. This is surprising, to say the least, since contemporary Basque nationalism contained several elements that would have appealed to him.[20] In the Carlist Wars, Euzkadi had displayed commitment to a dynastic cause that would have delighted the heart of any Jacobite. In addition, Basque nationalism was even more clearly defined than its Breton equivalent. The emphasis on race would have pleased him, directed as much of it was against the working class of the state's general population. The championing of territorially-focused, prescriptive rights ought to have interested him, but, curiously enough, Cornwall's legal and constitutional status does not for him merit more than a couple of sentences.[21] Despite the long legal disputes between the Duchy and the Crown, and despite its being resolved in favour of the Duchy on the grounds of continued Cornish sovereignty, Jenner appears quite uninterested.

Since he was not aware of Cornwall's legal personality, the high probability is that he simply did not think it relevant to his project. A further clue lies in his one foray into electoral politics in Cornwall when he stood unsuccessfully for Hayle Town Council. None of the electoral material among his papers makes any reference to the issue of Cornish nationality. It is hard to avoid the conclusion that Jenner never intended the Cornish language, or any element of Cornish nationality, to be a premise for political action.

This is not inconsistent with a cautious and empirical scholarly method. Jenner bases his standard on the most recent forms of Cornish to be used as a community language. These were the dialects of Kerrier and Penwith in the seventeenth and eighteenth centuries. In the absence of a written standard, such as that provided in Welsh by the Bible, spelling and morphology could vary considerably, especially as Cornish speakers had little practical choice but to adopt contemporary English orthography. This had the additional drawback that the graphemic repertoire of English does not always correspond particularly well with the sound system of Cornish. Jenner solves these two problems, in part at least, by following the lead of Edward Lhuyd in adopting particular spellings, and also in using certain graphemes. Beyond that, he takes the common path of following the example of related languages in a stronger position, just as Occitan has followed Catalan, or Faroese has adapted from Icelandic. For Jenner, Breton is the closest model to follow, and then Welsh.

Jenner's analysis of the language adapts the traditional categories of Western grammar. A consensual repertoire of parts of speech is presented, together with a basic outline of sentence formation and the functions of the most important idioms. His strategy for dealing with the initial mutations consists in alerting the learner to their existence at the beginning, presenting specific instances as they arise in the course of exposition, and then summarising rules at the end of the section on syntax. His terminology of 'States' is in use today, with the radical form termed the First State, Lenition the Second State, Aspiration the Third, and Devocalisation the Fourth (Since Nance's intervention, a Fifth State is recognised).[22] Like many grammarians of the Classical languages, Jenner includes a chapter on prosody. Using copious examples mainly from Middle Cornish literature, Jenner demonstrates the existing techniques for verse composition. Not understanding the classical Welsh prosody, he does no more than refer to it, mentioning some forms common to many European languages, that might be adapted to Cornish.

Two particular inclusions are specific to Cornish. One chapter discusses Cornish names. Discovering the meaning of their house's name is often a motive for many people wishing to learn Cornish. In addition, many toponyms have become family names, apart from surnames derived from epithets and callings. Books on names remain popular,[23] and Jenner recommends caution both in the interpretation of names, and also in the confidence with which once accepts the authority of such books. A short chapter on 'Swear-Words and Expletives' explains how to express strong emotions without recourse to physiological or anatomical terminology. The force of oaths is sometimes derived from mild blasphemy, specifically of a pre-Reformation cast. This ambience is confirmed in an appendix on the vocabulary of the Calendar, where a full page is given to Christian feast days. An extensive bibliography for Cornish leads into the publisher's list of Celtic scholarly and literary books and periodicals.

What Jenner is doing is unprecedented in Cornish, but a standard trope in language generally. The first part of this observation I must qualify. Nobody had written a normative grammar of Cornish as far as we know. There are several references to men very learned in the Cornish language, men who wrote in a period when traditional Latinate grammar went unchallenged. Edward Lhuyd made a careful description of Cornish,[24] with an emphasis on the contemporary spoken language. The preface to the Cornish section of his *Archæologia Britannica* is, like the respective Welsh and Irish prefaces, and, indeed, like his elegy on William III, in an elevated, ornate style.[25] Both Welsh and Irish possessed such a register, but by the time of Lhuyd's field trips in Cornwall, Cornish had lost the more formal domains. Lhuyd's original texts were therefore by way of being the analogue of the philologist's 'starred form'. Jenner's project is to make such a register operative.

Jenner's Achievement

Jenner's achievement was threefold: to formulate a standard form for Cornish, to make that standard accessible to a general public, and to link the language indissolubly with Cornish nationality. Modern Cornish has evolved considerably since Jenner's initiatives. The modifications proposed by Robert Morton Nance in the 1920s and 1930s brought the standard closer to the forms of Middle Cornish.[26] The changes associated with Brown and George in the 1980s and 1990s incorporated the developments and insight of the intervening two generations.[27] Richard Gendall's initiative ostensibly rejected all forms of standardisation since the Early Modern period, but in practice has moved closer to Jenner in recent years.[28] All have accepted Jenner's first premise, namely that it is both possible and right to establish for Cornish a standard facilitating the generation of original texts as opposed to an exegesis of existing ones.

In effect, Jenner was proposing Cornish as what sociologists call a classical language. This means, in the first place, that the language is learned from written texts as opposed to being acquired orally in the domains of the home, neighbourhood and workplace. Secondly, a classical language is reserved for such dignified domains as worship, study, law and administration. Except sporadically, it will not be used in the most common transactions of daily life. Thirdly, a classical language changes little, if at all, since the texts which are its source express and embody an overriding world-view lying above the constant change and decay of an unruly world. Unsurprisingly, Jenner's *Handbook* is shaped on a pattern familiar from the old kind of Latin or Greek textbook.

Classical languages are often linked with a particular religion: Hebrew with Judaism, Arabic with Islam, Sanskrit with Hinduism, Greek and Church Slavonic with Eastern Orthodoxy, and so on. Latin was, for centuries, associated with Roman Catholicism, but after the Reformation became more a generalised vehicle for the higher domains of Western culture. (Indeed, there is scarcely a school of thought in the West that has not expressed itself in Latin.) Since knowledge of the language is a prerequisite for access to sacred texts, learning it will be a crucial process if a person wishes to advance that religion. The process of learning the language becomes a crucial marker between the educated and the uneducated. Techniques, forms and genres in classical languages take effort to acquire. That effort consecrates them as norms for other tongues.

The third part of Jenner's achievement, making Cornish a keystone of Cornish nationality, is conceptually the most intriguing. Jenner was the first to offer a coherent theory of Cornish nationality.[29] Where previous commentators had either taken Cornish identity as read or else posited such unconnected factors as territory, language, laws and descent without any attempt to explain their relationship or account for their form, Jenner offers precisely such an explanation but, paradoxically, for him language is not the crucial element in nationality. That is reserved for race, which is by implication a set of immutable biological characteristics, not being sex or age, transmitted hereditarily. Following this, again by implication, is territory. A single race may inhabit more than one territory, but geographical separation can bring about the emergence of a new nationality. Language on the other hand, can change in a generation, and be shared across several territories. Jenner knew this about language, and proved it to be so in his *Handbook*. He also believed it to be potentially very dangerous. That is why he posed the question, and that is why the answer he provided was so simple.

Notes

I am grateful to Alan M. Kent and Derek R. Williams in the preparation of this chapter:

1. Henry Jenner (1904) *A Handbook of the Cornish Language*, London: David Nutt, p.xi.
2. Ibid., p.v.
3. Ibid., p.11.
4. Ibid., p.xii.
5. For a history of philosophical thought on Cornish, see Alan M. Kent and Tim Saunders (ed.) (2000) *Looking at the Mermaid: A Reader in Cornish Literature 900–1900*, London: Francis Boutle, pp.263–338.
6. Jenner, op.cit., p.3.
7. Ibid., p.5.
8. Ibid., pp.5–6.
9. Ibid., p.7.
10. Ibid.
11. Ibid., p.9.
12. Ibid., p.12.
13. A term sometimes used in Cornwall to describe the series of conflicts variously known as the Civil War, Great Rebellion, Wars of the Three Kingdoms (1642–1654).
14. Ibid., p.xii.
15. Ibid., ppxi–xii.
16. Ibid., p.4.
17. Ibid.
18. See P.A.S. Pool (1982) *The Death of Cornish*, Redruth: Dyllansow Truran.
19. Henry Jenner (n.d.) *Who are the Celts and what has Cornwall to do with them?* St Ives: Federation of Old Cornwall Societies, p.3
20. For background, see Luís Nuñez Astrain and Meic Stephens (ed. and tr.) (1997) *The Basques: Their Struggle of Independence*, Cardiff: Welsh Academic Press.
21. For an understanding of the legal system, see G. Harrison (1835) *Substance of a Report on the Laws and Jurisdiction of the Stannaries of Cornwall*, London: Longman, Rees, Orme, Brown, Green and Longman.
22. See Robert Morton Nance (ed.) (1990) *A New Cornish Dictionary/Gerlyver Noweth Kernewek*, Redruth: Dyllansow Truran, pp.1–12.
23. See for example (1984) *Names for the Cornish: 300 Cornish Christian Names*, Redruth: Dyllansow Truran.
24. See Derek R. Williams (1993) *Prying into Every Hole and Corner: Edward Lhuyd in Cornwall in 1700*, Redruth: Dyllansow Truran.
25. See Kent and Saunders, op.cit., pp.232–6.
26. See Nance, op.cit.
27. See Ken George (1986) *The Pronunciation and Spelling of Revived Cornish*, Cornwall: The Cornish Language Board; Wella Brown (1984) *A Grammar of Modern Cornish*, Cornwall: The Cornish Language Board.
28. See R.R.M Gendall (ed.) (1997) *A Practical Dictionary of Modern Cornish: Cornish-English*, Menheniot: Teere ha Tavaz.
29. For a wider contextual background, see Richard Weight (2002) *Patriots: National Identity in Britain 1940–2000*, London: Macmillan.

Preface to 'A Handbook of the Cornish Language'

Henry Jenner

This book is principally intended for those persons of Cornish nationality who wish to acquire some knowledge of their ancient tongue, and to read, write, and perhaps even to speak it. Its aim is to represent in an intelligible form the Cornish of the later period, and since it is addressed to the general Cornish public rather than to the skilled philologist, much has been left unsaid that might have been of interest to the latter, old-fashioned phonological and grammatical terms have been used, a uniform system of spelling has been adopted, little notice has been taken of casual variations, and the arguments upon which the choice of forms has been based have not often been given.

The spelling has been adapted for the occasion. All writers of Cornish used to spell according to their own taste and fancy, and would sometimes represent the same word in different ways even in the same page, though certain general principles were observed in each period. There was a special uncertainty about the vowels, which will be easily appreciated by those who are familiar with Cornish English. Modern writers of all languages prefer consistent spelling, and to modern learners, whose object is linguistic rather than philological, a fairly regular system of orthography is almost a necessity. The present system is not the phonetic ideal of "one sound to each symbol, and one symbol for each sound," but it aims at being fairly consistent with itself, not too difficult to understand, not too much encumbered with diacritical signs, and not too star-

tlingly different from the spellings of earlier times, especially from that of
Lhuyd, whose system was constructed from living Cornish speakers. The writer
has arrived at his conclusions by a comparison of the various existing spellings
with one another, with the traditional fragments collected and recorded by himself in 1875, with the modern pronunciation of Cornish names, with the
changes which English has undergone in the mouths of the less educated
Cornishmen, and to some extent with Breton. The author suggests that this
form of spelling should be generally adopted by Cornish students of their old
speech. The system cannot in the nature of things be strictly accurate, but it is
near enough for practical purposes. Possibly there is much room for controversy, especially as to such details as the distribution of long and short vowels, the
representation of the Middle Cornish *u, ue, eu* sometimes by *î*, sometimes by *ê*,
and sometimes by *eu* or *ew*, or of the Middle Cornish *y* by *i*, or *y*, or occasionally
by an obscure *ă, ŏ*, or, *ŭ* and it is quite likely that others might arrive at different conclusions from the same evidence, though those conclusions might not be
any the nearer to the sounds which the Cornishmen of the seventeenth and
eighteenth centuries really did make. As for grammatical forms, it will be seen
that the writer is of opinion that the difference between Middle and Modern
Cornish was more apparent than real, and that except in the very latest period
of all, when the language survived only in the mouths of the least educated persons, the so-called "corruptions" were to a great extent due to differences of
spelling, to a want of appreciation of almost inaudible final consonants, and to
an intensification of phonetic tendencies existing in germ at a much earlier
period. Thus it is that inflections which in the late Cornish often seem to have
been almost, if not quite, inaudible, have been written in full, for that is the
author's notion, founded on what Middle Cornishmen actually did write, of
what Modern Cornishmen were trying to express. For most things he has prece-
dents, though he has allowed himself a certain amount of conjecture at times,
and in most cases of difficulty he has trusted, as he would advise his readers to
do, to Breton rather than to Welsh, for the living Breton of to-day is the nearest
thing to Cornish that exists.

Why should Cornishmen learn Cornish? There is no money in it, it serves no
practical purpose, and the literature is scanty and of no great originality or
value. The question is a fair one, the answer is simple. Because they are

Cornishmen. At the present day Cornwall, but for a few survivals of Duchy jurisdictions, is legally and practically a county of England, with a County Council, a County Police, and a Lord-Lieutenant all complete, as it were no better than a mere Essex or Herts.[1] But every Cornishman knows well enough, proud as he may be of belonging to the British Empire, that he is no more an Englishman than a Caithness man is, that he has as much right to a separate local patriotism to his little Motherland, which rightly understood is no bar, but rather an advantage to the greater British patriotism,[2] as has a Scotsman, an Irishman, a Welshman, or even a Colonial; and that he is as much a Celt and as little of an "Anglo-Saxon" as any Gael, Cymro, Manxman, or Breton. Language is less than ever a final test of race. Most Cornishmen habitually speak English, and few, very few, could hold five minutes' conversation in the old Celtic speech. Yet the memory lingers on, and no one can talk about the country itself, and mention the places in it, without using a wealth of true Cornish words. But a similar thing may be said of a very large proportion of Welshmen, Highlanders, Irishmen, Manxmen, and Bretons.

Omnia Graece,
Quum sit turpe magis nostris nescire Latine.[3]

The reason why a Cornishman should learn Cornish, the outward and audible sign of his separate nationality, is sentimental, and not in the least practical, and if everything sentimental were banished from it, the world would not be as pleasant a place as it is.

Whether anything will come of the Cornish part of the Celtic movement remains to be seen, but it is not without good omen that this book is published at the "Sign of the Phoenix".

A few words of comprehensive apology for the shortcomings of the handbook. When the writer was asked by the Secretary of the Celtic-Cornish Society to undertake a Cornish grammar, which was the origin of this book, it was more than twenty years since he had dropped his Cornish studies in favour of other and more immediately necessary matters. Much of what he once knew had been forgotten, and had to be learnt over again, and the new grammar was wanted quickly. There must needs be, therefore, inaccuracies and inconsistencies, espe-

A HANDBOOK OF THE CORNISH LANGUAGE

CHIEFLY IN ITS LATEST STAGES WITH SOME ACCOUNT OF ITS HISTORY AND LITERATURE

BY

HENRY JENNER

MEMBER OF THE GORSEDD OF THE BARDS OF BRITTANY
FELLOW OF THE SOCIETY OF ANTIQUARIES

" Never credit me but I will spowt some Cornish at him.
Peden bras, vidne whee bis cregas."
The Northern Lass, by RICH. BROME, 1632.

LONDON
DAVID NUTT, AT THE SIGN OF THE PHŒNIX
57-59 LONG ACRE
MCMIV

Title page from Henry Jenner's
A Handbook of the Cornish Language

cially with regard to the spelling, which had to be constructed, and he is conscious also that there are at least two living men, if no more, who could have made a far better book. Of either of these two, Dr Whitley Stokes and Prof. Joseph Loth, Doyen of the Faculty of Letters in Rennes University, who probably know more about Cornish between them than any one else ever did, the writer may well say, as John Boson of Newlyn said of Keigwin two centuries ago, "*Markressa an dean deskez fear-na gwellaz hemma, ev a venja kavaz fraga e owna en skreefa-composter, etc.*"[4] For, indeed, even in that same *skreefa-composter* is there much scope for argument, and Boson's "et cetera" stands for a good deal besides.

It is not given to a grammar-writer to strive after originality. If he did so, he would probably not be the better grammarian. The writer therefore has no hesitation in acknowledging to the full his many obligations to previous workers on the subject. To Lhuyd and Pryce, to Gwavas, Tonkin, Boson, and Borlase he owes much (and also, parenthetically, he thanks Mr John Enys of Enys for lending him the Borlase MS.). But it is to the workers of the second half of the nineteenth century, living or departed, that he owes most, and especially to Dr Edwin Norris, Dr Whitley Stokes, Prof. Loth, Canon Robert Williams, and Dr Jago. Of the works of these writers he has made ample use, though he has not necessarily agreed with them in every detail.

The well-known work of Edwin Norris has been of the greatest value in every way, and the copious examples given in his "Sketch of Cornish Grammar" have frequently saved the writer the trouble of searching for examples himself. Dr Whitley Stokes's editions of two dramas and a poem have been of great assistance, the notes to the *St Meriasek* being especially valuable in collecting and comparing the various forms of irregular verbs, etc. Without Canon Williams's Lexicon nothing could have been done, and though some amount of friendly criticism and correction has been given to it by Dr Stokes and Prof. Loth, neither of whom, of course, really undervalues the Lexicon in the least, no one can fail to appreciate that excellent work. Prof. Loth's articles are mostly on details. A more general work from his hand is much to be desired, and every Cornish student must look forward to the forthcoming volume of his *Chrestomathie Bretonne*, which will contain the Cornish section. It would have been better for the present work if its author could have seen that volume before writing this.

But Prof. Loth's articles in the *Revue Celtique* have been full of suggestions of the greatest value. Dr Jago's English-Cornish Dictionary has also been most useful. In a somewhat uncritical fashion, he has collected together all the various forms and spellings of each word that he could find, and this rendered it possible to make easily comparisons which would otherwise have given a good deal of trouble. Even the somewhat unconventional lexicographical arrangement of the book has had its uses, but, if one may venture an adverse criticism, it was a pity to have followed Borlase in including without notice so many Welsh and Breton words for which there is no authority in Cornish. It is on this account that the work needs to be used with caution, and may at times mislead the unwary.

The author begs to thank very heartily Mr E. Whitfield Crofts ("Peter Penn" of the *Cornish Telegraph*) for his great service in making this handbook known among Cornishmen.

Perhaps a subject in connection with Cornish which may be of greater general interest than anything else is the interpretation of Cornish names. It is for this reason that a chapter embodying shortly some general principles of such a study has been added, and for those who would try their hands at original verse composition in Cornish a chapter on the principles of Cornish prosody has also been given. The composition of twentieth-century Cornish verse has already begun. Dr C.A. Picquenard of Quimper, well known as a Breton poet under the title of *Ar Barz Melen*, has produced several excellent specimens, Mr L.C.R. Duncombe-Jewell published the first Cornish sonnet in *Celtia* in 1901, and the present writer has contributed a sonnet and translations of the Trelawny Song and the National Anthem to the *Cornish Telegraph*, besides writing two Christmas Carols, one in *Celtia* and one printed separately, and the dedication of this book, which, he may remark, is not meant for a sonnet, though it happens to run to fourteen lines.

The writer had originally intended to add some reading lessons, exercises, and vocabularies, but it was found that the inclusion of these would make the book too large. He hopes to bring out shortly a quite small separate book of this character, which may also include conversations, and he has in preparation a complete vocabulary, though he has no idea as to when it will be finished.

Notes

1. Cf. "Ista sunt nomina corrodiorum et pensionum *in Anglia et Corubia* quae sunt in dono Regis Angliae." Harl. MS. 433, f. 335, temp. Ric. iii.

2. The Bretons of to-day habitually speak of Brittany as "notre petite patrie," and France as "notre grande patrie," and none have fought and died for France more bravely than these. As soldiers (and still more as sailors) they are to France what the Highlanders are to Britain, and avenge the atrocities of 1793 in the same noble fashion as that in which the Gaels have avenged the horrors of Culloden and its sequel. Loyalty is in the blood of Celts, whether to clan, or to great or little Fatherland.

3. 'Everything is Greek,
   When it is more shameful to be ignorant of Latin.' (editor's note)

4. "If that learned wise man should see this, he would find reason to correct it in orthography, etc." – *Nebbaz Gerriau*.

Cornwall: A Celtic Nation

[A paper read before the Pan-Celtic Congress at Caernarfon in August 1904 and published in the *Celtic Review* in January 1905]

Henry Jenner

The history of Cornwall proves it to have been a separate nation in the past – separate from England on the one side and from the rest of Celtia on the other, ever since the progress of the Saxon conquest separated the Britons into different nationalities. No doubt the Cornish on occasions joined with Cambria and Armorica under one leader against their common enemy. They did this under their own Arthur in the sixth century, and under Rhodri Molwynog of Gwynedd and Ivor map Alan of Brittany in the eighth century; but these were temporary military emperors, and Cornwall continued to be governed by its own kings, Constantine ap Cador, Conan, Gerrans, Teuder, Blederic, Duniert, Hoel, and the rest, until Athelstan in 935 drove the Cornish out of Devon and set the Tamar for their boundary. This is what the Saxons called 'conquering' Cornwall, but as a matter of fact they never did conquer it. From Athelstan's time the rulers of Cornwall seem to have been called Earls, and to have generally allied themselves with the Saxons against a new common enemy, the Danes; but the last native earl, Condor, made common cause with William of Normandy and his army of Bretons and Normans against the Saxons, who were holding out in Devon, and especially at Exeter, and was tricked out of his earldom for his pains. But Cornwall did not become a part of England. It became an appanage of the Norman dynasty, and no more a part of England than Ireland became a century, or Wales two centuries, later. The dukes of Normandy, who happened to be also kings of the English, for the turn of the *Sows Meleges* was over, appointed earls of Cornwall generally of their own near kin. The Conqueror appointed his brother, Robert of Mortain; some time after came Reginald de Dunstanville, appointed by Stephen. Henry II appointed his son John, afterwards king, and he in turn appointed his son Henry, afterwards Henry III. Perhaps the most distinguished earl was Richard, brother of Henry III, who was elected King of the Romans, and, had he lived, would have been Emperor. Edward II appointed that dreadful 'bounder', Piers Gaveston, to be earl, but he came to a bad end, and again the earldom was merged in the Crown. Edward II then gave it to his son, John of Eltham, who died young, and Edward III erected it into a dukedom and bestowed it upon his eldest son, Edward the Black Prince, since which time it has been the inherited title of the eldest son of the reigning sovereign. Unlike other British territorial titles of nobility, the dukedom of Cornwall really means something, for even now it involves certain jurisdictions which elsewhere fall to the Crown – foreshore rights, escheats, and other things, and, what is perhaps of more importance to the holder, a very considerable income. It was thus put into the same position as Wales, which, like Cornwall but unlike Ireland, was not included in the style and title of the king himself, but in that of his eldest son. Even the English did not consider Cornwall to be a part of England, but a separate earldom or duchy attached to the English Crown. All through the middle ages the official expression *in Anglia et Cornubia* was as common as *England and Wales* is now. I have found it as late as 1484. Even now certain laws, especially those relating to mining, are peculiar to Cornwall, and we still have our Cornish acre and our Cornish bushel. As late as the seventeenth century the separate nationality is clearly recognised. Thus we find John Norden saying of the Cornish about 1620, 'And as they are among themselves litigious, so seem they yet to retayne a kind of concealed envy against the English, who they yet affect with a desire of revenge for their fathers' sakes, by whom their fathers received their repulse.'

During the Civil Wars (in Clarendon's *History* and elsewhere) one finds the 'Cornish host,' the 'Cornish troops,' the 'Cornish army' under that grand Cornish hero, Sir Beville Granville, spoken of as quite distinct from the English

Henry and Katharine Jenner with Rev P. Treasure at the Celtic Congress,
Caernarfon 1904. Gwynedd Archives Service

cavalier army; as distinct as the 'Highland host' of the greatest of all Royalists, James Graham of Montrose. And splendid service they did too!

> 'Aye, by Tre, Pol, and Pen ye may know Cornishmen,
>   'Mid the names and nobles of Devon;
> But if truth to the King be a signal, why then
>   Ye can find out the Granville in Heaven.'

And to them the noblest of kings addressed that beautiful Letter of Thanks which Cornishmen may still read with pride on the walls of their old churches. He calls them a 'county,' no doubt, but a county may be a separate nation as well as an empire; besides, it is *Our* loyal County of Cornwall,' his in an especial way, not as a mere shire of England. Some shires of England were fairly loyal at times, but he could not differentiate between them and the disloyal parts of England, or at any rate he did not, and I am disposed to consider that the opinion of King Charles is better worth taking than that of most people. And they were worthy of his thanks. Except Raglan, also a Celtic stronghold, Pendennis Castle was the last fortress to surrender to the rebels, and Cornwall might have held out almost indefinitely, had not most of the flower of Cornish chivalry fallen around the Granville in Landsdowne fight. As a nation the Cornish were loyal to the sons of the Martyr King, as a nation they refused to give up their loyalty at England's bidding, and when, in 1715, James Paynter had proclaimed King James III at St Columb, a Cornish jury refused to find him guilty of treason, and his countrymen gave him a triumphant progress through the length of Cornwall from Launceston to Trelissick. Which was a bold thing to do about that time.

These are a few of the things which show that the separate nationality of Cornwall has been recognised. There can be no question that as Scotsmen, Irishmen, Welshmen, and Manxmen recognise, quite apart from governments and jurisdictions, and without any necessary wish to alter existing conditions, their separate nationality from Englishmen, so do the Cornish, only perhaps rather more so. Go to any part of the British Empire, and even outside it to the United States and to South America, and everywhere, especially where there is mining to be done, you will find Cornishmen. They do not merge themselves in the people of the land, often they do not even bother to take up the franchise of a colony, or to make themselves American citizens. They and their children after them do not call themselves Australians, New Zealanders, Canadians, or Americans, but Cornishmen. They form Cornish associations, they stand together 'shoulder to shoulder' like Highlanders, and 'One and All' they hope to make enough to retire from exile and end their days in peace in their own dear land, perhaps in their native villages, for they have the homing instinct as well as the clan instinct of the Celt. Yet they have done as good service in peace and in war to the British Empire as any nation of their size, especially, like their Breton brethren, as sailors; but if going to a colony meant never coming back to Cornwall, they would not go at all.

Not long ago I was talking to a Scottish minister of the name of Macgregor, who told me something that reminded me of the Cornish. He said that his clan until about a century ago had had a religion of their own. He could not tell me any details, for it was just out of reach. 'What sort of thing was it?' I asked. 'Were they Catholics or Protestants?' 'No,' he answered, 'they were neither Catholics nor Protestants. They were just Macgregors.' And we may say the same sort of thing of the Cornish. They are British subjects, no doubt, and loyal ones at that, but they are neither Englishmen, Welshmen, Irishmen, nor Scotsmen, they are just Cornishmen.

And if Cornwall is a nation, is it a Celtic nation?

If he is a Celt who speaks a Celtic language, then Mr Rudyard Kipling's Nova Scotian Negro, who 'called himself Macdonald and swore in Gaelic,' was a Celt, while thousands of Irishmen, Highlanders, Welshmen, and Bretons who speak only English or French are not Celts. If you say that a Celt is a person of Celtic blood who belongs to a nation that has preserved its Celtic language, then you must needs be intricately ethnological, and will exclude the Silurian or Iberian element in South Wales, the pre-Celtic element in parts of Ireland, and the Bigaudens of the Penmarch district of Brittany, and you must measure a man's skull and decide whether he is brachycephalic or dolichocephalic before he is admitted to the Celtic fraternity – and that way madness lies. If, however, you define a Celtic nation as one which, mainly composed of persons of Celtic blood and possessing Celtic characteristics, and having once had a sep-arate national existence, has preserved a separate Celtic language and litera-

Pan-Celtic Congress, Edinburgh, September 1907.
Henry Jenner 8th from left, 2nd row. By permission of Mary Beazley

ture, I am not disinclined to agree; and I am prepared to show that Cornwall fulfils those conditions.

The Cornish are mainly of Celtic blood. They are probably of more unmixed Celtic descent as a whole than any of the other Celtic nations, except perhaps the Bretons of Leon. There is little or no Scandinavian element among them, as in the Isle of Man, the Highlands and Islands of Scotland, and parts of Ireland. There is little or nothing of the pre-Celtic element, as in parts of Wales, parts of Ireland, and in the Bigauden district in Brittany. The shape of the country made it impossible for the Saxons to surround it and to absorb the inhabitants, as they did elsewhere. Indeed, the Saxons never settled Cornwall at all to any extent. Certain great Norman houses – Arundels, St Aubyns, Granvilles, Bevilles, and others – acquired estates there, but like the Normans in Ireland who, as Giraldus says, became *ipsis Hibernis Hiberniores*, these were absorbed by the Celts and became as Cornish as any of them. As for Celtic characteristics, who can deny them to the Cornish? The imaginative temperament, the poetic mind, the superstitions, if you like to call them so, the religious fervour, the generosity of heart, the kindly hospitality, the passionate nature, the absolute honesty, the thirst for knowledge, the clan spirit, the homing instinct, all these are there. Like the Macgregors whom I have mentioned, the Celt may be a Catholic or a Protestant in the outward form of his religion, but below and beyond the outward form he is just a Celt, and the Wesleyanism of Cornwall and its offshoots, when you get below the surface and the mere outward expression, is nearer akin by far to that most beautiful of religions, Breton Catholicism, than the former is to English Protestantism or the latter to English Catholicism. There is no questioning the fact that the Cornishman himself recognises too that he is a near relation of the Welsh and the Bretons.

I think I have shown satisfactorily that the Cornish are mainly of Celtic blood (which I do not think any one has ever seriously denied), and I have pointed out that their known and recognised characteristics are eminently Celtic. It remains to show that they possess, and that they have preserved a Celtic language and literature.

And now some definitions must come in, and we must ask what is meant by 'preserving a language' or by an 'extinct language,' which is a shorter way of saying a language which has not been preserved. There are more ways of preserving a language than by talking it. Who shall say that Latin, Hebrew, and Sanskrit are extinct languages, and yet no one of them has been for centuries any one's mother-tongue? If our modern knowledge of those languages, however complete now, had been laboriously revived by archaeologists, as Assyrian was revived, by the discovery of ancient documents and bi-lingual inscriptions, and there had been no continuity of knowledge, one might call them 'extinct' languages, but that is not the case, for these three have been continuously preserved, by the Latin Church, the Jews, and the Hindus respectively, ever since the time when they were the literary forms of a spoken language.

I admit that the preservation of Cornish has been far less in degree than that of Latin, Hebrew, and Sanskrit, but I doubt whether there ever was so very much of it to preserve. It was the least cultivated of the Celtic languages, except perhaps Manx, and has the least copious vocabulary; but one may fairly say that most of what there was of it has been preserved, and that it has been continuously preserved, for there has never been a time when there were not some Cornishmen who knew some Cornish; and though others have helped them and have written learnedly about the language, the preservation has been mainly the work of the Cornish themselves.

Probably until the time of Elizabeth the language was spoken over the whole duchy from the Tamar to the Land's End. The Reformation dealt it a hard blow, when the Bible and Prayer-book were used in English and were not translated into Cornish, but the people remained largely Catholic well into the seventeenth century, so that troubled them less than it might have. In the seventeenth century it began to recede, and in the Civil War period it was spoken from Truro westward, but very little to the east of that town. In 1700 it was still general among the working-classes in the western hundreds of Penwith and Kerrier, but the young people spoke it less and less, and though there were people who habitually used it down to the last quarter of the eighteenth century and persons who could speak it, and had done so in their younger days, survived till nearly the middle of the nineteenth century, it would seem to have ceased to be any one's mother-tongue before the nineteenth century began. But the work of preservation began before 1700, and though most of those who worked at the subject were very ill-equipped philologists, they did succeed in preventing the language from being quite lost. Moreover, apart from the literary work of educated men, there has been a continuous tradition among the less educated of the people, by which words, numerals, and phrases, which once were in common use, have been handed down as parts of the old language without the aid of books, and this tradition continues to this day. I myself received some of it from old people in Newlyn and Mousehole in 1875, so did Mr Lach Szyrma, who found these people for me, so did Dr Jago, the author of the English-Cornish Dictionary. Once there was more of it. It is said, though I do not vouch for the truth of the story, that there were old people in the early nineteenth century who habitually recited the Lord's Prayer and Creed in Cornish at their private prayers as they had been taught to do as children. Be this as it may, there were people who could have done so, and one instance came under my observation. My own mother-in-law (the late Mrs Rawlings of Hayle), when she was a child, that is to say somewhere before 1830, had learned these two things in Cornish, though of course not as part of her religious instruction. Unluckily she had quite forgotten them in later life. Mr Norris records also that he had heard an old man recite the Creed in Cornish, probably somewhat later. Beside the definite tradition of a small amount of Cornish as a separate language may be set the existence of a considerable number of Cornish words that are still in use in the mouths of the Cornish working-classes. There are perhaps a hundred or more of them, mostly, as may be supposed, the names of things. Thus a cow-shed is a *bowjy*, a pig-sty is a *crow*, a mine is a *bal* or a *wheal*, heather is *grig* or *griglans*, a broom (the plant) is *banal*, an elder-tree is a *skow*, a newt is a *pajerpaw* (four feet), a frog is a *quilkin*, ants are *murrians*, a toad is a *cronack*, to swallow is to *clunk*, to break is to *scat*, a milking-pail is a *lattis*, a dug well is a *peeth*, while a natural well or spring is a *venton*, a fiddle is a *crowd*. These are only a few taken at random, and of mining terms a very large proportion are Cornish, and so are many fishing terms. The names of places in the west of Cornwall are almost wholly Cornish, generally intelligible late Cornish, and not only the generic prefixes *tre, chy, pen, bos, zawn, porth, enys, carreg*, and the rest, but also such differentiating epithets as *wartha* and *wollas*, for upper and lower, *gwidn* and *dew*, for white and black, *mear* and *bean* for great and little, are very generally understood. Indeed *vean*, little, is a common term of endearment, as *bach* is in Welsh – *cheeld vean*, little child, is very common. But all this survival, though it constitutes in my opinion a faint flicker of actual life, is as nothing compared to the

Breton gathering, early part of the twentieth century. By permission of Mary Beazley

literary work of preservation, which began, as I have said, somewhere about 1700 and has continued to this day. It began with the copying and translating into English by John Keigwin of the old Cornish literature, the Trilogy of the *Ordinalia*, the Drama of the Creation, the Poem of the Passion, the collecting of proverbs, verses, epigrams, and phrases, the translating of chapters of the Bible and other things into Cornish, and the collecting of words into vocabularies, besides the composition of a few original pieces by the same John Keigwin, by William Gwavas, William Kerrow, Thomas Tonkin, John Boson, and others. In the middle of it all to them enter Edward Lhuyd, a Welsh genius and a skilled philologist and grammarian, as philologists went in those days. He put their information into shape for them, and the result was his Cornish Grammar, published in 1707. But he could have done nothing without his Cornish helpers, who taught him the language (and his proficiency did them credit), translated the literature for him, and put all their knowledge at his disposal. In point of fact he supplied the artistic finish to their unskilled work. Later on the same work was taken up by others. Dr William Borlase published a very copious vocabulary in 1759. William Pryce republished Lhuyd's Grammar, with a vocabulary substantially by Gwavas and Tonkin, and a considerable quantity of minor pieces from the collections of Gwavas and Borlase in 1790. Polwhele, Whitaker, and Davies Gilbert continued the work well into the nineteenth century. They did not do it very well, but that is not the point – they did it. Polwhele and Whitaker published fragments, specimens, and a short vocabulary. Davies Gilbert printed the Drama of the Creation and the Poem of the Passion, and a number of scraps of one sort and another, the latest appearing in 1827. From that time until 1853 very little appeared except occasional articles in magazines, though even then there were several Cornishmen who had some knowledge of the language. Then foreigners began to intervene. Hitherto, with the important exception of Lhuyd, the whole work had been done by Cornishmen. But the intervention of the foreigners, and highly skilled foreigners too, was no misfortune.

In 1853 appeared the first edition of Zeuss's *Grammatica Celtica*, which included the Cornish vocabulary of the twelfth century and a good deal more, chiefly Davies Gilbert's publications. In 1859 Edwin Norris published his excellent edition of the *Ordinalia*, three fifteenth century dramas, *Origo Mundi*,

Passio Christi, and *Resurrectio Domini*, with an equally excellent and learned essay on the grammar and literature generally. Then Dr Whitley Stokes published his new editions and translations of the later drama of the Creation in 1864, and the Poem of the Passion in 1862, and Robert Williams of Rhydycroesau his splendid Cornish Lexicon in 1865, but it is not taking away from the credit of either of these to say that they could have done comparatively little without the work of those Cornishmen of whom I have already spoken, to whose efforts, faulty and unlearned as they may have been, the preservation of the language is due. In 1872 Dr Whitley Stokes published the Drama of St Meriasek, a new discovery which added a fair number of words and forms. Then the natives took up the subject again. In 1876 I published the results of my enquiries into the Traditional Relics of Cornish, and in 1877 a fragment of a late fourteenth, or early fifteenth, century poem or play discovered by me on the back of a charter in the British Museum, and much about the same time I also wrote two general papers on the language. The late Mr William Copeland Borlase, who had published a few scraps from his ancestor's collections as early as 1866, edited John Boson's account of the Cornish language (in Cornish and English) in 1878, and ten years later appeared Dr Jago's English-Cornish Dictionary. Meanwhile the 'foreigners,' Dr Whitley Stokes and Professor Loth, have been adding greatly to our knowledge at intervals in the *Revue Celtique* and elsewhere, and up to the present time I have had the last word in my *Handbook of the Cornish Language* which has just now appeared.

The position of Cornwall as regards its language and literature in 1700 was very like that of the Isle of Man now, and the results of the efforts to preserve them will probably be repeated in the latter case, making allowance of course for the great advantage that the Manx people have in an improved knowledge of how to do it. I should like to illustrate what I mean by a reference to that language. It was only the other day that I came upon a remarkable opinion in the most widely circulated Guide-book to the Isle. It is interesting as an evidence of the ordinary cheap tripper's view of the matter; but then one knows very well what sort of illiterate unobservant idiot the cheap tripper is. And this is what is good enough for the cheap tripper in the Isle of Man. 'There is no occasion for the tourist to trouble himself about the Manx language. Early in the present century' (he means the last century, for the book is dated 1904, but he can't even get his chronology right) 'the then bishop spoke of it thus in a letter to his wife: "It is an unmitigated portion of the curse of Babel."' What the Bishop of Sodor and Man said is not evidence, but to one who considers the Manx language to be the most interesting thing in that most interesting island, this opinion sounds curious. Yet it is probably well suited to the readers of the book, which, after all, does tell you where the golf links are, so what more can any reasonable man expect? There were people, and Manxmen too, I fear, a century ago, who would have been glad to get rid of Manx as an obstruction. Now, as Cornishmen did two centuries ago, they are eagerly preserving every bit that is left of it. They will succeed in preserving it on paper; they will prolong its life as a spoken language a little longer; they will preserve, and perhaps add to, its little literature, but that is all. When the present old people are dead, it will cease to be any one's mother-tongue. I do not want to throw cold water on the laudable efforts of the Manx Language Society. Let them aim high; let them set before themselves the object of preserving it *in saecula saeculorum*, and they will probably preserve more of it for a longer time than if they made languid efforts. The Cornish, even those who loved their language most, saw that as a spoken tongue it was doomed, and it is possible that their efforts were marred by that knowledge. But though the Manx may preserve the whole of their speech as a literary language, and even as an artificially spoken language, they can seriously hope for no more.

The Cornish are again beginning to show their interest in their old language. I do not say that they are likely to introduce it as a spoken language to the exclusion of English, but I think a good many of those who do not know it will repair that defect, and will learn certainly to read it, probably to write, and possibly to speak it. That it can be spoken intelligibly by modern people was proved very clearly last year at the Breton Congress at Lesneven. At the dinner which ended the Congress I made a speech of about four or five minutes' duration in Cornish, and – much to my astonishment, for I must confess that I did not think it would be so – I was very well understood by my Breton audience. I spoke fair Cornish, and did not 'fake' it to suit Breton, and I pronounced it as I supposed a seventeenth century Cornishman would have pronounced it. Of course I spoke slowly and distinctly, and it is possible that, having been for the previous fortnight in the middle of Breton-speaking people, I had caught something of the

Breton intonation unawares; also it was not very difficult to conjecture what I was likely to talk about; but making all due allowances for these things, it is a remarkable fact that a speech in Cornish was understood by an audience of Bretons, only one of whom had studied Cornish.

And I have good reason to know that the awakening of Cornwall has begun. Since, some six months ago, the *Cornish Telegraph*, a local paper of Penzance, began to make known my Cornish Grammar, I have received many letters from intending subscribers. They are of all classes of the community, no doubt, but certainly a very large proportion belong, not to the rich and leisured class, who might take up Cornish as a fashion, as they take up golf or motoring, but to the classes of hard-working clerks, small business men, shopkeepers, and artisans, the classes that form the backbone of Cornish Methodism – a very different sort of people from the same classes in a non-Celtic country – and I found that perhaps the most intelligent of these letters was from an ordinary walking postman. People of that class in Cornwall want to know things, and, what is more, they generally succeed.

Henry Jenner, F.S.A.: City Scholar and Local Patriot

Derek R. Williams

Introduction: Remain Forever Cornish

Sixteen months before his death on 8 May 1934, Henry Jenner, in a New Year message to the Cornish people on behalf of the Federation of Old Cornwall Societies and the Cornish Gorsedd, used a phrase that has become a watchword for Cornish patriots everywhere – 'Remain forever Cornish'. He went on to prove that he had lost none of his devotion to the homeland that had inspired him throughout his life:

> Cornwall is not merely a county. It is a country with its own history, and its own language, which is by no means a lost one, and can easily be learnt. Hold fast to your heritage, resist the monotonous "standardization" which is being forced upon the world, and preserve your individuality. It is not enough to treasure the past. Look forward to the future ... The other Celtic nations have unreservedly recognized Cornwall as a sister nation. Recognize it yourselves and be loyal to our little Motherland, without prejudice to your loyalty to King and Empire.[1]

Jenner's intense loyalty to his homeland is all the more poignant because he spent over sixty years of his long life east of the Tamar and yet still chose to define himself largely by what he achieved for Cornwall after coming home in

1909. Indeed, on his deathbed he dismissed in no uncertain terms his work at the British Museum – work that had brought him into contact with many of the leading literary, political and royal figures of his day:

> I regard that as nothing. It is only since then that I have been able to do anything that really pleased me, and seemed to me of worth.[2]

Jenner was a colossus, not only physically big, but the guiding force behind so many organisations that had worked – and continue to work – to establish the identity of Cornwall as a Celtic nation. He has been variously called 'Father of the Cornish Revival',[3] 'Leader of the Cornish Movement'[4] and 'Leader of the academic circles of Cornwall',[5] and Brian Sullivan's description of him – 'a figure of almost messianic significance in the renascent Cornish culture of the early decades of this century'[6] – can hardly be bettered for conveying something of the great sense of awe and respect in which he was held.

Early Years
Henry Jenner had 'the good fortune to have been born in Cornwall',[7] at St Columb Major on 8 August 1848, the son of the Rev Henry Lascelles Jenner, who was at the time a curate in the town, and Mary Isabel Finlaison. As Jenner himself acknowledged, he was not of Cornish ancestry, but 'rather "mixed" – partly English, partly Highland Scottish, with a dash of Irish and Welsh'. Despite this, he remained, in his own mind, a Cornishman and felt a very strong sentiment of patriotism towards Cornwall from his earliest days.[8] His paternal grandfather, Sir Herbert Jenner Fust, was Dean of Arches and the chief ecclesiastical judge in the kingdom, while his maternal grandfather, William Finlaison RN, was sometime governor of Ascension Island. Henry Lascelles Jenner, the seventh of eight sons, was born at Chislehurst in Kent and the curacy of St Columb in 1846 was his first appointment. He was subsequently curate of Maryfield, then the estate church for Anthony House, the ancestral home of the Pole-Carews [now the Carew-Poles] with whom the Jenners became close friends. His father's rapidly declining health forced him to resign the curacy in 1851 and, after a brief spell at Leigh, near Southend, he moved to east Kent where he was successively a minor canon at Canterbury and, from 1854

Oil painting of Bishop Henry Lascelles Jenner, Henry Jenner's father.

By permission of the Canterbury Cathedral Archives

onwards, vicar of Preston-next-Wingham where Henry's sisters Mildred and Elizabeth were born. Wherever he was stationed, the Rev Jenner undertook the restoration of the church and introduced ritual according to the principles of the combined Oxford and Cambridge Movement. These 'ritualistic tendencies' would feature in the controversy surrounding his nomination in 1865 as the first Bishop of Dunedin, New Zealand[9] and help explain his son's own High Church views.

It is to two of the many talks that he gave in the late 1920s/early 1930s when he was a visiting lecturer at the then University College of the South West, Exeter that we must turn in order to glean anything substantial about Jenner's childhood, schooldays and working life. One of his earliest memories concerned his paternal grandfather, Sir Herbert Jenner Fust, who was sufficiently famous as an international lawyer for Dickens to include him in his description of a visit to the Arches Court in Doctor's Commons, near St Paul's Churchyard. Furthermore, the judgement that Dickens' 'very fat and red-faced gentleman, in tortoise-shell spectacles'[10] made in 1845 in a celebrated case about a restored Cambridge church led to him being mentioned by name in *The Ingoldsby Legends*.[11] For the young three year old, though, who was known always in the family as Harry, he was never anyone other than the 'grandpapa' whom they visited every year in his large eighteenth-century house at Chislehurst, one of the three that his family deemed him to be 'quite satisfied with'.[12] 'I remember going there by sea once,' Jenner wrote, 'and that is connected with one of my memories of my grandfather, for I had evidently learnt at least one nautical term on that voyage. I used to come down to dessert ... and was put to sit by my grandfather. He quite politely asked me which wine I would take, and when I answered "port", which pleased him greatly, for he was a great connoisseur of port, it was part of the "good living" which Dickens noted, he solemnly poured me half a glass – fancy giving half a glass of port to a child of three – it wouldn't be done now! Then, and I remember this quite distinctly, I sent him into a fit of delighted laughter by asking quite seriously, "Is the other called starboard wine?" I chiefly remember him at dessert, but I also remember standing in the waste-paper basket by the side of the very same table at which I have written these words, while he and my father talked together. He seemed to me to be very stout and red-faced – Dickens was right there – and much shorter than my father. I can also remember the tortoiseshell spectacles, not necessarily the same ones, of which Dickens spoke.'[13] As John Pearce says, boys in those days were little men and Harry was, it seems, able to recite a good deal of Longfellow, compare the fairy tales of Andersen and Grimm, and repeat an ode of Anacreon in Greek without knowing what a word meant.[14] Not long after this – towards the end of 1851 – the Jenners left Cornwall for Essex and it would be sixteen years before Henry set foot again in his native land.

Harry the Harlovian

Although he would later express his sorrow at leaving Cornwall, these were exciting times for a young boy growing up in a well-to-do family, whatever the setting. He recalled, for instance, a visit to the Great Exhibition in Hyde Park during which he drank from what was known as the 'crystal fountain' – 'probably a very insanitary performance,' commented Jenner, 'but nobody bothered about pure drinking water in those days.'[15] On the international stage, a series of bloody conflicts in the 1850s and 1860s captivated the boy. During the Crimean War he went down to Deal to watch the British fleet sail through the Downs on its way to the Baltic, his family, especially his maternal grandmother who lived with them, taking great care that he should follow events as they unfolded. The relief of Lucknow during the Indian Mutiny was greeted with excitement, while the constant changes in Italian stamps during the wars of the Risorgimento served to direct the attention of the young philatelist to what was going on. Although he was not particularly interested in the American Civil War, Jenner did go on board the Federal warship 'Kearsarge' as she lay within the three-mile limit at Dover, watching a Confederate ship at anchor in French waters off Boulogne. And later still there were the German wars. 'I was only a boy in those days,' he wrote many years later, 'but I rather fancied myself on my knowledge of history – I always used to get the history prize at school, if that counts for anything – but I am inclined to believe that I don't know as much history now as I *thought* I knew then.'[16]

In May 1857, nine months before he began attending St Mary's College, Harlow, Jenner had his first taste of foreign travel when, during the course of a holiday in Dover, he was taken by his father on a two-day visit across the Channel. He either kept a diary that remains to be discovered or his memory, seventy years or so after the event, was extremely good, for his lecture 'Foreign Travel' contains a vivid description of 'workmen in blue blouses, queer caps and wooden shoes, blue-coated soldiers with baggy red trousers [and] military-looking policemen with cocked hats and swords'. Most intriguing of all, though, was the fact that everyone, even the children, actually spoke French![17] In due course Jenner would become an accomplished traveller, going abroad no less than twenty-eight times between 1867 and the early 1930s, as well as exploring much of England, Wales and Scotland and reacquainting himself with Cornwall.

In 'Some Reminiscences of Notable People' we get one or two glimpses of Jenner the schoolboy at Harlow, where he attended St Mary's College between 1858 and 1865. One day in 1862, for instance, he and some other boys were in the local post office which doubled as the school tuckshop, when a large, burly man with a big beard rode up to the door on a large horse and fastened his bridle to a ring in the wall before entering and having a short conversation with the post-master. It was none other than Anthony Trollope and the first in a succession of well-known writers, artists, politicians and 'royals' whom Jenner would see and, more often than not, meet either socially or professionally. This, of course, is Jenner the octogenarian remembering an incident suitable for inclusion in a public lecture. Far more revealing – and redolent of boarding-school life – are three diaries from this period, which also contain basic accounts and lists of letters sent and received.[18] 'Fine day,' begins the entry for 18 November 1863. 'Wrote to Mama asking for some tins, also wrote to [?] saying I should be happy to change the stamp with him. Finished Paradise Lost and also read Paradise Regained. Wrote to Miss Paynter sending my photograph.'

In short, this is a picture of an eminently sensible young man who is, perhaps, about to taste the first fruits of romance. More representative, though, are the following entries from the diary for Michaelmas Term, 1864, which reveal another side to sixteen-year-old Harry:

> September 28th. Wednesday. Fine day. Went out in the afternoon with Watt and Hardy and smoked and got sick. Went to bed at 7.30.

> November 9th. Wednesday. Fine day. Went out with Hardy. Row about throwing a stone over the brewery wall. All the leaves stopped but got back again...

November 12th. Saturday. Cold day. Went out with Hardy. No end of a
row in the afternoon. Smoking, snuff, pistol etc. all found out. Had to
stop in bounds this afternoon for not being in at the bell.

Jenner and Hardy were obviously a pair to be reckoned with!

Cornish and Cornwall Regained

Although, according to Robert Morton Nance, as a small boy Jenner heard some
talk among his elders of a Cornish language and determined that henceforth it
would be his language,[19] Jenner himself gives a slightly different version, tracing his first contact with the language to his schooldays at St Mary's where, as a
12 or 13 year old, he was using Latham's *Smaller English Grammar*. In addition
to a lot of miscellaneous information about English, this contained specimens
of the Celtic languages, some in Cornish. 'At once I said, "I must learn this",'
wrote Jenner, 'and I learnt it all.'[20]

It is generally accepted that Cornish became extinct as a means of communication in about 1800, though it lived on into the nineteenth and twentieth
centuries in a number of ways before being revived, notably in hundreds of
place-names and in traditional fragments such as versions of the numerals. In
1859 Dr Edwin Norris published three Middle Cornish texts, known collective-
ly as the *Ordinalia*, which he had transcribed and translated. Another great
Celtic scholar, Dr Whitley Stokes, was preparing for publication the remaining
known Cornish texts, *The Passion* (1861), Jordan's *Creation* (1864) and *The Life
of St Meriasek* (1872). At about the same time, Prince Louis Lucien Bonaparte,
a philologist, came to Cornwall in order to search for remains of the language.
He was instrumental in erecting, in June 1860, a monument to Dolly Pentreath
who, erroneously, has gone down in history as the last of the native Cornish
speakers. Disparate though these events undoubtedly were, together they did
succeed in publicizing the language and a growing number of scholars, both
Cornish and non-Cornish, began to take a greater interest.

Another important stage in Jenner's own pursuit of his 'native' tongue
involved visiting the monument in Paul Churchyard – presumably, as we shall
see, early in 1867 – and learning the text of this and one or two other pieces. Two
years later, at the age of twenty-one, he applied for a British Museum reading

ticket, told the attendant that he wanted any books they had on the Cornish language, and spent the rest of the afternoon reading 'Norris's *Cornish Drama*'. Although he could not claim to 'have gone at it continuously ever since',[21] these early enquiries were to dictate the course of what would prove to be the core interest in Jenner's life.

In the meantime, on 24 August 1866 the Rev Henry Lascelles Jenner was consecrated in Canterbury Cathedral as the first Bishop of Dunedin, New Zealand,[22] a grand event that enabled his 18-year-old son to meet 'some very notable people' at both the service itself and subsequently at lunch in the Deanery and at Minor Canon Hirst's house. It was, too, a great social occasion for the family, and the six of Bishop Jenner's brothers who were present, together with his sisters Charlotte and Anne, all met up later at the Fountain Hotel.[23]

The following year was an exciting one for Henry himself. Not only did he make his first solo foray abroad, but he returned to what, sixty-five years or so later, he described as 'a tourist-ridden country', namely Cornwall. As the whole family were meant to be going out to New Zealand, this was part of a round of farewell visits. Having stayed with relations at Wenvoe, near Cardiff where, incidentally, a good deal of Welsh was still spoken,[24] Jenner travelled by train to Bristol in order to catch a steamer for Hayle. 'It was a very rough day,' he recalled, 'and I am never very happy at sea on a very rough day, but we got there eventually, rather late for the tide, and had to go in in boats. I remember seeing Godrevy Lighthouse, and Lelant Church, and a hill which I suppose was Trencrom, and I quoted to myself the words of Coleridge: "Oh dream of joy, is this indeed the lighthouse top I see? Is this the hill, is this the kirk, is this mine own countree?" ' Staying mostly with old friends in St Columb, Jenner explored antiquities such as the cromlech – then used as 'a pig's crow' – that once stood at a small farm called, after it, 'Quoit' on the slopes of Castle-an-Dinas.[25] He also visited the coast between what was then the tiny fishing hamlet of Newquay and Bedruthan, although, in so doing, he did not consider himself a tourist, but a native.[26]

He could hardly avoid being saddled with the 'tourist' epithet in June 1868 when he took a break from his teaching duties at a school in Rhyl in order to undertake a two-day walking tour of Snowdonia. He had, though, already learnt some Welsh. From Rhyl he travelled to Penmaenmawr and then on to

Caernarfon. Having reached the top of Snowdon in time to see the sun set in a perfectly cloudless and very clear sky, he spent the night in the Summit Hotel – 'a collection of wooden sheds' – before walking down the other side to Capel Curig and Betws-y-Coed and thence back to Rhyl by train. Two months later he spent a week in Paris, though he makes it abundantly clear that the noisy and crowded French capital, with its 'cafés, chantants [sic], music halls and things', was not really to his taste and that, thereafter, he generally avoided it.[27] On 18 November he travelled to Liverpool to see his father board the City of Boston on the first stage of his ill-fated visit to New Zealand.[28]

City Scholar

In January 1869 Jenner abandoned teaching and moved to London in order to take up a clerical post in the Principal Registry of the Court of Probate. Eighteen months later, at the instigation of Archibald Tait, the new Archbishop of Canterbury whom he had met at his father's consecration, he was appointed Junior Assistant in the British Museum's Department of Manuscripts. Thereafter, forays into the literary and social life of the city would combine with his philological and linguistic studies to set the pattern for much of the forty-year period that he spent in the English capital. As well as attending garden parties and other social functions at Lambeth Palace, he was a regular at the musical entertainments at St James's Hall known as the Monday Popular Concerts and at the recitals given at the new Albert Hall. At such gatherings or in the British Museum Jenner either met or got a glimpse of – 'vidi tantum' is a phrase he uses often in 'Reminiscences of Notable People' – such luminaries as Dickens, Thomas Carlyle, Swinburne, Jenny Lind, Charles Hallé, John Ruskin, Whistler, Ellen Terry, Charlotte Yonge, Edward Burne-Jones and William Morris, whom he describes as a 'poet, artist and high-class furniture dealer'! The latter proved a useful contact when Jenner and a colleague were planning a tour of Iceland:

> We had a long evening with Morris, who knew the country and its litera-ture well, and gave us a great lot of practical and literary information of great interest and value, and much of it very amusing, for he and his partner Burne Jones, whom I knew slightly, had a great sense of humour, though you wouldn't think it from their works.

In the event, the tour never came off.

Preferring the shilling orchestra seats behind the platform at the Monday Concerts to the extravagant five-shilling stalls, Jenner became familiar with the faces of many of the 'swells' who sat opposite him, among them 'an ugly woman with a face like a house'. This was none other than George Eliot whose 'very *dull* books' he felt obliged to read because everyone was talking about them. 'I think I liked *Silas Marner* best only because it was the shortest,' he wrote rather unkindly years later. 'But her face, ugly as it was, was a very striking one...'[29] Another encounter, this time at the British Museum, is best left to Jenner himself to describe:

> One day in 1872 there came into the ms. Dept ... a tall man with rather wild hair and beard and wearing a great cloak and picturesque broad-brimmed hat. He said that he was writing a poem about a tournament and had a line in which he described the ladies in their gay dresses as being like a rainbow on the ground. But he had a haunting misgiving that the lists were rectangular, and thought that the critics would be down upon him for a square rainbow. We got him out any number of miniatures representing tilting and in all of them the lists were rectangular, so he had to cut that line out. I knew exactly where it would have come – somewhere about line 148, so you can look it up if you like – for the poem was 'One Last Tournament' and the poet was Alfred Tennyson.[30]

'Cornish, thou livest yet!'

Rather surprisingly, the general lectures of Jenner's that I have perused contain virtually no references to fellow Cornish men and women. It is tempting to believe, for instance, that he must have met the Rev Mark Guy Pearse who was the Rev Hugh Price Hughes' right-hand man at the West London Mission which organised the Monday concerts at St James's Hall. As we have already seen, the seeds that were sown in early childhood or boyhood were already germinating and when he was not socialising or going to concerts, Jenner was studying the Cornish language and attending meetings of the Philological Society at University College. On his table at the British Museum he kept handy such texts as Pryce's *Archaeologia Cornu-Britannica* and Williams's

Lexicon Cornu-Britannicum, as well as those Cornish texts that Norris and Stokes had already transcribed and translated.[31] At home he was writing scraps of Cornish, sometimes in verse, but more often, perhaps, as comments in his note-books where they appear, too, in Latin, Greek, French, German or Hebrew which he began learning from a Jewish rabbi as early as 1871.[32] The first fruits of this research appeared in a paper – the first of many from his pen – that he read to the Philological Society on 21 March, 1873.[33] From this it is clear that not only was Jenner consulting any Cornish texts that he could lay his hands on, but he was also putting his leave to good use by carrying out research on the ground in Cornwall. He ends this general survey of the grammar, literature and history of the language on a seemingly rather despondent note:

> This, then, is all that can be found at present on the subject of the Cornish language. I have done much more in the way of *compiling* than of originating anything, for the subject has been pretty well exhausted by other writers; and unless some new book should turn up, very little of any importance remains to be done.

Privately, though, he seems to have regarded his lecture that day as something of a milestone, for in the evening he wrote the following poem entitled *A Dead Language*:

> They have seen thy last hours pass,
>   Those antiquary priests;
> They have sung thy funeral mass
>   And spread thy funeral feasts.
>
> They have traced thee to the tomb,
>   Have watched and seen thee dead,
> Driven from each hill and combe
>   Before the Saxon's tread.
>
> But, for all the learned throng
>   That round thy grave have met,

Or have heard thy dying song,
    Cornish, thou livest yet!

Livest, yes, thou art not gone;
    Old Cornwall holds thee still,
Naming every Druid stone,
    Each hamlet, moor, and hill.

Where green fields and homesteads stand,
    Where flows each holy fount,
All throughout the Cornish Land,
    From Bude to Michael's Mount.

And where'er the wild waves rear
    Their billows none can tame,
Still they strike on cliffs that bear
    Some grand old Cornish name.

They may lay thy dying head
    Where the white ocean foams,
But, if they can call thee dead,
    Thou'rt buried in our homes![34]

At Philological Society evenings he met with others who were establishing themselves in this particular field, such as Frederick Furnivall, James Murray and Henry Bradley, all of whom were heavily involved in the society's *A New English Dictionary on Historical Principles*, later the *Oxford English Dictionary*. The most interesting person, though, was 'that industrious philologist, Prince Louis Lucien Bonaparte, the nephew of the great Napoleon. He was a striking likeness of his uncle. I was quite startled by it when I first saw him. We got on very well and he was very kind and helpful to a young student of Cornish, as I then was.'[35] Another enthusiast whom Jenner would have met was the Rev W. S. Lach-Szyrma who was elected a member of the society in December, 1873.[36] In 1874, by way of preparation for a visit to the Isle of Man during which he would

Senior staff at the Department of Printed Books, c.1885.
Henry Jenner far left, second row. By permission of the British Library Archives

investigate the condition of the Manx language, Jenner sent questionnaires to the incumbents of all of the island's seventeen parishes. During the visit itself he attended a church service conducted in Manx and was welcomed into the homes of a number of local people, only one of whom, he found, could not speak English.[37] The results of his enquiries were presented in a paper to the Philological Society on 18 June 1875.[38] A month later he and the Rev Lach-Szyrma, who had the previous year become vicar of St Peter's, Newlyn, toured West Cornwall visiting elderly people in Newlyn and Mousehole who were still able to repeat the numerals in Cornish and who knew other words of the language. Jenner divided his findings into three groups: a) the numerals, which he compared to those listed by Pryce in his *Archaeologia Cornu-Britannica* (1790) and Norris in his *The Cornish Drama, with a Sketch of Cornish Grammar* (1859); b) detached words; and c) complete sentences. He argued that those who had learned English as a new language would have found it easier to count in Cornish and would have counted their fish in that tongue. Their children would have heard them and would have done so themselves with the result that the numerals as far as twenty would have survived long after the death of the rest of the language.[39] The extent of such survivals was, however, very limited:

> I only found that a few people of great age could repeat the numerals as far as twenty, and one or two knew a few detached words and two short sentences.[40]

Jenner has been criticised for failing to tap further what Ken MacKinnon calls 'the speech-community of the last semi-speakers' in the Newlyn-Mousehole-Madron area, especially such individuals as John Davey the younger (1812–1891), a farmer-cum-schoolmaster of St Just and Boswednack, near Zennor who, according to J. Hobson Matthews, had sufficient traditional knowledge of the language to be able to speak some. However, Davey's ability to converse in Cornish has been contested[41] and the results of Jenner's and Lach-Szyrma's interviews were not particularly encouraging. What is more, Jenner's personal circumstances were about to change.

In the meantime, on 19 August 1876 the British Archaeological Association met at Penzance. Jenner's contribution to a number of papers on various aspects of Cornish antiquities was 'The History and Literature of the Ancient Cornish Language' which was, in effect, an expanded version of his talk to the Philological Society three years earlier. There was, in his opinion, nothing very new to put forward, for the language had been

> I will not say thoroughly *worked* out, for much remains to be done, but very considerably *talked* out ... What originality it [this paper] may possess will be rather in the way of omitting oft-repeated nonsense than of adding facts already put forward.[42]

One such example of 'oft-repeated nonsense' was the story that the last old woman who spoke Cornish walked up to London in the Exhibition year of 1851 to see Queen Victoria! Madron-born 84-year-old Mary Kelynack's walk to London and her presentation to the Queen in September 1851 is well-documented, but Jenner's informant appears to have been alone in insisting that she was able to speak Cornish. Of particular interest in the paper is Jenner's criticism of the Ordnance Survey for the form of spelling they were using on their maps. Some names were apparently spelt phonetically, others

> according to a curious idea of assimilating Cornish to Welsh, and others after a wildly affected plan, with accents and strange philological tricks, based upon the system adopted (very usefully in *that* case) in Canon Williams' Cornish Lexicon.

He proposes that a committee be formed to decide all questions relating to Cornish spelling and that the form which the names should take be settled by them on principles consistent with the current sound, the derivation and the meaning, 'taking care in all cases in which the spelling has been already settled by anything like common usage, to preserve it as so settled'. He stresses that, should such a plan be adopted, he would be very willing to give any assistance that time allowed, subject to the following conditions:

> I give notice that I shall violently oppose any antiquated vagaries or unnecessary deviations from established usage, and shall try to get the

spelling settled in accordance with practical common sense, and not
with any design for cramming a smattering of ancient Cornish down the
throats of a number of people who do not in the least want to be bothered
with it.[43]

Such was the interest created by Jenner's paper that Lord Mount Edgcumbe,
who presided over the Penzance meeting, suggested that a society be formed to
ensure the publication of such remnants of the Cornish language as had not
already been printed. In this he was supported by William Copeland Borlase of
Laregan, Penzance, who was the great great grandson of the antiquary William
Borlase and, himself, a promising archaeologist.[44] A prospectus for the proposed
society was compiled by Borlase and Jenner and issued on 2 October.[45] It was
hoped that the Gwavas manuscript, which had been recently acquired by Louis
Lucien Bonaparte, would provide material for its first number and that subsequent issues would draw on the manuscript collection made about 1748 by the
Rev William Borlase. In the event, the Cornish Manuscripts Society never got
off the ground, possibly through lack of money, though Peter Berresford Ellis
suggests that a hostile reception from established societies such as the Royal
Institution of Cornwall and the Royal Cornwall Polytechnic Society may have
killed the idea.[46]

Harry and Kitty Lee

The following year was a busy one for Jenner. On Thursday 12 July 1877 he
married Katharine Lee Rawlings, the eldest daughter of William John Rawlings
of 'The Downes', Hayle in St Erth Parish Church.[47] That afternoon the newly-
weds travelled as far as Plymouth on the first stage of a six-week tour of France,
Switzerland, northern Italy, Austria and Germany. This was the first of numerous continental holidays that the couple would share and, incidentally, Kitty
Lee's first experience of foreign travel. All of them were planned down to the
last detail, including the probable cost, by Jenner, himself, who seemed inordi-
nately proud of his ability to keep to a budget. 'I thought it unlikely that we
should ever be able to afford to do it again,' he wrote, 'so we might as well have
a really good and representative one while we were about it, and, as I had the
run of the best library in the world, I was able to draw up [a] very thorough pro-

gramme. This was so successful that we never departed from it and the cost [£90] was within a few shillings of my estimate ... We did it, not regardless of expense, but quite well, going to good hotels everywhere, often travelling first class, for in those days it was not unusual for the long distance expresses, especially in France, to have no second-class, and having carriages when necessary. I think for a pair of utterly inexperienced travellers we did not do so badly.'[48]

The Jenners' courtship is dealt with elsewhere in this volume, but I think it is worth quoting in full Kitty's diary entry for New Year's Eve, 1877, if only as a counterpoint to the military efficiency with which Harry planned their honeymoon. In it she reveals the close bond between them – one that seemed to strengthen with the passing of the years – and explores her fears about her pregnancy:

> Yes, what I wanted last year has come by this one. I do love my husband very much better than I ever loved anybody – besides that we have got to a state of perfect oneness I never before contemplated as possible on earth. I can't write about that, words don't express it – This has been about the happiest year of my life. The tour which began with such a miserable wedding day, was simply 5 weeks of perfect happiness and delight and since then as far as we two are concerned life has been perfect – we have had troubles, Mother's illness, the Bishop's dreadful smash, my bad health, ugly uncomfortable rooms to live in – but somehow, except when I am ill, I am very happy, one could not be otherwise with such a husband. There is another thing to this year, at first I was wild at the thought, now I rather like the prospect, at least don't dislike it, except for the fear of the pain and the possible death of myself, that I do dread but more for my darling's sake than my own – we are both rather poorly only are beginning to take an interest in "the Baby" – now and not to mind it so much. I do hope I shall see next New Years Day, if I don't my boy will read this and know, only he knows it already that I love him beyond and above every other created thing, far more than I ever have or ever could love anybody anymore – we began this year with kisses (its past 2 now) and I only hope we shall do the same next year and have the baby to kiss as well.[49]

Wedding of Henry Jenner and Katharine Lee Rawlings at 'The Downes', Hayle, Cornwall, 12 July 1877. By permission of Mary Beazley

The 'Charter Fragment' and Dolly Pentreath

It was in 1877, too, that Jenner discovered a fragment of a play in Cornish that is now generally known as the 'Charter Fragment'. Cataloguing manuscripts acquired by the British Museum between 1854 and 1875 involved summarising charters, such as those granting lands in Melidor, St Stephen-in-Brannel that had been presented by Sir Charles Trevelyan in 1872. On the back of one Jenner discovered forty-one lines of a previously unknown Cornish play of about 1400. Having published his findings at the beginning of December,[50] he sent a copy to Dr Whitley Stokes who subsequently edited and translated them himself for the *Revue Celtique*.

Later that month, on the 27th, the centenary of the death of Dolly Pentreath was commemorated at Paul. The prime mover behind the celebrations seems to have been the Rev Lach-Szyrma. Some traditional scraps of Cornish were spoken by Mousehole fisherman Bernard Victor, whose grandfather George Badcock had been the undertaker who had buried Miss Pentreath, and by the folklorist William Bottrell, author of *Traditions and Hearthside Stories of West Cornwall* (1870–1880). Dr Edward White Benson, who eight months previously had been consecrated as the first Bishop of Truro, sent a message in Cornish, and the founder of the *Revue Celtique*, Henri Gaidoz, also sent an appropriate greeting, though not in Cornish. What Jenner made of the verbal part of the day's proceedings is hard to imagine, for, according to Robert Morton Nance, it was he who actually congratulated the Cornish people that they no longer had a second tongue, thus echoing sentiments expressed by Davies Gilbert in the 1820s. The general consensus at that time seems to have been that, for all but philologists, the Celtic languages were best forgotten.[51] Any proposal to revive Cornish would certainly not have won much backing!

The centenary, though, stimulated further discussion and research. Dr F. W. P. Jago's *Glossary of the Cornish Dialect*, for instance, was published in 1882 and his *English-Cornish Dictionary* five years later. Although in the latter Jago was intent on preserving what was left of the language rather than on encouraging Cornish people to use it again, he did open up the possibility of them learning it. In 1879, the *Cornishman* offered a prize for an essay about the language written by a layman. Two contributions, both with glossaries, were received and sent to John Rhys, who had recently been appointed the first Professor of Celtic at

Merton College, Oxford. Unable to decide on their merits, he suggested that the prize be divided equally between the two writers, a decision with which Jenner, when consulted, agreed.[52] Ironically enough, just when others were beginning to profit from and build on the increased interest in Cornish, Jenner suspended his studies for more than twenty years 'in favour of other and more immediately necessary matters'.[53] It was, in fact, the cultivation of what the late Royston Green disparagingly called 'feudal royalist politics'[54] that seems to have occupied him towards the end of the nineteenth century and on into the twentieth.

Changes

The late 1870s, too, saw a significant change in Jenner's situation at the British Museum and this, together with the demands of a busy social life, a liking for foreign travel and the birth of their daughter,[55] may well have left him with little time to pursue his Cornish studies in any concerted way. In 1879 he incurred the displeasure of Maunde Thompson, the newly appointed Keeper of Manuscripts, who refused to sign his diary for October because of the poor quality and quantity of his work.[56] There were, though, extenuating circumstances, as Kitty Lee makes clear:

> Hal has not been well for the winter. [?] has been promoted and Thompson behaves like a beast ... The room Thompson has put him into smells so terribly that he is always getting bad headaches and is unfit for anything in the evenings.

Indeed, his work situation was so bad that they were trying to find some way of getting him out of the British Museum. 'If only I can get money by writing we might afford to take a less paid place with less money,' agonised Kitty Lee.[57] Following a departmental row, however, the Museum's trustees decided that Jenner should be transferred to the Department of Printed Books where he was 'most enthusiastically received by keepers and men and will probably get on much better and have a much nicer time of it'.[58]

Although the Jenners did not anticipate going abroad again for some time, in June 1880 Henry was ill enough from 'a sort of brain fever' to need several months sick-leave and this, when added to his normal annual allowance of eight weeks, made for a long break. Letting their house to some Germans, the Jenners left for the Isle of Wight on 2 July. The glacial air of the Swiss Alps was strongly recommended and in due course the couple began a seven-week stay at 'a nice little mountain chalet hotel on top of the ridge between Lauterbrünnen and Grindelwald'.[59] Two years later they explored the Vosges mountains together on foot and 1883 saw them undertaking another 'cheap walking tour off the beaten track', this time through the volcanic Eifel range in the angle between the Rhine and the Moselle. Subsequent foreign holidays included Switzerland (1884 and 1889), Germany (1886) and Dalmatia, Montenegro, Herzegovina and Bosnia (1894), the latter 'a delightful tour in lands then unspoilt by hordes of tourists'.[60] Jenner wrote up a small part of this holiday for *The Royalist* as 'Three Days in a Legitimate Monarchy', a piece which reveals as much about his attitude to governance as it does about his and Kitty Lee's holiday habits.[61] He considered the early 1890s, by which time they had become both experienced travellers and better off, to have been their best period of travel, with their 'great Italian tour' of 1891 the highlight. Armed with valuable introductions to cardinals and other eminent people – 'If you don't have introductions,' wrote Jenner, 'you miss a lot' – they spent three weeks in Rome, where one of the cardinals got them an invitation to one of the smaller audiences of Pope Leo XIII. 'I got about five minutes pleasant conversation with him,' recalled Jenner, 'chiefly about the British Museum, which he knew … It was a most successful tour, we were away six weeks and though we did ourselves well, stayed at good hotels and had carriages when we wanted them, and went a considerable distance, it only cost £100.' In the autumn of 1895, they spent a week in Paris in order to take their daughter to school at the Sacré Coeur convent at Conflans. And towards the end of the century they took her with them on a trip up the Rhine and on a tour of Rome, Florence and Venice in order to give her some taste of foreign travel.[62]

Closer to home, Scotland was a favourite destination throughout the '90s. Although they had never visited their Celtic cousins before 1892, Jenner later declared himself to have been 'well up in Scottish history and geography, especially of the Highlands', having acquired a fair knowledge of Gaelic from books. They spent most of their time in the West Highlands and Skye following the course of Prince Charlie's wanderings, something that necessarily meant visiting the site of the battle of Culloden. While Henry tried to master colloquial Gaelic, Kitty Lee devoted herself to the sketching that occupied so much of her time during all these tours. Their Scottish visits followed much the same pattern in 1893 and 1895 when they made Inverie on Loch Nevis and the Outer Hebrides their bases.[63]

Meanwhile, in 1884 Jenner became 'Placer' in the Department of Printed Books where his work included 'the superintendence of the arrangement and classification of the whole library, as well as the keeping up of the Reading Room and Reading Room Gallery Catalogues, and the selection of books for the Reference Library in the Reading Room'.[64] One consequence of this was that he was constantly called upon to advise readers, many of them noted specialists, on the books relating to their particular subjects. Both at work and at the Society of Antiquaries, of which he was elected a fellow in March 1883, Jenner made the acquaintance of a host of celebrities, many of whom as we have already seen, grace the pages of his lecture 'Some Reminiscences of Notable People'. The novelist Sir Walter Besant lived near Jenner in Hampstead and was a close friend in the late 1870s/early 1880s when they would frequently spend evenings together 'in pipes and talks'. Although he had never had much to do with politicians, in 1889 Jenner's suggestion that movable presses be introduced at the library attracted the attention of Gladstone who came over specially to see how the work was progressing. The ensuing tête-à-tête Jenner remembered with pleasure, considering the once and future prime minister to have been 'one of the most delightful personalities that I have ever met, though I had not the slightest sympathy with his politics'.[65] Aundell Esdaile, who was a junior colleague in the early years of the last century, recalled that Jenner's own talk was not always without a touch of malice and was made livelier by his gift for producing the apt Biblical quotation. In particular, '[h]is abundant conversation on these topics [Celtic gatherings] was a delightful passing (who said waste?) of time to his younger colleagues in the Library.'[66]

Jacobite and Royalist

Jenner was always, as he himself put it, 'an irreconcilable Jacobite and Royalist' and his substantial involvement in the production of 'a sort of amateur magazine entitled 'The Royalist', which was devoted to the history, etc. of the Royal

House of Stuart and its adherents, and of the Stuart and Jacobite period generally', allowed him between 1890 and 1905 to give free reign to his sympathies
for the cause.[67] A very close relationship existed between *The Royalist* and the
Order of the White Rose which was re-constituted in 1886, not to set 'Dynasty
against Dynasty, but the True against the False ideal of Sovereignty', arguing
that 'Obedience to the Throne (without question of its occupant) must needs be
more truly rendered by those who hold it a sacred Duty, than by such as pretend
that the People gave, and that the People can take away'.[68] One contemporary
journalist put it rather differently when he wrote that the ambition of such lat-
ter-day Jacobites was 'to pack Queen Victoria off to Hanover and establish the
heiress of the Stuarts upon the throne in her stead'![69] Jenner was in 1889
Chancellor and later Recorder of the order that the same journalist dismisses as
'a sleepy society' of Jacobite 'bookworms recruited mainly from suburban draw-
ing-rooms' who 'read dreary papers on unimportant details of history, and
indulge in harmless ceremonies with parchments and rose-water.'[70] He contributed to *The Royalist* from its first appearance in April 1890, with articles
such as 'The Macdonalds at Culloden' and 'A Record Reign and a Diamond
Jubilee' being read as papers to sessions of the Order of the White Rose. The
central premiss of the latter, which was read in the French Room, St James's
Hall, on 1 June 1897, Jenner described as a reminder of ' "what might have
been", if "what hadn't ought to be", viz, the Revolution of 1688, had not been'.[71]
Two years previously the magazine had carried a long and complimentary
review of Kitty Lee's last novel *When Fortune Frowns*, which it described as '*the
novel of the Forty-five: and of the White Rose*'.[72] Another link with the family is
apparent from the obituary of Jenner's father who, though not himself a member of the Order, was 'the father, grandfather and father-in-law of members of it,
and … always took a great interest in its proceedings and was a constant reader
of THE ROYALIST'.[73]

It is clear from the pages of the magazine that the Order of the White Rose
had a hand in organising the first, at least, of a series of historical exhibitions
that were held at the New Gallery, Regent Street between 1889 and 1901–1902.
Jenner had originally suggested that the Stuart Exhibition of 1889 would be a
way of taking the wind out of the sails of those who were likely to want to
express their approval of the Glorious Revolution of 1688 – Jenner deemed it

Cover of The Royalist *magazine, November 1903*

'Inglorious' – by commemorating it. The exhibition was, therefore, intended as a glorification of the House of Stuart and, as such, was a great success. Particularly impressed one Sunday afternoon were the then Prince and Princess of Wales, later Edward VII and Queen Alexandra, and their children. 'I don't think I ever met a more satisfactory person to show things to than the prince,' wrote Jenner, 'and I have done a good deal of showman work in my time.' The family also came to the Tudor, Guelph and Victorian Exhibitions in succeeding years and in 1902, Coronation year, attended the Monarchy of Great Britain and Ireland Exhibition. Queen Victoria, herself, attended the Tudor and Guelph, but not, according to Jenner, the Stuart. 'On both occasions she was in a very good humour,' he recalled, 'and, after we had been solemnly presented, talked to us quite freely and pleasantly, but I think we were all a good deal afraid of her – she was such a very impressive person.' An entirely different slant on one of these meetings was provided by B. Waters who claimed that Queen Victoria was following the Jabobite movement closely and knew the names of its leading lights. 'One of them, a Mr Jenner,' he continued, 'was presented to her, in company with other promoters of the Stuart Exhibition, but she at once turned her back on him, saying curtly: 'I have heard of Mr Jenner.'"[74] Despite the apparent rebuff, Jenner was undoubtedly in his element on such occasions!

Other well-known individuals whose acquaintance he made during the period of the exhibitions included the historian James Anthony Froude, the Scottish man of letters Andrew Lang, who shared his interest in the Jacobite rising of 1745, and the critic Walter Pater. Jenner recalled a dinner party chez Pater, where the only other guests apart from Kitty Lee and himself, were Daniel Latbury, the editor of the *Guardian*, and Mr & Mrs Oscar Wilde. 'As you may suppose,' he wrote, 'the talk was brilliant, and, except when Stuart history came up, it was as much as I could do to hold my own. Wilde and Pater were both uncommonly good talkers and the former, whom I never met before or since, contrary to what I expected, talked seriously and was not always firing off epigrams and smart paradoxes.'[75]

Cornwall: A Celtic Nation

In the 1870s Jenner, Lach-Szyrma and many others viewed the Cornish language as antiquarians and philologists. By the beginning of the twentieth century, however, when he was once again beginning to focus more on Cornish matters, Jenner's ideas appear to have changed, although, as we shall see, in essence he would remain, until his death, ambivalent about the role of revived Cornish as a spoken language. Throughout the late nineteenth century an awareness of what had hitherto been either suppressed or forgotten concerning their history, customs, languages and literatures began to take hold among the Celtic peoples generally.[76] By 1901 a wave of this Celtic revival had at last reached Cornwall and on 15 August the *Cowethas Kelto-Kernuak* was formed. This Celtic-Cornish Society put the revival of spoken Cornish at the heart of its programme, together with the re-establishment of a 'Cornish Gorsedh of the Bards at Boscawen-Un', the preservation of Cornish antiquities and the encouragement of Cornish sports. Among its Council members were Jenner (Vice President, Cornish Language), Thurstan C. Peter, A. T. Quiller Couch and L. C. Duncombe Jewell (Secretary) who was undoubtedly the society's driving force and who had, in the mid 1890s, edited *The Royalist*.[77] Although its existence proved to be brief and Jenner himself claimed that his role did not go much beyond translating its prospectus into Cornish,[78] the Society was instrumental in bringing its members into contact with kindred spirits in Wales and Brittany, and in fostering a conviction that there really was something lasting in the Celtic Revival.

Over the years Henry Jenner had established himself as something of an authority on the Cornish Language and in September 1903 he was admitted as 'Gwaz Mikael' (Servant of Michael) to the recently formed Gorsedd of Brittany. When, many years later, he recalled the honour that had been bestowed on him, he expressed the opinion that perhaps it had been rather presumptuous of him 'to nobble the patron of all Cornwall' for himself.[79] He went on to excuse himself, however, on the grounds that he was the first native of Cornwall to be made a bard. This was not strictly true, for the historian John Hobson Matthews, Reginald Reynolds and Mrs Hettie Tangye Reynolds had all been made bards of the Welsh Gorsedd in 1899. During their time in Brittany, Henry and Kitty Lee attended the Congress of the *Union Régionaliste Bretonne* at Lesneven, Finistère as 'quite self-appointed' representatives of Cornwall. Jenner himself takes up the story:

Nothing could have been kinder and more cordial than these Bretons, all of whom, except one, with whom I had had some correspondence, he writing in Breton and I in Cornish, which he had studied, were perfect strangers to us. The case was that I knew that at the concluding dinner, I should certainly have to make a speech. I can *talk* French fairly fluently, but to make a speech in it is quite another matter, and my Breton did not extend to more than reading it and following, more or less, a distinctly spoken sermon or speech. So I made up and learnt by heart a speech in Cornish with a preliminary apology in Breton that as I could only speak bad Breton, I would therefore use the old language of my native land, Cornish. My Cornish speech took four to five minutes to deliver, and to my astonishment I found at once that the audience, only one of whom had studied Cornish, were taking all the points, applauding in the right places, and evidently understanding me fairly well.

Jenner was at pains to stress that he did not 'fake' his speech – on why Cornwall should be recognised as a Celtic country – to suit Breton, although it was possible that, having been in the midst of Breton speakers for about a fortnight, he might perhaps have caught something of the intonation unawares. As far as pronunciation was concerned, he tried to re-create that of a seventeenth century Cornishman. Before then, the language had not been officially heard for well over a century – indeed, Jenner thought that it was probably the first set speech that had been made in Cornish for two centuries.[80]

A year later Jenner travelled to Caernarfon to deliver an address entitled 'Cornwall: A Celtic Nation' to the Pan-Celtic Congress which had been established in Dublin four years previously. Hitherto, Cornwall was thought of as too Anglicised to be considered one of the Celtic nations and a formal application for membership at the second Congress in Dublin in 1901 had been rejected by 34 votes to 22. Since then, however, leading members of the *Cowethas Kelto-Kernuak* had worked hard to impress upon their fellow Celts that Cornish was not dead and that enough people spoke it as a revived language for Cornwall to be considered a Celtic country. Indeed, Duncombe Jewell revealed that since the Congress he had been overwhelmed by applications for membership of the *Cowethas Kelto-Kernuak* and by offers of subscriptions towards publishing 'the new Grammar and Dictionary'.[81] In his paper, which was published in *The Celtic Review* in January 1905, Jenner presented a

potted history of Cornwall, drawing particular attention to events that underlined its separateness:

> There can be no question that as Scotsmen, Irishmen, Welshmen, and
> Manxmen recognize, quite apart from governments and jurisdictions,
> their separate nationality from Englishmen, so do the Cornish, only per-
> haps more so.[82]

Having established that Cornwall was indeed a nation, he needed to prove
that she was a Celtic nation in accordance with the linguistic criterion of the
Congress. He defined a Celtic nation as 'one which, mainly composed of persons of Celtic blood and possessing Celtic characteristics, and having once had
a separate national existence, has preserved a separate Celtic language and literature' and proceeded to present arguments to show that Cornwall fulfilled all
these conditions. He concluded his presentation of the facts and of his own
understanding of Cornwall's status by tracing the work that had been done to
preserve the language from about 1700 up to the present day when he himself
had the last word with his *Handbook of the Cornish Language*, which he described
as having 'just now appeared'. As far as the future was concerned, Jenner introduced his customary note of caution:

> I do not say that they [the Cornish] are likely to introduce it as a spoken
> language to the exclusion of English, but I think a good many of those
> who do not know it will repair that defect, and will learn certainly to
> read it, probably to write, and possibly to speak it.[83]

His impassioned arguments for Cornwall's inclusion were seconded by the
Revs Percy Treasure and W. S. Lach-Szyrma and when it came to the vote, the
majority of delegates at the Congress supported the motion and Cornwall was
admitted to membership on 31 August.[84] The following day a delighted Jenner
produced a telegram of congratulations in Cornish from Dr Hambley Rowe
that read:

> Hutyc [huthyk?] of godhfos Kernow hy bos drehedhys arte the y wyn

[wyr?] trig un mysc tues Celtic. Yn on [ow?] colon assyw lowene. Kernow bis vicken. Tintagel byth agan cres agan fenten a breder! Onan hag ol – J. H. R.

[*Happy am I to know that Cornwall is raised again to its true place amongst Cornish people. What a joy in my heart. Cornwall forever. May Tintagel be our centre, our fountain of the brothers! One and all.– J. H. R.*][85]

'If the Post Office can send that by wire in Cornish, then Cornish cannot be a dead language,' cried Jenner to his fellow Celts amid vociferous applause.[86] At the plenary meeting of the Congress at Caernarfon Guildhall on the Friday evening, Jenner sang the Cornish version of the Welsh anthem Hen Wlad fy Nhadau (Land of my Fathers) that had been adopted as the anthem of the Celtic peoples. And on the following day, 'attired in a Gorsedd robe, and carrying the Cornish flag', he directed – in Cornish – the removal of the topmost fragment of the Lia Cineil (Logan Stone) that had been added three days earlier in honour of Cornwall's admission to the fold.[87]

A Handbook of the Cornish Language

The decision of the Congress must have come as a boost to Jenner's recently published *Handbook* ... which had been publicised in the *Cornish Telegraph* six months previously when Hambley Rowe had appealed to readers of *Notes and Queries* to do their bit for the language by subscribing and endeavouring to get their friends to do the same.[88] The response was encouraging, coming, as it did, from all classes of the community. Jenner was particularly pleased that he had received so many letters from clerks, small businessmen, shopkeepers and workmen – those he described as 'the classes that form the backbone of Cornish Methodism...'[89] It was at the suggestion of Dr Hambley Rowe that the *Cowethas Kelto-Kernuak* had asked Jenner to make the learning of Cornish a more realistic proposition by producing a grammar. As we have seen, this request came at a time when he had long since dropped his Cornish studies, with the result that much of what he once knew had been forgotten and had had to be re-learnt. As well as providing an outline of Cornish grammar based on the language found in sources written between c.1558 and the end of the eighteenth century (Late Cornish) and chapters on versification and the interpretation of Cornish names, the *Handbook* set out all that was known at the time about the history and literature of Cornish 'for those persons of Cornish nationality who wish to acquire some knowledge of their ancient tongue, and to read, write, and perhaps even to speak it'.[90] Although it has long since been superseded as a manual, it did encourage others to learn the language.

A.S.D. Smith later criticised the *Handbook* for failing 'to give enough of the language itself for the learner to get a real grip of it',[91] but, to be fair to Jenner, he had intended to add some reading lessons, exercises and vocabularies, but had found that their inclusion would have made the book too long. In order to make it more complete as a means of instruction, he hoped to issue a small book containing these elements, together with conversations.[92] A complete vocabulary was also planned, but neither came to fruition, partly because the *Handbook*'s publisher, his friend Alfred Nutt, was, in Jenner's words, 'the most unbusinesslike man that I ever met with' and produced a book that was too sumptuous for the agreed price.[93] There were no profits and author and publisher alike were probably out of pocket. Another factor was the uncertainty surrounding the future of the *Cowethas Kelto-Kernuak*. In response to a question in the *Cornish Telegraph* as to whether or not the society was still in existence, Jenner confirmed that it was not dead. However, owing to illness and a variety of other circumstances, the secretary, Mr Duncombe Jewell, had found himself unable to continue his work and had asked him to act as temporary secretary. 'As I am rather a busy man and do not live in Cornwall,' continued Jenner, 'I should be very glad if someone would take the work off my hands.'[94] On the language front, though, Jenner did his best to encourage those who had already started to learn the language, from time to time sending Cornish verse to local newspapers in order to provide students with something new. He also wrote to them in Cornish.[95] The publication of the *Handbook* certainly put Jenner at the forefront of the Pan-Celtic movement. It would be a few years, though, before he would be free to devote himself completely to the homeland.

The Local Patriot
On his retirement from the British Museum in May 1909, Jenner returned to Cornwall where he and his wife bought a house near Kitty Lee's family home in Hayle, naming it 'Bospowes' (House of Peace). He promptly joined in the activ-

ities of those societies concerned with Cornwall's past or tending to draw Cornish people together in a common interest.[96] In due course he would make many of their scattered studies 'one in the university of his own mind', as Pearce so succinctly put it,[97] and 'Bospowes' would become the hub of the burgeoning Cornish movement. In these pre-'Old Cornwall', pre-Gorsedd days, the main instigators of research were the Royal Institution of Cornwall and the Royal Cornwall Polytechnic Society. Jenner joined the former in 1909, was elected a Council member in 1911, served as its secretary between 1912 and 1920 and its president from 1922 to 1923, as well as being the editor of its journal from 1919 until his death. In a move that echoed his earlier criticism of the Ordnance Survey, he proposed at the Institution's annual meeting in December 1909 that it should 'take some steps towards promoting a systematic general survey and collection of Cornish place and family names, with a view to their correct interpretation'.[98] Much of his research on the subject, together with his mixed views on the language revival, is contained in 'Cornish place names' in which he wrote:

> Our old language is gone and we cannot revive it as a spoken language, but its ghost still haunts its old dwelling and we cannot talk much about the county or its inhabitants without using plenty of Cornish words, so that in a sense we do talk some of it still.[99]

Jenner's ambivalence resurfaced in 1912 when the *Western Morning News* for 8 January carried a report of a paper on the Cornish language that had been read by Dr F. V. Bice at St Columb Institute – a report which also mentioned that Jenner had referred to 'the revival of Cornish as a spoken language'. His reply, printed in the next day's issue of the newspaper, constituted his most unequivocal and forthright statement to date concerning the revival:

> Sir,
>
> Please let me correct a mis-statement in the paragraph in today's 'West of England Views' on Dr Bice's lecture on the Cornish language at St Columb. I did not say a single word in any way referring to 'the revival of Cornish as a spoken language'. I cannot imagine what I can have said to lead your reporter to think that I was referring to anything

so fantastic and impossible. Most of my remarks were about its survival in the form of place-names and I recommended the study of the language from that point of view as an interesting and perhaps a patriotic subject for Cornish people.

Hayle, January 8th.[100]

In spite of such outbursts, Jenner never let slip an opportunity to inform the world of the existence of a Cornish language. When, for example, in 1916 the *Daily Mirror* published the soldiers' marching song 'It's a long way to Tipperary' in the languages of the Empire, he supplied a Cornish version.[101] Similarly he provided a Cornish version of the text of St John's Gospel, chapter 5, verses 1–14 which, in various languages, used to line the walls of the entrance porch of the Pool of Bethesda in Jerusalem.[102] 'I shall feel very proud if a translation of mine shall find a place in the Holy City,' he wrote on 10 January 1919 to Donald Attwater who had suggested that a Cornish version be added.[103] By 1921, he was optimistic that before long he would be able to converse in Cornish with Robert Morton Nance, a fellow member of the Royal Institution of Cornwall.[104]

Jenner became a member of the Royal Cornwall Polytechnic Society in 1911 and was elected a vice-president the following year and honorary librarian and editor of its journal in 1913. In the course of returning thanks for the honour of being elected president on 15 February 1916, he promised not to be an ornamental president, but one who would try to do as much as he could for the Society, for in so doing he would be serving Cornwall – something that every Cornishman must always wish to do.[105] In 1919 he was re-elected for another term and at the Society's meetings between those years he also carried out the duties of the secretary who was away on war service. The Society published his research on a number of subjects. Other bodies that benefited from his scholarly guidance included the local branch of the Society of Antiquaries, the Cornwall Music Competitions, the Cornwall Folk Dance Society, the County Wrestling Association, the County Committee charged with the preservation of Cornwall's ancient monuments and the Penzance Library where the naturalist and writer W.H. Hudson saw him every week. 'He is an interesting man,' wrote Hudson in February 1920, 'and knows more than anyone else in the universe about Cornish history and antiquities and language.'[106] Another feature of Jenner's work at this period was his encouragement of younger workers, notably Charles Henderson, who from boyhood profited from his friendship, and Robert Morton Nance who considered himself the recipient, over a period of twenty years, of 'quite literally all his [Jenner's] knowledge of Cornish'.[107]

As one of the leaders of a 'revivalist' movement, Jenner was ever keen to foster in his fellow Cornish 'the sentiment of local patriotism'.[108] He was, however, totally opposed to any wider political expression of Celtic nationalism. His response, for instance, to the call of Irish and Welsh delegates attending the Celtic Conference at Birkenhead in September 1917 for 'Celtic Union' was unequivocal:

> I am sure that if it keeps clear of all taint of politics, as I am confident that it will, Cornwall will be happy to join in...[109]

Seven years later a report of an address that he made to Truro Rotary Club made his position amply clear and echoed what he had written in the preface to his *Handbook*:

> After discussing what nationality amounts to, he said that Cornwall, by reason of its history, its position, and its individuality, had every bit as much right to call itself a nation as had Scotland, Wales, and England. In saying that he was not advocating Cornish independence, or even 'Cornish Home Rule', nor did he wish to translate the Irish words Sinn Fein into Cornish – their version of them was 'One & All', a better motto ...[110]

Bilbao and 'Bospowes'

The Jenners' appetite for foreign travel continued unabated after 1918, even though Henry was now in his 70s. Kitty Lee was five years his junior. In February 1919 he was considering the possibility of visiting Egypt in order that Kitty Lee might bathe at what is now Hulwān, near Cairo, where there were said to be healing waters good for rheumatism and gout. 'Do you know the place? and is it a pleasant place to stay at?' he inquired of Donald Attwater with his customary eye for detail. 'Are the hotels good and not too prohibitive in price? Or would it be better to stay in Cairo and go there by train for the baths?' So as to be able to 'play about with the Coptic Church and its Liturgy' during the planned stay, he was, he revealed, learning Coptic. For a 70-year-old, though, it was no easy task, his memory not being what it was.[111]

Of the six holidays they enjoyed abroad in this period, the most significant as far as Cornish is concerned took place in 1924. 'It occurred to me,' Jenner explained to the autumn meeting of the R.I.C. on his return, 'that I might as well go and see it [the Cornish Manuscript at Bilbao] myself. I do not mean to say that I went all the way to Bilbao and back for nothing else, but I thought that west-French cathedrals and the Pyrenees would make very good objects for our holiday of this year, and having got as far as the Spanish frontier, it was not far to go to get to Bilbao...'[112] Leaving Kitty Lee at San Sebastian, he duly set off for 'the rather unattractive seaport' that housed the manuscript. Once there, he had a rather curious experience:

> The librarians were most kind and let me examine the ms. as long as I liked – I had four hours of it – but they could talk nothing but Spanish, and I, though I can read it readily enough to enjoy Spanish novels, had never heard it spoken or tried to speak it till the day before. I found myself always trying to run off into Italian, which is more misleading than you would think. But we got along somehow with good humour, and smiles.[113]

The momentum in the re-awakening of the Cornish people to a sense of their nationhood and their cultural and linguistic difference was sustained throughout the 1920s and came to a climax with the establishment in 1928 of the Cornish Gorsedd, the story of which is told elsewhere in this volume. The extent to which 'Bospowes' was throughout the 1920s and early 1930s a magnet for those involved in the Cornish revival is evident from Erma Harvey James' recollections. It was here, too, that Jenner, ensconced in the study that according to Mrs James contained 'a delirious selection of books',[114] could indulge his passion for reading. 'Everyone has a right to a certain amount of enjoyment and amusement in life,' he wrote round about this time, 'and if one pleases to take it out in reading novels instead of going to theatres, cinemas, or concerts, playing bridge, chess, cricket, tennis or golf or looking on at football matches – none of which happens to appeal to me much – why not?' He had even written a novel himself at the age of 19, 'though luckily it was never published'.[115] Although nothing matched the golden age of the Victorian novel, he was keen to keep up with modern trends and developed a liking for 'fantastic impossible stories made convincing like those of Jules Verne and H. G. Wells'. He loathed what he called the propaganda or problem novels that were becoming increasingly common in the mid 1920s. In 'Novel Reading [with some Reminiscences]' he revealed how he had taken home one by G. K. Chesterton, normally a most amusing writer and, as Jenner had discovered when the author had taken tea with them in 1926, equally amusing as a conversationalist. 'The moral of this book,' he complained, 'was the evils of capitalism and that all the really good people in the story must necessarily become Catholics. I have no objection to the second proposition,[116] but I don't want it in a novel, and the first proposition is simply boring...' The current fad for detective stories, he thought, would be short-lived because, before long, everyone would have discovered 'the trick' and would know how it was done. In spite of his criticism of some aspects of modern novels, he asserted in 1927 that he fully intended to go on reading them for as long as his eyesight would allow him.[117]

A Gorsedd too far

Jenner's decline in the early 1930s is chronicled in the minutes of both Hayle Old Cornwall Society[118] and the Gorsedd Council.[119] He was unable, for health reasons, to attend the AGM of the former on 16 March 1931, although he had recovered sufficiently to chair the members' evening on 22 April and a Gorsedd Council meeting at 'Bospowes' three weeks later. He was unable to make the journey to Trencrom to be present at the annual mid-Summer bonfire in 1933, but was well enough to witness another landmark event. On Sunday 27 August the first church service in Cornish for 250 years was held at Towednack. Organised by the first Cornish Youth Movement, Tyr ha Tavas (Land and Language), with the assistance of the Rev L.V. Jolly, it used a Cornish version by Morton Nance of the Form of Evening Prayer from the Anglican Prayer Book. The congregation that took part in this service in which everything was in Cornish was a large one, consisting of Cornish folk from many parts and of all denominations.[120] Jenner would later emphasise how much importance he attached to Tyr ha Tavas and its work:

> When I reflect on the Tyr Ha Tavas, the Land and Language, movement, I feel that my work has not been in vain. What I have been trying to do, that movement will carry still further. The service they held at Towednack was attended with remarkable success, as you know. That, I believe, is a good sign. If there is one thing that I should like to say before I die, it is that I hope the Tyr Ha Tavas will prosper.[121]

His attendance at both the church service and the Gorsedd at Roche Rock on an inclement afternoon proved too much for the Grand Bard, as he himself acknowledged:

> The Gorsedd did it in the beginning. It is that – the crown of my labours – which has meant my end. I should not have gone, but I could not resist it.[122]

He was 'too fatigued' to take part in the annual meeting of bards[123] and rheumatism kept him in bed for several days. Thereafter, his health began to fail and during his final six months he was attended by two nurses from the Blue Nuns order. The chair at the Hayle Old Cornwall Society meeting on 20 November was taken by Mr C. Ellis 'in the absence of Mr Jenner who was seriously ill'. The Society's minutes for 18 December mention 'the continued serious illness of our esteemed President' and on 6 January 1934 a committee meeting was called '…to consider the advisability of cancelling or postponing the Federation social owing to the grave illness of Mr Jenner'.[124] At a Gorsedd meeting a month later the secretary, Walter Eva, was instructed to write to him in order to convey the Council's sympathy.[125]

During the past decade Cornish had come more and more into use in writing, speech and print, and Jenner lived just long enough to see the publication, in April, of *Kernow*, the first Cornish language magazine. On Tuesday 8 May he sank into a coma and died at home at 11pm. Requiem Mass was celebrated on the morning of Saturday 12 May at St Michael's Roman Catholic church. When the coffin containing 'Cornwall's foremost patriot' left the church, the sword of the Cornish Gorsedd was placed upon it and members of the Gorsedd, of Old Cornwall Societies and of many learned institutions from all over Cornwall accompanied it to Lelant Cemetery.[126]

Notes

1. Henry Jenner (1932) 'Old Cornwall' in *The Western Morning News* 31 December.
2. *The Cornishman & Cornish Telegraph* 9 May 1934.
3. A.S.D. Smith (1947) *The Story of the Cornish Language: its extinction and revival*, Camborne: Camborne Printing & Stationery Co. Ltd., p.13.
4. R. Morton Nance (1935) 'The Jenner Memorial Fund' in *Old Cornwall* vol. 2, no. 9, Summer 1935, p.40.
5. J[oseph] H[ambley] R[owe] and R[obert] M[orton] N[ance] (1934) 'Henry Jenner, M.A., F.S.A.' in *Royal Cornwall Polytechnic Society* 101st Annual Report, new series vol. 8 1934, p. 59.
6. Brian Sullivan (1984) 'Hayle Old Cornwall Society and Henry Jenner' in *Old Cornwall* vol. 9, no. 11, Autumn 1984, p.522.
7. 'Royal Institution of Cornwall, Annual Meeting 1921: The New President' in *Journal of the Royal Institution of Cornwall* vol. 21 (Pts. 69–72), 1922–25, p. 28.
8. Ibid. The name itself, found in early forms as L'Ingenieur, Le Geneur, Gynner and various other spellings, is of Norman-French origin and means 'architect' or 'engineer'. Jenner researched his family's history throughout his life, committing genealogies, cuttings and correspondence with relatives to a notebook that is now in the possession of Mary Beazley, Kitty Lee Jenner's step-niece. See also Henry Jenner (1917) '[Portrait Gallery] III Henry Jenner, F.S.A., President, 1916' in *Royal Cornwall Polytechnic Society* 84th Annual Report, new series vol. 3, 1917, pp. 165–166.
9. For full details of the career of Henry Lascelles Jenner see John Pearce's introduction to *Seeking a See: a Journal of The Rt. Revd. Henry Lascelles Jenner D. D. of his visit to Dunedin, New Zealand in 1868–1869*, Dunedin: Standing Committee of the Diocese of Dunedin, 1984.
10. Charles Dickens (1957) *Sketches by Boz*, Oxford: O.U.P., p. 86.
11. Thomas Ingoldsby (Rev Richard Harris Barham) (1890) *The Ingoldsby Legends*, 4th edition, London: Ward, Lock & Co., p. 266.
12. Pearce (1984), p. 18.
13. Henry Jenner, 'Some Reminiscences of Notable People', unpublished (?) lecture, Nance Collection Box 3: Jenner Essays and Lectures, Courtney Library, Truro. In his 'Recollections of Henry Jenner' (*An Baner Kernewek* 34, November 1983), E. G. R. Hooper asserts that Mr Palme[r] of the *Western Morning News* persuaded Jenner to write about his *Handbook* and the people he had met at the British Museum and enquires, 'I wonder if anyone has these news cuttings?'
14. Pearce (1984), p. 25.
15. Jenner, 'Some Reminiscences of Notable People'.
16. Ibid.
17. Henry Jenner, 'Foreign Travel', unpublished lecture, Nance Collection Box 3: Jenner Essays and Lectures, Courtney Library, Truro.
18. These diaries form part of Mary Beazley's Jenner archive.
19. R. Morton Nance (1934) ' "Gwas Myghal" and the Cornish Revival' in *Old Cornwall* vol. 2, no. 8, Winter 1934, p. 1; R. Morton Nance (1958) 'Cornish Beginnings' in *Old Cornwall* vol. 5, no. 9, 1958, p. 368.
20. *Journal of the Royal Institution of Cornwall*, 1922–25, p. 29.
21. Ibid.

22. The Revd. Jenner was consecrated only to discover that there was disagreement in the diocese over his appointment and that he was not wanted. Although he visited his see in 1868–9, he eventually resigned any claims to it on 16 June 1871. It is clear from correspondence in the Canterbury Cathedral Archives that the 'old controversy' – in particular the question of his late father's richly jewelled, silver and ivory coloured crosier – was still a major issue for Henry Jenner and for his mother and sisters in 1900. For the background to the controversy, see Pearce (1984). See also 'A Bishop Resurrected' in *Outlook*, December 2001, p. 5.

23. Jenner, 'Some Reminiscences of Notable People'; Pearce (1984), pp. 37–38.

24. Henry Jenner (1928) *Who are the Celts and what has Cornwall to do with them?* St Ives: Federation of Old Cornwall Societies, p. 28.

25. Henry Jenner (1921) *The Preservation of Ancient Monuments*, Falmouth: 'Cornish Echo', p. 2.

26. Jenner, 'Foreign Travel'.

27. Ibid.

28. Pearce (1984), p. 81.

29. Jenner, 'Some Reminiscences of Notable People'

30. Ibid.

31. Nance (1958), p. 368.

32. Ibid; Jenner, 'Some reminiscences of Notable People'. On his application form for the post of Senior Assistant in the British Museum, Jenner specified that he could read, write and speak French, read and write Latin, Greek, Spanish and German, and had some knowledge of Italian, Hebrew and Persian. I am grateful to David Everett for supplying me with this information.

33. Henry Jenner (1873–74) 'The Cornish Language' in *Transactions of the Philological Society*, 1873–74, Pt. 1, pp. 165–186.

34. Henry Jenner (1953) 'A Dead Language' in *Old Cornwall* vol. 5, no. 4, Winter 1953, p. 159.

35. Jenner, 'Some Reminiscences of Notable People'.

36. See Margaret Perry (2000) 'Eminent Westcountryman, Honorary Cornishman' in *Journal of the Royal Institution of Cornwall*, new series 2, vol. 3, pts. 3 and 4, 2000, pp. 154–167.

37. Jenner, 'Foreign Travel'; David Everett (2001) The Celtic Revival and the Anglican Church in Cornwall from 1870 – 1930, M.A. Dissertation, University of Wales, Lampeter, p. 4.

38. Henry Jenner (1875–6) 'The Manx Language: its grammar, literature and present state' in *Transactions of the Philological Society*, 1875–6, pp. 172–197.

39. Henry Jenner (1875–6) 'Traditional relics of the Cornish language in Mount's Bay in 1875' in *Transactions of the Philological Society*, 1875–6, pp. 533–542.

40. Henry Jenner (1877) 'The History and Literature of the Ancient Cornish Language' in *Journal of the British Archaeological Association*, June 1877, p. 145.

41. Peter Pool (1975) *The Death Of Cornish (1600–1800)*, Penzance: Peter Pool, p. 30. For the position of Cornish in the 19th century, see also P. Berresford Ellis (1974) *The Cornish Language and its Literature*, London: Routledge & Kegan Paul, pp. 125–146; A. S. D. Smith & E. G. Retallack Hooper (1969) *The Story of the Cornish Language*, Camborne: An Lef Kernewek, pp. 15–18; Craig Weatherhill (1995) *Cornish Place Names and Language*, Wilmslow: Sigma Leisure, pp. 147–149; [Kenneth MacKinnon] (2000) *An Independent Academic Study on Cornish*, SGRUD Research, http://www.gosw.gov.uk/Publications/Independent_Cornish_Language_Study, accessed 21 December 2003.

42. Jenner (1877) p.145.

43. Ibid.

44. Of Borlase's subsequent change of career, Jenner had this to say: '[I]n an evil hour in 1880 he was persuaded to take up politics and go into Parliament – such a waste of a good man…' Jenner (1921), p. 3.

45. G. C. Boase and W. P. Courtney (1882) *Bibliotheca Cornubiensis* ... Supplementary Catalogue ... and Index vol. 3, London: Longmans, Green, Reader & Dye.
46. Ellis (1974), p. 143.
47. Rawlings took a keen interest in the Cornish dialect and supplied information to phonologist A. J. Ellis. See Martyn F. Wakelin (1975) *Language and history in Cornwall*, Leicester: Leicester University Press, p. 29.
48. Jenner, 'Foreign Travel'.
49. Diary in the possession of Mary Beazley.
50. Henry Jenner (1877) 'An early Cornish fragment' in *The Athenaeum*, December 1877, pp. 698–699.
51 Nance (1934), p. 2.
52. Ellis (1974), p. 145.
53. Henry Jenner (1904) *A Handbook of the Cornish Language*, London: Nutt, p. xiii. With the exception of 'Cornwall in 1715' which was published in *The Royalist* in 1890, there would be no more substantial Cornish-interest articles until 1902.
54. Royston Green [c. 1980] *The National Question in Cornwall* (Our History 74), History Group of the Communist Party, p. 23.
55. Cecily Katharine Ysolt, the Jenners' only child, was born on 21 June, 1878. Katharine Lee Jenner's diary for that year contains a vivid description of her feelings at the time of her daughter's birth.
56. P. R. Harris (1998) *A History of the British Library, 1753–1973*, London: British Library, p. 368.
57. Diary of Katharine Lee Jenner.
58. Harris (1998), p. 369; Diary of Katharine Lee Jenner
59. Jenner, 'Foreign Travel'; Diary of Katharine Lee Jenner
60. Jenner, 'Foreign Travel'
61. H[enry] J[enner] (1894) 'Three Days in a Legitimate Monarchy' in *The Royalist*, vol. 5, no. 6, September 1894, pp. 89–93.
62. Jenner, 'Foreign Travel'.
63. Ibid. It is clear from the pages of *The Royalist* that Jenner's knowledge of Scottish Gaelic became substantial. Indeed, the anonymous author of an article about an Order of the White Rose evening in June 1898 asks: 'When will some competent person – Mr Henry Jenner for choice, who not only "has the Gaelic", but the poetic faculty besides – give us some accessible edition of the poetical and musical Jacobitism of the Highlands?' See 'A Session of Song' in *The Royalist*, vol. 9, no. 2, July 1898, p. 25.
64. Henry Jenner, Letter to the Archbishop of Canterbury 19 July 1900, cited in Heather Eva (1970), [*Henry Jenner, librarian and Cornishman*]? A.L.A. dissertation submitted to the College of Librarianship Wales, p. 16.
65. Jenner, 'Some Reminiscences of Notable People'.
66. Obituary in *The Library Association Record*, June 1934, p. 184.
67. Jenner (1917), p. 167.
68. *The Royalist* vol. 12, no. 4, April 1905, p. 82; *The Royalist* vol. 5, no. 9, December 1894, p. 131.
69. B. Waters 'New Kings on Old Thrones' in *Pearson's Magazine*, February 1898, http://homepage.ntlworld.com/forgottenfutures/kings/kings.htm, accessed 10 December 2003.
70. *The Royalist* vol. 13, September 1905, p. 49; Waters (1898).
71. H[enry] J[enner] 'A Record Reign and a Diamond Jubilee' in *The Royalist* vol. 8, no. 2, July 1897, p. 19.
72. *The Royalist* vol. 6, no. 1, April 1895, p. 19.
73. *The Royalist* vol. 9, no. 3, November 1898, p. 35.
74. *The Royalist* vol. 13 September 1905, p. 49; Waters (1898).
75. Jenner, 'Some Reminiscences of Notable People'.
76. Ellis (1974), p. 151.
77. *Celtia*, vol. 2, no. 5, May 1902, pp. 78–79.
78. Jenner (1917), p. 167.

79. Henry Jenner (1928) 'The Gorsedd of Boscawen-Un' in *Old Cornwall*, no. 7, April 1928, p. 5.
80. Henry Jenner (1910) 'Cornish Place-Names. A lecture given at the Truro Church Institute, 6 December 1910', Nance Collection Box 3: Jenner Essays and Lectures, Courtney Library, Truro; Henry Jenner (1905) 'Cornwall: A Celtic Nation' in *The Celtic Review*, 16 January 1905, p. 245; H[enry] J[enner], 'A Recent Speech in Cornish' in Peter Penn (ed) (1906) *Cornish Notes & Queries*, Penzance: Cornish Telegraph, p. 106.
81. *Celtia*, vol. 1, no. 9, September 1901.
82. Jenner (1905), p. 236.
83. Ibid, p. 245.
84. *Celtia*, vol. 4, no. 6, Congress Number 1904, p. 102.
85. 'Telegram to the Pan-Celtic Congress' in Penn (ed) (1906), p. 117; Hugh Miners and Treve Crago (2002) *Tolzethan: The Life and Times of Joseph Hambley Rowe*, Cornwall: Gorseth Kernow, p. 16.
86. *Celtia*, 1904, p. 109.
87. Ibid, p. 108. 'Lia Cineil' literally means 'tribal or racial stone'.
88. J. Hambley Rowe (1903) 'Jenner's Cornish Grammar' in the *Cornish Telegraph*, 2 December 1903. My own copy of the *Handbook* bears the inscription: 'Auntie Lil from Harry 23.7.03.'
89. Jenner (1905), pp. 245–246.
90. Jenner (1904), p. ix.
91. Smith (1947), p. 13.
92. Jenner (1904), p. xvi.
93. Henry Jenner, 'Projects and suggestions for a Cornish Dictionary. Presidential Address to the St Ives Old Cornwall Society', Unpublished lecture, Nance Collection Box 3: Jenner Essays and Lectures, Courtney Library, Truro.
94. Henry Jenner, 'The Cornish Celtic Society … still in Existence' in Penn (ed) (1906) p. 125.
95. Nance (1934), p. 4.
96. Ibid.
97. Pearce (1984), p. 15.
98. Henry Jenner (1910–11) 'Cornish place-names' in *Journal of the Royal Institution of Cornwall*, vol. 18, 1910–11, p. 140.
99. Jenner (1910).
100. Brian Murdoch (1992) 'Henry Jenner in a Scottish Library' in *An Baner Kernewek* 68, May 1992, p. 23.
101. Ellis (1974), p. 157.
102. Donald Attwater (1961) 'Cornish in Jerusalem' in *Old Cornwall* vol. 6, no. 1, Autumn 1961, p. 39.
103. Henry Jenner, Letter to Donald Attwater in the latter's *A Handbook of the Cornish Language* in the Morrab Library, Penzance.
104. *Journal of the Royal Institution of Cornwall*, 1922–25, p. 29.
105. Rowe and Nance (1934), p. 61.
106. *Letters from W. H. Hudson to Edward Garnett*, London: Dent, 1925, p. 199. I am grateful to Audrey Pool for supplying me with this reference. The Jenner Room for Celtic Studies at the Penzance Library was opened on 2 December, 1995.
107. Nance (1934), p. 4.
108. This phrase occurs again and again in Jenner's writings.
109. Henry Jenner 'The Present Position and Prospects of Celtic-Cornish Studies in Cornwall' in D. Rhys Phillips (ed), (1917) *The Celtic Conference, 1917: Report of the Meetings held at Birkenhead, September 3–5…*, Perth: Milne, Tannahill & Methuen, p. 114.
110. *People's Weekly* 23 August 1924, cited in Philip Payton [1993] *The Making of Modern Cornwall*, Redruth: Truran, p. 160.

111. Henry Jenner, Letter to Donald Attwater dated 8 February 1919, Morrab Library, Penzance. There is no indication that the planned visit was ever made. There is certainly no mention of it in 'Foreign Travel'. I am grateful to Catherine Rachel John for drawing my attention to Jenner's letters to her father.

112. Henry Jenner (1925) 'The Cornish Manuscript in the Provincial Library at Bilbao in Spain' in *Journal of the Royal Institution of Cornwall*, vol. 31, 1925, pp. 423–424.

113. Jenner, 'Foreign Travel'.

114. Erma Harvey James (1976) *A Grain of Sand*, London: William Kimber, p. 71. Erma Harvey James' description of a visit to 'Bospowes' is reprinted elsewhere in this volume.

115. Henry Jenner, 'Novel Reading, with some Reminiscences', Unpublished lecture, Nance Collection Box 3: Jenner Essays and Lectures, Courtney Library, Truro.

116. Chesterton became a Roman Catholic in 1922 and Jenner himself, always of High Church views, was received into the faith a few months before his death.

117. Jenner, 'Novel Reading…'

118 Sullivan (1984), pp. 523–525.

119. The Gorsedd Kernow Archive Survey [n.d.] *A Summary of the Minutes of the Cornish Gorsedd (August 1928–September 1939)*, passim.

120. Ellis (1974), p. 166.

121. *Cornishman*, 9 May 1934.

122. Ibid.

123. Miners (1978), p. 26.

124. Sullivan (1984), p. 524.

125. The Gorsedd Kernow Archive Survey, p. 12.

126. *Royal Cornwall Gazette* 9 and 16 May 1934.

Visiting 'Bospowes'

From Erma Harvey James' *A Grain of Sand* (London: William Kimber, 1976)

Erma Harvey James, author of A Grain of Sand: Memories of a Cornish Childhood, *describes 'Bospowes', near Hayle in Cornwall, the house Henry and Katharine Jenner retired to in 1909. She was about five when she, her mother and her elder sister arrived in Hayle from Liverpool late one summer evening in 1920. A week later they moved into a cottage 'in the hills behind the town', a cottage that looked out over Copperhouse Pool to Rivière House directly opposite. Her mother always referred to the world beyond their garden gate as 'the Outside' and divided its inhabitants into 'Very fine people' and 'Rotters', amongst whom she placed all the neighbours. It is not surprising, therefore, that the family 'didn't fit in, simply didn't belong'. One of the few visitors to cross the cottage's threshold was Father Berry, the Vicar of St Elwyn's, Hayle, where the family worshipped. One day he brought with him another clergyman, a Mr Doble 'who at that time was diverting congregations at Redruth where he was curate, with stories of the Celtic Saints and early missionaries'[1] and who would later acquire an international reputation as a hagiographer.*

Mr Doble I felt sure had not liked my mother smoking and he certainly didn't like me,[2] but something of interest to him must have transpired for very soon after his visit we were all invited to tea at the Jenners' house on Foundry Hill. To my surprise my mother made considerable preparation for this event, even going to the length of removing the tell-tale stains of nicotine from her fingers. And when the actual afternoon arrived both she and Mabel wore gloves and straw hats trimmed with little glazed fruits and I was crammed into cherry-red and new shoes with steel buckles.

Henry Jenner looked like Michel Angelo's 'God creating Adam' from the ceiling of the Sistine Chapel, of which I had seen a photograph in *My Magazine*. He came out of his study into the hall as the black-and-white cap-and-apron maid opened the front door, and shook hands with me as well as with my mother and Mabel which pleased me, and looked down from what seemed to be a great height. My attention however was almost immediately diverted from his magnificence by the (to me totally unexpected) behaviour of the maid who had moved away and was now standing in an open doorway behind us apparently reciting, and I suddenly realised that we were being announced!

Mrs Jenner, the novelist and poet Katherine Lee, was a small kind-looking lady with tortoiseshell combs in her hair. Mr Doble was there and a tall very fine looking young man who turned out to be Charles Henderson the historian,[3] already regarded as a successor of Borlase and Carew, and a dark woman wearing Liberty silk and a lorgnette on a long chain which flashed whenever she raised it.

It was still an age in which children were expected to be seen and not heard and to speak only when spoken to, and apart from Mrs Jenner's, 'would you like to sit here by me dear?', no one took the slightest notice of me; which was really just as well, for in addition to my unfortunate stammer, now doubly unfortunate, considering Mr Doble's presence, I usually only heard about half of what was said to me.

The talk was principally about the recently formed Old Cornwall Society[4] and Charles Henderson's new appointment to the University of the South-West at Exeter and the great Parochial History on which he was working and Mrs Jenner's recently published book of poems *Songs of the Stars and Sea*.[5] When tea was over Mrs Jenner asked me to ring the bell for the maid to come and clear away; she had to repeat it twice. My new shoes were beginning to hurt; and in addition, the leather soles unworn until today squeaked as I walked, sent up at each painful step a high-pitched rasping note. Unaware of the glory of scholarship which was blazing above the porcelain and the seed-cake like an untempered light, I made for the bell-pull conscious only of the sound of my own footsteps and the dangers of the journey to the far side of the room. First I had

'Bospowes', Hayle, Cornwall, July 1972.
Former home of Henry and Katharine Jenner.
By permission of Brian Sullivan

to negotiate Charles Henderson's considerable length which stretched like a perilous reef across the carpet from one end of the sofa, and then I was afraid of colliding with the table itself with its load of silver and egg-shell china, or worse still with the fragile cake-stand which at one point loomed up straight ahead of me.

As I crossed the beautiful room, out of the corner of one eye I saw the lorgnette flash like a signal at sea, heard far off, the question 'And where does she go to school?'

Presently the conversation took a turn which quite interested me for I heard one of my favourite fairy tales mentioned. They were talking of the widespread primitive belief in the relation between name and destiny. As well as *Rumpelstiltskin* there were other stories in which power could only be broken by the discovery of a secret name.

There was a Cornish folk-tale where the Devil or Bucca-boo sang a song ending:

> Tomorrow she shall ride with me,
> Over land and over sea,
> Far away! Far away!
> For she can never know
> That my name is Tarraway!

There was even an Orcadian version,

> Little kens my dame at hame
> That Whuppity Stoorie is my name.

On my mother quoting these lines Mrs Jenner asked her how the words were spelt and Mr Doble rashly attempted to say them. I would never have attempted it myself and was delighted to hear his struggles with the funny little name. It was at this point that 'talking of stories' and taking pity on the apparently deaf mute by her side that Mrs Jenner asked me if I would like to look at some books and without waiting for a reply, briskly led the way from the room.

The hall ran through to the back of the house where French windows opened into the garden. The study was on the right of the front door and the drawing room on the left, and beyond the drawing room door was another leading into what turned out to be a large book cupboard with shelves up to the ceiling and all loaded with books which had belonged to the Jenner children when they were young.[6] There was a large armchair on castors by the door and when I sat in it Mrs Jenner pushed it into the cupboard, and pointing out that when I wished to emerge I could reverse back into the hall by simply pushing on the shelves in front of me with both feet, she left me.

I had never seen so many books in my life; on every side and well within reach was a delirious selection. Lamb's *Tales from Shakespeare*, Kingsley's *Heroes*, *The Story of Gilgamesh*, *The Voyage of Bran*, Baring Gould's *Old English Fairy Tales*, *Mother Bunch's Closet*, *A Peep at the Pixies*, Andrew Lang's fairy books, the whole range of Arthuriana and many others besides.

Many of them were beautifully bound with the title on the cover in silver or gold, and most were illustrated; some with colour wood-engravings, and there was something about the formal outline and the colours, red, green, mustard, pale blue and brown and the fact that the landscape they depicted always looked so parched and the flowers about to wither that, though I didn't like them, fascinated me.

Henry Ford's illustrations in the Andrew Lang books were really more to my taste though, for there were so many details to be lingered over; like a border with four corners – a butterfly, a skull, a cherub's head, a snail shell. Blue Bull and Dapplegrim were barely two inches high yet they towered, and the colour plates had a melting quality as though the paint had only just been applied and was still wet; and trees, garlands, golden hair, crowns, embroidered robes, all floating, wavering, seen at a distance, seen softly. I had never seen illustrations like these before, and at the end of the afternoon was delighted at being allowed to borrow some of the books to take home.

We went to the Jenners' on several other occasions after that, and I enjoyed going partly because they were the only times I ever heard my mother talk of her childhood, and it put her in a new light. Even then she spoke of places not of people, except vaguely like the time when she lost the others in St Magnus' Cathedral in Kirkwall and had stood in the triforium while the verger in the nave below called up directions on how to get right up to the top where 'the others' had gone, and she had climbed up past openings to mysterious passages and the hangman's ladder still lying there after all those centuries. It made one shiver to think of it.

As a child she had been taken to the island of Stenness to see Maeshowe, the grass-covered mound with an entrance just high enough for a child, and had gone down the narrow passage inside where it was always dark except at the Winter Solstice when the rays of the setting sun shone down the long tunnel right into the heart of the darkness. A few fields away was the Ring of Brodgar, the neolithic Standing Stones. And at one time there had been a holed-stone as well, the Stone of Oden, through which people passed their children as a protection against illness or the 'evil eye', after having first dipped them in the water of an underground spring. And when lovers had joined hands through the stone the simple ceremony was considered sacred and binding.

Mrs Jenner sometimes spoke of parallels in Cornish folklore. The Men-an-Tol near Morvah through which the country people passed their children as a cure for rickets. And the Orcadian 'peerie folk', as their name implied, were very like the Cornish 'little people', and lived in the green mounds, the fairy hills, and sometimes helped a human in return for a gift or a service rendered. And there were the 'trows' belonging to Winter and darkness and the underworld; and who every year as the light faded grew stronger, and stole children from their cradles leaving their own weak, pale offspring in their place so that anyone suffering from a lingering illness or even thought to be sickening for one was said to be 'trowie'. I tried to imagine the strange northern land with its long Summer twilight (six weeks when it was never really dark even at midnight), and the *Aurora Borealis* and the great cartwheels covered in straw rolling blazing down the hills from the midsummer bonfires.

A subject often discussed was the legend of Joseph of Arimathea, the metal merchant related to the Virgin Mary, who had come to Britain originally in search of Cornish tin and Somerset lead and returned later in his own ships bringing Jesus and his mother with him. There was a deeply rooted tradition linking certain places in Cornwall with this story. Notably St Michael's Mount where they were supposed to have landed, Marazion, Nancledra and Ding Dong mine all in the extreme west, as well as Falmouth, St Just-in-Roseland, Creeg Brawse an ancient mine near Redruth, and Looe Island farther east. And

Mr Jenner said that he had been surprised to find similar legends in the Outer Hebrides. He told a story of how the friend of someone he knew had gone to an organ-builder's workshop in London to see how the pipes were made and had noticed that at a certain stage when, in order to obtain a perfect surface, shovelfuls of molten metal were poured onto a tightly stretched linen cloth, each man as his turn came said very softly, 'Joseph was in the tin trade'.

The foreman explained that this invocation was traditional among the metal workers because, 'Joseph, the rich man in the gospels, made his wealth from the tin trade with Cornwall.'

As well as 'a rich man' he was of course also referred to as a 'councillor of honourable estate' and 'a good man and righteous', and Mr Jenner said that in the Latin version of the Gospels he was called *nobilis decurio*, which was the Roman title for officers in charge of the metal mines and that in the British Museum he had found an account of his having gone with St James the Great to Galicia in Spain which was the other largest mining area. A *decurio* was appointed to every mining district in Spain and would also have been in charge of the farms and fortifications.

The saying 'Joseph was a tinner' was common in both Cornwall and Somerset. And in Somerset there was a song

> O Joseph came a-sailing all over the sea,
> A-trading of metal, a-trading came he
> And he made his way to Mendip
> O Joseph came a sailing all over the sea
> And Joseph was a merchantman, a tinner was he.

And there was the carol of the three Josephs.

> Here came three Josephs, three Josephs are here,
> All for to bring 'ee the Luck of the Year.
> One he did stand at the babe's right hand,
> One was a lord in Egypt's land,
> One was a tinner and sailed the sea.
> Good keep you merry, say we.

There had been many Jewish settlements in the west at one time. Once a lead figure had been discovered inscribed with the letters of the Hebrew alphabet, and in the museum at Truro there was a little bronze bull with a human face and plumes and a double crescent on its side, which had been found near St Just and which Mr Jenner said could have been a version similar to those that bore up the brazen sea in Solomon's temple. It was just the sort of little image that might have been carried by a metal merchant on his journeys. The Cornish miners spoke of 'Jews' leavings' and 'Jews' pieces'; and 'Jews' houses' was the name given to the old heaps of mine waste which contained the fused metal known as 'Jews' house tin'. And then there was the mystery as to the origin of names like Market Jew and Marazion[7] which sounded more like districts of Jerusalem.

Naturally these discussions were far above my head but I enjoyed listening to them and absorbed what I understood of them along with the flavour of the apricot jam and China tea. Mrs Jenner was always very nice to me and ignored my stammer without ignoring me, and as soon as tea was over I was always allowed to go to the book-cupboard, and before we left to choose what I wanted to read at home.

Notes

1. Doble's adaptation of the Cornish miracle play *Beunans Meriasek* was performed at St Andrew's Church on 12 June 1924.
2. Doble had previously misinterpreted Erma's stammer as an imitation of his own affliction and therefore in pretty bad taste.
3. From an early age, Charles Henderson, 1900–1933, benefited from close contact with Jenner.
4. The first Old Cornwall Society was founded at St Ives in the spring of 1920. Truro and Redruth followed suit in 1922. Hayle Old Cornwall Society was formed on 10 February 1923.
5. *Songs of the Stars and the Sea* was published by Erskine and MacDonald in 1926.
6. The Jenners had only one child, Cecily Katharine Ysolt who was born on 21 June 1878.
7. It is surely inconceivable that those present would not have known that Market Jew and Marazion are derived from the Cornish for 'little market' and 'Thursday market'.

'Song of our Motherland': Making Meaning of the Life and Work of Katharine Lee Jenner 1853–1936

Alan M. Kent

Introduction: Myth and Woman

I will begin this chapter by making several contentious points relevant to our understanding of Kitty Lee Rawlings, later Katharine Lee Jenner or 'Mrs Jenner', not to mention the main subject of this volume: Henry Jenner himself. Katharine Lee Jenner was perhaps more famous in her lifetime than her husband, although after their deaths, a reversal occurred; it was her reputation that was eventually to be overshadowed by her husband's. Indeed, even a cursory study of her career tells us that Mrs Jenner was a more prolific and confident writer than her husband, with a pan-British reputation, and as I will argue here, her Cornish activism, though hidden and eclipsed by her husband, was nonetheless as central in shaping the cultural politics of the late nineteenth- and early twentieth-century Cornish Revival as many more famous and oft-quoted figures.[1] In essence, it was Katharine Lee Jenner who most vocally formed the female conscience of that Revival, even if it was not so self-consciously constructed in the Cornish language as her husband. By understanding, however, the ideological and the religious commitment of Katharine Lee Jenner's work, we are not entirely able to disassociate her career from her husband's, since it crossed at so many points, but we are at least able to hear her voice more clearly.

Crucially, we need to note that for much of his life Henry Jenner followed Davies Gilbert's line (that Cornish should not be revived and was best replaced with English), and was initially not keen to commence any kind of large-scale revival of the language; his investigations initially were either antiquarian, historical or for fun. In the Jenner 'mythos', the more or less twenty-year suspension of his studies on Cornish is not much mentioned. From the outset then, we should realise that we are dealing with a monolith of commentary and scholarship on the Cornish Revival and those active within it, which on occasions, repeats a tested, not to mention near-mythical narrative.[2] My examination of Katharine Lee Jenner will therefore necessitate not only an approach which acknowledges the progress of feminist scholarship in literary and cultural studies,[3] but also one which seeks to negotiate a revised narrative within a paradigm shaped by wider Catholicism, Pan-Celticism and Orientalism. I have already made some preliminary studies of the life and work of Katharine Lee Jenner, and have edited her poetry,[4] but the place of this scholarship, within a wider framework of attempts to unravel the continuities and discontinuities of Cornish, Anglo-Cornish and Cornu-English literature, demanded brevity and a consideration of her place within 'imagined' and 'written' Cornwalls. The alternative methodology here will allow a much-needed multi-disciplinary approach to her life and work.

Family History: The Rawlings and the Hambleys
Katharine or 'Kitty' Lee Rawlings, the eldest daughter of William John and Catherine Rawlings of 'The Downes', Trelissick Downs, Hayle, was born on 12 September 1853,[5] and was christened at St Erth Church on 9 January 1854.[6] Her father, William John, was born at Marazion in 1815, but the only christening for this name is actually found at Marazion in St Hilary Parish for 9 August 1812, his parents being Abraham Shorland and Susanna Rawlings. His father was christened at St Mary's Church in Truro on 25 September 1784, the son of Thomas and Jane Rawlings. The marriage register states that Abraham Shorland Rawlings, agent, was his father. Kitty Lee's grandmother was one Susanna Roskilly and in 1851 she was living with her son at St Erth, when she

'Gwithian'. Watercolour by Katharine Lee Jenner. By permission of Mary Beazley

was aged seventy-nine.[7] Like many Cornishmen of the time, William John started young in engineering and shipping. He began his career with Harvey's of
Hayle, aged ten, becoming an accountant and an agent, though on 29 March
1854 he brought cash into the firm and was initially created a director with two
shares.[8] Rawlings stayed a director gaining some forty-two shares until his
death in 1890.[9]

By all accounts, at least something of Kitty Lee's innate literary talent had
come from her father. According to the *Bibliotheca Cornubiensis*, in 1868 he wrote
*A Letter on Present Stannary Court Practises and Laws with suggestions for alter-
ations*, published by the major Cornish publisher W. J. Netherton of Truro, and
then a year later, *On the Stannary Amendment Act of 1869 and the Cost Book
System*, this time published by W.J. Heard and Sons of Truro.[10] Not only this, but
Rawlings himself had an amateur interest in Cornu-English dialect and supplied information on West Cornwall to the phonologist A.J. Ellis (1814–90),
author of the influential four-volume study *On Early English Pronunciation*
(1869–74),[11] a link which had been noted by Henry Jenner. Rawlings was clearly a man of taste. A funeral report stated that his house above the Foundry
'abounded in works of art and contained a fine library'.[12] The report continues
by mentioning the 'charming' gardens at 'The Downes', commenting that 'this
lovely spot and the exquisite manner in which the gardens were arranged attest-
ed the possession of rare artistic tastes by the deceased'.[13] No doubt, it was these
elements which were critical in the early life of Katharine Lee – she was to
inherit her father's interest in art and literature, as well as his aesthetic tastes.

Katharine Lee's mother, Catherine Hambley, was the daughter of John
Hambley – an engineer and ironmonger – and Catherine Gilbert Hoskin.
William John Rawlings married her on 6 January 1848 at Phillack Church.[14]
Initially, William and Catherine lived at the Foundry in Hayle, but by 1867 had
moved to 'The Downes'.[15] As well as Katharine, they had another daughter,
named Edith Mary Giddy, who was christened at Phillack Church on 17 July
1857.[16] Catherine died on 7 July 1879 only a couple of years after the marriage
of Katharine and Henry Jenner.[17] Considering his time of life, this must have
been a devastating blow to William John, who at this time was living with his
youngest daughter Edith and had his niece Lucy Gibson to support. Financially
though, the family was well off: he kept a cook, a parlour-maid and a house-

maid. A second marriage came sometime around 1887 when he married the singer Marion Florence Hughes. She was the daughter of Henry Hughes, the Pre-Raphaelite artist and stained glass painter who was living in Green Street, near Park Lane in Mayfair. The likelihood is that she met William John through Kitty since she had been studying in London. William John and Marion had two sons – John Claude (known as 'Jack'), born on 6 July 1888, and Henry Bernard Hughes born in 1889 and christened at St Elwyn's, Hayle on 23 October of the same year. William John himself died on 12 August 1890 as a result of pneumonia, and was buried at Phillack.[18] Both of Kitty's parents' families were Protestant and members of the Church of England, and we have no record of when she converted to Catholicism, but clearly it was before she left Cornwall. Indeed, such was her interest in Christianity that often she attended Church of England services as well, although throughout all her letters and diaries there is a sense that she found the latter dull. Clearly, however, Kitty Lee Rawlings was a committed churchgoer, as was Jenner himself.

Despite reading all their correspondence, it has not been possible to discover the precise date of Henry Jenner's first meeting with Kitty Lee Rawlings, although given the circumstances, it would seem likely that Jenner made early contact with William John Rawlings over his knowledge of language survival in west Cornwall, and that having travelled to Hayle, he then met Kitty and began his friendship with her from London.[19] Their correspondence begins in 1873, therefore indicating this year as the possible start of their relationship. Some four years of letters pass, however, before Kitty Lee Rawlings married Henry Jenner on 12 July 1877 at St Erth Parish Church. The reason for this, as I shall later explain, is outlined in Jenner's correspondence to Rawlings. He had earlier embarked on an unhappy engagement. It was Rawlings who was both his shoulder to cry on, the woman whom he eventually fell in love with, and his intellectual partner. They became devoted to each other.

In 1877 Rawlings was twenty-four years old, Henry twenty-nine. 1877 was therefore a momentous year for Jenner. It was also, as myself and other scholars have noted, the year of the discovery of the Charter Endorsement from Meledor, St Stephen-in-Brannel,[20] as well as the commemoration of the centenary of the death of Dolly Pentreath at Paul which many observers are now understanding as a crucial marker in the revival of Cornish.[21] By the 1881 Census, Kitty and

Henry were living at 18 John Street, Hampstead, Middlesex; Henry is listed as an Assistant Librarian at the British Library and Kitty as a Novelist. With them was their daughter Cecily Katherine Yarlton [*sic*], aged two years old (she was born in June 1878), and an eighteen-year-old domestic servant living in, named Elizabeth Sophia Snelling. The astute reader will note the strange spelling of Kitty and Henry's daughter, which was actually Ysolt (from the Cornish legend of Tristan and Ysolt), and was either taken down incorrectly by the London Census recorder, or at some point mistranscribed.[22]

The Making of a Marriage: Celts and Courtship

Much of the information about Rawlings' and Jenner's relationship can be found by studying the collection of several hundred letters in the British Library Manuscript section from Jenner to Rawlings, mostly written in the four years or so before their marriage in 1877.[23] I have read all of this correspondence, and in my view, such is the significance of these letters on subject matter ranging from Christianity, to philosophy, philology and Celtic Studies, that they actually necessitate a separate study, and time and finance permitting these ought to be properly edited and published. There is indeed, such a wealth of material in this correspondence that I would recommend any scholar seriously interested in Jenner's life and work to study them in detail; in particular those interested in Breton and Cornish Studies. For the most part, I have tended to focus here on the early correspondence, since, in my view, it is the most relevant to our purposes here. The interested reader may, of course, go to the full correspondence of the immediate period before their marriage.

Brevity, and the need in this chapter at least, to focus on the life and work of Kitty Lee means that I am only able to offer the reader a selected range of that correspondence, though I still hope that this will be useful. Frustratingly, despite my efforts to find more of Rawlings' return correspondence I have been unable to do so (some selected diaries do survive, but are mainly concerned with Christianity, church-going, social life in London, her love for Cornwall and the need to write novels and earn some money), and I am coming to the opinion that most of it has not survived. Therefore, in dealing with Jenner's letters to Kitty Lee, I first offer the important caveat that we are dealing with a 'filter' of Rawlings' life – it is how Jenner sees it, and therefore we must be sceptical of it. At times, he shows signs of being very patronising and sexist, although we may put this down to Jenner's slight advantage in age and fashionable male attitudes of the era, and not treat him too harshly.

The correspondence was also conducted over a very delicate and difficult period of both of their lives. Jenner, one senses, was very unhappy in his engagement to another girl, whilst Rawlings knew the attraction the two of them had, but was unsure which way Jenner's mind was working. Given the social circumstances it was unlikely that either was going to quickly confess their love for each other – things had to be carried out in the proper way. For the modern reader, this 'dancing around' the issue can seem acutely frustrating, accustomed as we now are to text messaging and mobile phones, although the dance and its completion actually show how, to use a contemporary expression, 'in tune' the two of them were. The making of their eventual marriage makes fascinating reading.

The correspondence opens on 27 August 1873, while Jenner was back in St Columb Major on summer vacation. It seems Jenner had visited William John Rawlings at Hayle, and there had met Kitty. Jenner had been in correspondence with her father and had recently been on a trip to the nearby hill of Trencom. He addresses Kitty very formally: 'My dear Miss Rawlings' and comments 'I believe that with a telescope I might almost have been able to see your house, and had the telescope been still stronger, I might have seen you yourself, perhaps enjoying a pipe in the upper room of the summer house'.[24] In this striking comment, we perhaps see the origins of Jenner's interest in Kitty. In this and early letters, there is much discussion as to whether Kitty should attend the Bloomsbury or South Kensington Art Schools. Jenner apparently has doubts over Bloomsbury, and it is interesting that by 14 October, Kitty had selected the National Art Training School in South Kensington.[25] His influence on her was already marked. The initial correspondence also relied much on Jenner's own translation work, as well as their shared interest in the academic sphere of Celtic Studies. The following section from a letter dated 17 September 1873 is particularly interesting:

> I am pleased that you approved of my compositions. There were no more of those particular dialogues, but there is a good deal more of the same

sort of literature still existing in the Breton language, some of it being very good and some of it being like most modern Celtic so-called poetry, excellent as to verse but most idiotic as to matter. I think however, the Bretons being more thoroughly Catholic than any other Celts (even than the Irish, who are more politically, than devotionally so) are by far the best as to their religious poetry though judging from what remains of their literature, the Cornish might have run them very close if they had gone on a little longer. The author of those dialogues, whoever he may have been (they were written in the 16th century) must have been a man of considerable poetic and devotional feeling. My translation is not always literal – some of it was a little too quaint for English readers and I didn't wish to give it a comic element, though among the primitive folk of Brittany, comicality in religious matters didn't by any means mean irreverence and to laugh about religious things didn't mean to ridicule them, but our gloomy Saxon religionists wouldn't see the difference, so I thought it best to modify some passages.[26]

In the background of this early correspondence is the figure of Nellie, to whom Jenner is engaged. Their relationship is not an easy one, and as we shall see, Jenner had to surreptitiously write to Rawlings in code in order for Nellie not to become jealous and suspicious. By modern standards their engagement appears 'arranged', as if the families thought it would be a good thing, but as their relationship progresses, clear cracks begin to show. This is perhaps why, initially, Jenner plays the role of the father figure to Kitty while she is residing at 30 Richmond Terrace, West Brompton in London. He advises her: 'I would not let any girl whom I could prevent doing so walk along Regent Street, Oxford Street or any street in Bayswater alone after 8 pm.'[27] No doubt Rawlings ignored him. Already, however, Jenner and Kitty Lee are meeting up in London. Their first encounter, suggested by Jenner is at the Doré Gallery on Bond Street, and two days later it is agreed that she will meet him in the Antiquities room at the British Museum (a place where they were often to meet over the years).[28] At this stage their relationship is purely platonic since Jenner suggests that as Kitty is initially quite lonely in London, that she should meet Nellie. Cryptically though, he warns Kitty: 'Don't scare her with extreme theology or Catholicism, for she won't understand a word of it.'[29] The meeting with Nellie appears to have gone well, but by 3 December, Jenner is beginning to realise the problem with her, and confides his thoughts to Kitty, who he is beginning to realise is his intellectual equivalent:

> I am not so certain about everything as I was. She seems very change-
> able. Last night we had a terrible scene, such hysterical crying as I never
> saw. She can't make out for certain what she wants, and is very happy
> and very miserable by turns. When I got to their lodgings, she greeted
> me most lovingly and was to all appearance (and indeed really) perfect-
> ly happy. But in a little while before I went, she became very gloomy and
> after the others had gone to bed we had this strange scene. She declares
> that she did not really care for me and that she couldn't make out why
> she had said what she did, and that she had been very happy indeed at
> one time but that now she was utterly wretched and hated herself and
> should never be happy again.[30]

He concludes the letter by worrying about the social repercussions, yet questions, 'Why on earth should lives be utterly spoiled for nothing?' This debate
forms the central issue of Jenner's letters for the rest of the early months of
1874.[31] By 20 February, Jenner confides to Rawlings that he has received a letter,
which he has not opened. He is certain that it is about breaking off the engagement.[32] The difficulties for both Jenner and Rawlings are emphasised on 9 April
1874, while Jenner and Nellie are on holiday in Clifton, Bristol. In order to
express himself, Jenner resorts to a Runic alphabet so that Nellie won't be able
to read what he is writing.[33] This mechanism of code-writing, which allocates
most of the symbols their Roman equivalent, is now perhaps more famously
associated with the works of J.R.R. Tolkien,[34] but in their correspondence this
proved essential to maintaining confidentiality. Reflecting on Jenner's achievement from the twenty-first century, and in what I have termed elsewhere, the
'Celtic Nirvana' phenomenon where the appropriation and mingling of Anglo-
Saxon, Celtic and Runic is often now the convention,[35] it perhaps seems even
apt that the two of them choose this method to communicate, even more so
when Jenner is associated with ancient British languages.[36] By the summer,
Kitty had moved to 14 Euston Square and significantly Jenner not only used a
Runic script but he had begun to write to her in Cornish:

Kerra Maghteth,
    Ymma yu an lyvaz neb my a levyras ma my a vynnas dry tha why. My
a vedn bos tha'n escol Slade worth an tryssa ur aforow, ha ny a vedn
mones tha Verulam. My a rig anvyth scriven-danvoon a Nellie hythen,
nag yu drog.
    Benary thi' ys

Henry Jenner
Hem yu yn an tavaz agas gulas

[*Beloved Maiden,*
    Here is the book which I said that I would bring to you. I will be at the
school of Slade by the third hour tomorrow, and we will go to St Albans. I have
had a letter from Nellie today. It was not a bad one
    Forever thine,

    Henry Jenner
This is in the language of your country.][37]

This is vital, since it is a very early piece of Revived Cornish, and Jenner
clearly favours using 'Late' Cornish, adding much weight to Jenner's original
view that the language ought to be picked up from its last speakers. From now
on, Jenner continues to use occasional Cornish and encourages Rawlings to
learn it, even though through the summer of 1874 he is very unwell, 'drinking
large quantities of brandy' and suffering from neuralgia. In the same letter he
writes:

I hope the Cornish is progressing. I recommend it as a good cure for neuralgia. I look forward to the time when we shall be able to correspond
and talk fluently in our own language. I shall work at Breton a good deal
now that I have got books therein. It is much nearer to Cornish than
Welsh is, especially the Vannes dialect though I believe the dialect of the
Breton Cornouailles is curiously still nearer. Cornouailles is the southern half of what is now the Department of Finisterre containing all of
that Department south of Brest. Leonais or the dialect of the N. half of
Finisterre is the standard Breton I think. This letter seems to be resolving itself into a lecture on Celtic philology...[38]

Jenner's letter of 18 July 1874 indicates how close Rawlings and he had become. One can see their minds and hearts coming together, though perhaps at this stage, they were still unwilling to verbally and physically share those feelings. Jenner tells Rawlings that she 'would be right to make painting the real object of your life. Do it. We want Catholic artists and we haven't got many of them.' He then debates a Parliamentary Bill to crush 'Ritualism' and asks her 'What was the book of Cornish plays you mention?'[39] Yet curiously, by the late summer Jenner has still not resolved the situation with Nellie. Rawlings had written to him confessing her despair in her life in general. It is not explicitly linked to the Nellie situation, but we might well deduce that Kitty was waiting for him to make up her mind. Jenner's response is rather harsh. He tells her that despair is the 'unpardonable sin' – effectively a sin against the Holy Ghost – which must not have helped Kitty's situation, nor have made her feel better.[40] Jenner here seems heavy-handed and insensitive.

Things appear to have changed however by 4 September 1874, where Jenner is now calling Rawlings 'my darling' and refers to 'our pleasant few minutes in the summerhouse before breakfast'.[41] We now begin to see that the two are falling in love, yet Jenner is still engaged; a massive social dilemma. Though Rawlings' correspondence from this time has not survived, it is possible to understand her frustrations. What follows on 4 October 1874 is a confession from Kitty: 'You say you would not be able to get on without my letters ... I should gladly tell you the innermost thoughts of my heart.' Jenner responds romantically, but then characteristically adds:

When Lach-Szyrma goes back home off the Brighton congress do ask him to show me his old Cornish speakers and to go down to Newlyn to see them. I think it is really important for my grammar that I should see them before I get any further on with it so as to really settle the pronunciation and if I went there, I might possibly find time to spend a day at Hayle. These old folk are very aged and might die before I can see them, such is the uncertainty of human life, so it will be a case of 'What thou doest do quickly'. It will depend on the state of my finances. I like your notion about angels and memory ... If I wrote a book on comparative philology I shouldn't talk about the tower of Babel but should only concern myself with how and not why God confused the languages and

shouldn't even say that He did do it, taking it for granted that only readers would believe that all nature is the work of God.[42]

Curiously, or perhaps rightly, it is during this phase, where Jenner becomes
more enthusiastic about his interest in Cornish, that he also becomes more
enthusiastic about Rawlings. She and language seem tied together, highly likely considering Jenner was stuck for the most part in 'unromantic' central
London. At the same time, their correspondence deals with issues such as the
philosophy of John Locke, the poetry of Sir Philip Sidney, Faust, the Cabbala,
Anglo-Catholicism as well as Celtic Studies. By 7 November 1874, it seems as if
Jenner has told Nellie that he no longer wishes to be with her, and writes poeti-
cally to Kitty:

> [I have] terrific remorse and horrid feeling that I have done wrong to
> her. I am rather bewildered by it and feel rather as if I had got into the
> middle of one of those enchanted cities or forests full of wild glamour
> and magic that one reads of in delightful medieval romances. There are
> things quite like this fanning the medieval surroundings in the
> Mabinogion (a Welsh book of romances) and in some of Youqué's stories
> – the enchanted forest in "Jeudine" for instance, and Ferda's castle in
> the "Magic Ring". It is only the Celtic element in my nature that enables
> me to stand it, for it would turn any solid Saxon brain long ago, and I
> shall begin to have a better opinion of my powers in the future.[43]

Apparently, however, the relationship with Nellie drags on into the autumn.
At this point, Rawlings becomes more involved in helping Jenner with his work.
Jenner writes and asks her to write and send out some letters to the clergy on the
Isle of Man since, for a while, his scholarship had turned on to the Manx language. However, the questions he asks are not only relevant to all other Celtic
languages, but perhaps if they had been asked a hundred years before in
Cornwall, then more of the language might have remained. Even so, the list is
an interesting insight into the mindset of researchers like Jenner during this
period:

1. Which is the prevailing language in your parish – English or Manx?

2. If English, how many Manx speaking people (i.e. speaking it as their mother tongue) are there in your parish?
3. Of what class are they?
4. How many can speak no English, and of what ages and professions are they?
5. Do you ever preach or say the service, or any part of it in Manx, and if so, how often and what parts of the service?
6. Do children as a rule at present learn Manx or English first, or do they grow up knowing both?
7. Can you pick up any information relating to traditional songs, poems or stories in Manx still prevalent among your parishioners?
8. Can you tell me of any books, pamphlets, tracts etc (besides the Bible, Prayerbook, and the Manx societies publications) published in Manx, and if so, where they are obtainable?
9 Is there much important difference between the Manx at present spoken, and that of the Manx Bible and Prayerbook, and of Kelly's Grammar and Dictionary, or are these still easily intelligible to the lower classes?[44]

Some letters of the British Library collection have been lost, even though the envelope remains. The growing closeness between Jenner and Rawlings is established in the postscript of a letter on 27 November 1874. Jenner writes: 'I dreamt last night that you and I were rowing in a boat together along a river with wooded banks on both sides.'[45] The letter of 5 December 1874 is not in its envelope, while on 7 December 1874 he writes: 'I should do anything on earth for Nellie – except two things – marry her and give you up.'[46] By 19 December, he addresses Kitty as 'my love' and by the end of the month writes sonnets to her, at the same time closely indicating his own ideology: 'While writing it, I felt as if I was really living in the pre-Reformation (say about 1500 or so) and the next day I found myself really bringing expressions of that sort of English in my conversation.'[47]

The winter of 1874/75 is a crucial period in their relationship and it seems that rather than Jenner dumping Nellie, there was a time-led, 'natural' falling off of emotions, in particular on Nellie's side. The letters the next year are more concerned with issues of Catholicism, upon which Rawlings' fears about her relationship were most likely to have been founded. During this time period, we should acknowledge that their relationship was highly unusual and resolving the issues of Nellie took a lot of careful negotiation as well as, one imagines, some often heartbreaking decisions. It is to Rawlings' and Jenner's credit that they resisted following society's convention and dared to make their relationship work. Even though their letters are romantically frustrating for the modern reader, there is a sense that their love will win out. One of the few pieces of correspondence written by Kitty Lee Rawlings that has survived dates from 23 November 1875, when the issues had been resolved. Like many other pieces of correspondence between them, it was written in Runes, and an attempted translation is offered here, confirming their love:

> You are such a darling to send me such a long letter, you deserve one in return my own treasure, as soon as I can manage, so I shall only send you a postcard in the mean time. I have read your letter through twice already, there is a great deal to answer in it.[48]

This almost concludes my analysis of Jenner's correspondence to Kitty Lee Rawlings during this period. From the outside, and from our present perspective, the making of their eventual marriage did not look easy, considering the social circumstances aligned against them. However, through the combination of their interests it won through. During the correspondence, it is clear that Kitty Lee Rawlings was making her first steps forward into the literary world. Despite Jenner's view that she ought to become a Catholic artist, it was towards fiction that Rawlings' heart was drawn. As early as 12 October 1874, Rawlings had asked Jenner for a critique of her writing. He comments: 'I shall say what I think whether complimentary or not.'[49] The critique obviously served her well, since through the late 1870s she was developing several manuscripts which were to be published in the opening years of the next decade, and it is to that period of Kitty Lee Jenner's life that I now turn.

Mrs Jenner, Novelist

While Jenner made his initial surveys of enduring Cornish and investigated the surviving manuscripts, not to mention academic pursuits in other fields,

Katharine Lee Jenner developed her own novel-writing career, though initially, she used her nickname 'Kitty Lee' as her *nom-de-plume*. Though it had been in draft for a couple of years, her first success came in 1882 with *Western Wildflowers*.[50] She was twenty-nine years old. Two years later came *In London Town* (1884), followed by *Katherine Blythe* (1886) and *An Imperfect Gentleman* (1888).[51] Titles then appeared less frequently. 1891 saw the publication of *Love or Money*,[52] but it was to be a further four years before the 1895 publication of *When Fortune Frowns: Being the Life and Adventures of Gilbert Cosworth – A Gentleman of Cornwall*.[53] One senses that her career as a novelist was on the wane by now, perhaps because of shifting public taste. As I have argued elsewhere, there was serious Pan-British interest in novels with Cornish themes during late nineteenth-century Britain, despite their at times extraordinary artificiality.[54] As a woman writing during this phase, Kitty Lee was breaking new ground; there were few other indigenous Anglo-Cornish female novelists (an exception is Salome Hocking Fifield,[55] who ironically was writing at the opposite end of the Christian perspective) and her work became well-known. At the start of this chapter, I mentioned how Katharine Lee Jenner was at this point more significant in a Pan-British context than her husband. This was because Jenner's work was academic; hers was populist. Her stories, though containing strongly Cornish characters and settings, appealed not only in that territory, but because of a wider middle to late nineteenth-century British interest in the romance of the periphery (in both landscape and people),[56] and from the 1840s onwards, in Arthuriana and the Celtic Twilight.[57]

The two most interesting of Kitty Lee Jenner's novels are *Love or Money* and *When Fortune Frowns: Being the Life and Adventures of Gilbert Cosworth – A Gentleman of Cornwall*. *Love or Money* was originally published in three volumes – standard publishing format for this time – and is set in the Cornish coastal village of St Mervain, where the English Reverend Wilbraham Ferrars is unpopular amongst local people, not only because of his ethnicity, but also because he takes too much in tithes. The action begins with a battle against Nonconformity: a dead woman's family turns to the Little Bethel rather than the church,[58] prompting Ferrars to say: 'God forgive me! I have been thinking more of the Vicarage than the church, of my children's comforts before the souls of His poor'.[59] Kitty Lee Jenner develops two other central male characters,

Lord Roscarrock (a Cornish Catholic name), a young, modern man, apparently more interested in drains and sewerage than anything else, and the clumsily-named Darwin Bampton – scientist and atheist – who exclaims, 'You don't believe a word of the whole exploded rubbish of Christianity.'[60] Into this cultural vortex is thrown the heroine of the novel – Gabrielle – whose efforts are spent curbing the ambition of these three men.

The problem with the text is that it is too often a novel of manners alone, and reads rather like a Cornish Jane Austen, yet Jenner is not sophisticated enough a novelist to handle the subtleties of the 'showing' and 'telling' of Austen-like dialogue. Too often, then, the book reads as a set of ideas in search of a novel, and over three volumes, the narrative's concerns with class and manners drag. One of the central themes is that of Christian persecution, and though it may well have been an issue in Jenner's day (the threat of persecution of Catholics was still very real during the nineteenth century), it now reads more like science fiction. There are, however, some moments of clarity and understanding of Cornish ethnicity such as are hard to find in most other Anglo-Cornish nineteenth-century fiction:

> A Cornishman is the easiest-going creature in existence if you only let him have his own way. Give him his head, and let him feel that he is going of his own accord, and he will do anything that you insinuate. Once try to coerce him, and no more unreasonable, hot-headed, fanatical man is to be met with anywhere.[61]

Typically, after a canter across to Calais (many Anglo-Cornish novels during this phase have pan-European settings, demonstrating Cornish internationalism), it is Roscarrock, the Catholic hero, who saves Gabrielle from drowning.[62] Ideologically, there are points in the text where Kitty Lee specifically slows down the narrative to somehow show the reader that if Cornwall had, like Brittany, remained Catholic, then all would be fine. There is, however, no mention of the Cornish language, aside from place-names: Ferrars, for instance, lives at Lansladron Vicarage. Quite how hard-line Protestant Cornish writers like Silas Kitto Hocking or Joseph Hocking would have responded is best left unsaid. Interestingly, however, both Silas and Joseph used exactly the same technique as Kitty Lee Jenner – that of pausing the narrative for religious instruction, though obviously to very different ends.[63]

While the weaknesses of *Love and Money* are relatively easy to spot, they are less visible in perhaps Kitty Lee Jenner's greatest prose masterpiece *When Fortune Frowns: Being the Life and Adventures of Gilbert Coswarth – A Gentleman of Cornwall*. Such is the importance of this work in understanding Kitty Lee Jenner, and her husband, that I would like to devote a considerable amount of time to discussing it. As the subtitle of the novel makes clear – 'A Story of how Gilbert Coswarth fought for Prince Charles in the years of 1745 and 1746 and what befell him after' – the narrative is set around the events of 'The Forty Five'. At this time the exiled Stuarts continued to claim the British throne even after their abortive rebellion of 1715. Their supporters, mostly Roman Catholics, became known as Jacobites, from the Latin name for James, *Jacobus*. The exiled James II died in 1701, leaving his claim to his son James, known as the 'Old Pretender', but he failed to secure the support of the French. In 1745, James's son, Charles Edward, the 'Young Pretender', landed in Scotland with a handful of followers. He quickly raised an army among the Highland clans and entered Edinburgh with 2000 men. Defeating a British army at Prestonpans, Charles marched into England, but the support on which he counted was not forthcoming. In Scotland the Stuart forces were crushed in April 1746 at Culloden by an army led by the Duke of Cumberland. Charles fled to France and frittered away the rest of his life until his death in 1788.[64] Ellis makes some important observations on this conflict and its aftermath, issues which clearly Henry Jenner and Katharine Lee Jenner found intriguing:

> The insurrections between 1708 and 1745 have been passed off by historians as Jacobite manifestations. The point is that the Stuarts would have had no support in Scotland had they not made the dissolution of the Union in 1707 one of their prime policies. When the Stuart cause failed, the new creed of republicanism pointed the way for the Scots ... After the 1745 rebellion a 'pacification' of the Gaelic speaking areas, whose support for the insurrection had been total, was carried out with extreme ruthlessness. Not only the language was vigorously crushed but the visible signs of Celtic culture, such as the wearing of the kilt, the tartan and the playing of bagpipes.[65]

It is in these epic events that Katharine Lee Jenner decides to set the narrative of *When Fortunes Frowns*.[66] Interestingly, however, it is more Cornish material which appears to initially inspire the fiction – in particular, the connection
she now had with St Columb Major – the town her husband was born in:

> In this story I have not set before myself the task of writing up any par-
> ticular side, but rather of representing truly and faithfully the events of
> the period which I have selected from the point of view of a quiet, stu-
> dious country gentleman, whose conscientious principles, inherited
> from his nonjuror mother, impelled him, sorely against his inclinations,
> to take part in political strife. It began early for him in the proclamation
> of the King by James Paynter at St Columb, which is an historical fact,
> as is also the subsequent trial and acquittal of Paynter ... One name may
> need explanation. "Demonfryat" is a real name, and is found not infre-
> quently in the registers of St Columb. Judging from the local pronunci-
> ation of such Norman-French names as "De Dunstanville," I should
> imagine that its original form was something like "De Monfriart".[67]

Further justification for the historical accuracy of her text is given explicitly
by reference to a paper of her husband's, and implicitly by the fact that it was
probably he who checked not only the Cornish names and place-names of the
novel,[68] but also the Gaelic. Her comments back up the observations of Ellis,
and she is clearly aware of a multi-lingual Britain:

> Donald Dubh an t-Ephiteach was a real man, who fought in 1745, and
> not as Mr Allardyce in his "Balmoral" has made him, in the Fifteen. The
> conduct of the Macdonalds at Culloden is related in a manner which dif-
> fers from the usually received story. In this I have followed the theory set
> forth from contemporary accounts, some of them published for the first
> time, in a paper by my husband in *The Royalist* of April last. The charac-
> ters and fate of James Dawson and the fair Kitty are, alas, only too true;
> and I regret to say that the details of the harrying of the Highlands and
> the scenes in Inverness gaol are not only not exaggerated, but rather
> understated. This however, is a well known matter of history ... Of the
> dialects used in this book, one, the Cornish, I can warrant, but in the
> case of the Lowland Scots, I do not pretend to any pedantic accuracy,

and can do no more than give a "foreigner's" impression of that language. The Gaelic, however, is correct enough.[69]

The novel begins with a grand description of Celto-Catholic Cornwall in full flower, name-checking holy wells and famous Catholic locations and families:

> 'Tis sure that the votive rags fluttering still on the bushes that surround the wells of Madron, St Kevern, and many others, and the ceremony of named pins and pebbles, cast for augury upon the waters, belong not to Christianity, but have come down to us from the pious fears and trembling awe of older and ruder times. Albeit, in my time, save among such few folk, chiefly dwelling in Lanherne valley under guardianship of the great house of Arundel, as still held to the old religion, all thought of godliness and healing had fled from people's minds in connection with the arched and canopied well in our ancient garden.[70]

Though narrated by Coswarth's son, the novel's focus falls early upon Gilbert Coswarth. Perhaps the most interesting aspect of this is that father and son meet at the transition point of language in Cornwall. Gilbert Coswarth is presented to us as a natural Cornish speaker, who comes from a Cornish-speaking family. He has to undergo tuition from a mystical retainer, Mr Hoblyn – perhaps based on some of those last speakers whom Henry Jenner had read about and had been so interested in – yet given 'oriental' spin by Katharine Lee Jenner:

> Wild, strange, and fantastic were the stories told of the owner of the property of Nanswhyden, or the White Vale. He was known to have travelled much in strange countries in his youth, had been resident for some time in the East, where he acquired the knowledge of the strange and mysterious things.[71]

As for the Protestant succession, this is linked to the Stannaries, and in Katharine Lee Jenner's mind, the Stannaries, far from being indicators of Cornish particularity, not to mention jurisdiction and nationalism, are viewed as part of the oppression:

> The change of dynasty of 1714 was not accomplished as regards
> Cornwall without a murmur of protest, muttered under breath from
> gentry and common people alike, against the introduction of a foreign
> ruler into England ... These with a few families who were worldly-wise
> enough to see their way to advantage at the new court, were lusty in
> praise of the Hanoverian dynasty, and the Protestant succession ... These
> all being to a man, staunch supporters of the new dynasty. But over-top-
> ping all these in energy, though not living in our neighbourhood was Mr
> Hugh Boscawen, of Tregothnan, now appointed Controller of the King's
> Household and Lord Warden of the Stannaries.[72]

The oppression she clearly believes occurred is also given voice in the
Cornu-English dialogue of the novel. One Abraham Demonfryat who has
accepted this new combined Hanoverian and Stannary rule is at one point con-
fronted by one of the more comic characters, Molly:

> "Hark to 'un," cried Molly, exultingly. "Stuarts and Popery! and what
> was Queen Anne but a Stuart? an' I wish, weth all my soul, the old Popes
> had burnt out all such long-faced, kill-joy, bigoted old Puritans as thee
> art always praatin' about, Abraham Demonfryat."[73]

The work progresses at quite a pace, and though a historical work, Katharine
Lee Jenner clearly had her eye on the kind of books with Cornish subjects that
the reading public were buying – rollocking historical romances. By a third of
the way through we are transported to Scotland, where the real ideological
agenda of the book becomes apparent. This comes not before, however, a section
where the Reverend Dr Borlase is incorporated into the narrative as an expert
on the 'lore of his native county' which allows for a sideways step into 'wild
Celtic speech',[74] and presumably via his integration into the narrative shows
how highly Henry Jenner – and therefore Katharine Lee – valued his contribution to the preservation of the language. Though this might appear clumsy, in
the course of the novel, it actually works well, and is another example of how
the works of husband and wife meet.

The Scottish sections involve a number of battles, punctuated by passages of
ethnic fusion between the Cornish and the Scots. Lord George comments on

how 'the good folk of Cornwall are a canny race',[75] Malcolm MacErachar is described as having a 'dark eagle-like face, with eyes that shone with that strange glitter not uncommon in the Highlands and among my own Celtic Cornish'[76] while even Abraham Demonfryat tries to comprehend his dual nationality: 'I do knaw, I s'pose, that the English are the fust in the world, an' the Carnish the pick o'they...'[77] This fusion comes to ultimate fruition when the Cornish and other Jacobites escape capture by a clever union of their Celticity, in one of the finest sections of the novel:

> The captain jogged him with his arm.
> "Dedn't I tell 'ee," he observed, "that he was an unedjicated man, comes from Santust way an' can't speak no English. Here, you," and he poured out a rapid sentence in Cornish.
> The Ephiteach answered deliberately in Gaelic, bringing in the words Levan Pengellas.
> "He do tell 'ee as his name es Levan Pengellas, but he caan't speak no English," said the captain.
> The officer merely grunted, and took the name down; then interrogated the rest of the crew one by one, Zacky Trebilcock and I going through the same performance ... My not speaking any English hid any possible difference of accent.[78]

This fiction certainly backed up her husband's hard-line political and religious position. Jenner was a committed and nostalgic Jacobite, hence his later contribution to the 1889 exhibition based on the Royal House of Stuart, at the New Gallery in Regent Street, London and his 1903 publication of the *Memoirs of the Lord Viscount Dundee*.[79] Jenner had, however, already considered the potential ideological clash in the Cornish language 'X-Files' – writing which remained unused for some time by the early Revivalists, because the work did not suit their agenda, which was Jacobite, Catholic and Celtic. When the St Just-in-Penwith writer John Tonkin wrote '*Menja Tiz kernuak buz gowes*/If Cornish people would but listen' (c.1693), he celebrated the re-establishment of constitutional monarchy with the defeat of James II by William of Orange. Jenner calls Tonkin 'a violent Whig' and while he was prepared to promote the linguistic context of such Cornish language texts, he was opposed to their political outlook, which is why they were not given the attention they perhaps merited from early twentieth-century Revivalists.[80] For the same reason, Jenner failed to see merit in the spirited elegy of developed *englyns* (or triplets) to the Protestant cause composed by Edward Lhuyd in 1704, the gloriously titled 'In Obitum Wilhelmi 3tii Carmen Britannicum, Dialectu Cornubiensis; Ad Normam Poetarum Seculi Sexti/On the Death of King William III, a British Song in the Cornish Dialect; according to the pattern of the poets of the sixth century'.[81] For these reasons, the narrative remains an important exploration of the ideology of both the husband and wife, and it is perhaps a pity that it was her final novel.

Art and Catholicism

Throughout her career, as well as fiction and poetry, her other principal interest was in Christian art, an interest that she shared with her husband, since he himself was an acknowledged authority on the study of liturgy. Henry Jenner and Katharine Lee Jenner both saw themselves as Christians claiming to be in possession of a historical and continuous tradition of faith and practice. This may seem an obvious thing to say but it is important in understanding this next phase of her career. As Williams has noted,[82] 1879 saw the publication of Walter de Gray Birch and Henry Jenner's *Early Drawings and Illuminations: An Introduction to the Study of Illustrated Manuscripts with a dictionary of subjects in the British Museum.*[83] The parts of the work which referred to religious art and subjects of a theological or biblical nature were all completed by Jenner, who acknowledged the help he received from his wife 'chiefly in the branch of sacred art'.[84] This aspect of her career was borne out in three titles, all published in London by Methuen, which emerged in the early years of the twentieth century: *Christ in Art* (1903), *Our Lady in Art* (1907) and *Christian Symbolism* (1910).[85] The first two publications were part of a series of 'Little Books on Art' developed by Methuen's general art editor Cyril Davenport. The second, *Our Lady in Art,* is perhaps the most typical of her mature work. In the Introduction she outlines her topic, in so doing also revealing the essential nature of her own belief:

> Christian art is an expression of man's relation to God; thus it necessarily centres on the visible manifestation of God in the Person of His

Divine Son. Mary, as the human link between God, Who is a Spirit, and the human nature which He assumed, is thus invested with an awful dignity not attainable by any other created being.[86]

The book initially considers Mary in early Christian art as the great intercessor, through the Immaculate Conception, with detailed discussion on 'Our Lady as Intercessor' from a brasso-relief in St Mark's in Venice, then considers attributes and symbols, titles and votive pictures – among these the 'Virgo Sapientiae' from the painting by Van Eyck in the Church of St Bavo in Ghent. The most interesting part of the volume is where she considers the Virgin and Child in various kinds of art – beginning with enthroned Madonnas in early art, then considering domestic groups in the Middle Ages and finally a brief consideration of modern art. Thematically, the book covers core Catholic iconography – the Pietà – or Last Judgment, as well as Calvary, the Resurrection, Ascension and Coronation of Mary. Interestingly, there are no British examples, nor even any mention of Cornish ones, since she must by then have known of the depiction of Mary in the *Ordinalia*. Perhaps the focus was intentionally pan-Continental and non-British, and it was certainly not literary, but even so, the volume contains curious omissions.

Catholicism, Celticism, Orientalism

Much has been written by scholars such as Ellis, Miles, and Löffler on the importance of the Celtic Congress at Caernarfon in 1904,[87] which Henry Jenner and Katharine Lee attended, both having the agenda of making Cornwall's cause better known. As Löffler has shown, the photographer John Wickens lovingly details the Congress attendees who were all encouraged to wear Celtic national dress. Taking their cue from the Breton Goursez, Henry Jenner himself is in this Gorsedd's robes, while Katharine Lee and the Reverend Percival Treasure, though not barded, echo Jenner's design and colour-scheme. In Wickens' photograph, Jenner is seated, with Treasure standing, while Katharine Lee is crouched below them.[88]

In the same year Katharine Lee Jenner was made a bard of the Welsh Gorsedd at Rhyl where she took the bardic name *Morvoren* ['Sea Maiden']. She was not the first female Cornish bard of the Welsh Gorsedd – that position had gone to Mrs T. Reynolds back in 1899 – but she was the initial female activist in the drive towards the foundation of a Cornish Gorsedd. As Miners details, in 1928 it was Robert Morton Nance, the eight newly elected bards and Mrs Jenner 'who should constitute the Council of Gorseth Kernow'.[89] The full development of the Cornish Gorsedd is not something I wish to dwell on here, since it is more than adequately covered by Miners, Williams and others in this volume,[90] and yet if one analyses these accounts, it tends to be Nance and the other eight newly elected bards who are given credit. Kitty Lee's voice is perhaps lost in history, as the mantle of Grand Bard was transferred to Robert Morton Nance.

The period after the publication of her main works and her rise in the world of pan-Celticism and Cornish activism, saw Kitty enter her late fifties. With her initial novel-writing career long over, the works on Christian art had revived her literary aspirations, although the onset of the First World War seems to curtail them once again. She had to wait until 1919, for Penzance's Beare and Son to publish a short collection of poetry which she titled *Christmas Verse*.[91] The poems are not major works, and seem like they were only read in limited circles. Though certainly not as literary or philosophical as Jenner's earlier correspondence with Kitty, there is some limited material of interest held at the Courtney Library in the Royal Institution of Cornwall.[92] Some general trends and observations are perhaps useful on Kitty's correspondence during this phase, however. As we might expect, the volume of correspondence increases markedly around Christmas, as does the amount of material on the run-up to the first Gorsedd, though curiously, the event itself is not much mentioned in the letters and notes. Much also comes from Bernard Rawlings, Kitty Lee's half-brother who was serving in HMS Antrim during the period 1916–17,[93] to whom she remained very close, and her daughter Ysolt who had long since joined the Convent of the Visitation, Harrow-on-the-Hill.[94] At the same time, she engages in much correspondence with members of the St Ives and Newlyn artistic community – in particular with Katherine E. Sargent.[95] Many of these artists had 'Catholic' beliefs since the faith seemed to embody much of the romance of place they were trying to capture in their art – indeed it was Brittany's landscape and culture (and by implication Catholicism) that drove them.[96]

One interesting correspondent was the priest Adrian Fortescue, writing on 12 September 1916, from Letchworth in Hertfordshire, who typifies many friends and relatives who stayed with the Jenners during this phase, and was given the 'Cornish tour':

> Every bit of it was beautiful, but perhaps the jolliest memory of all is sitting on the Land's End and looking over the sea and at the lighthouse in its cloud of foam while we ate Cornish pasties. Hearing the story of Tristan and Ysolt as we drove through the Cornish valley with the sea in front and on either side was delightful too.[97]

And yet, the central thrust of Fortescue's letter to Kitty is actually to engage with her in a debate over Ritualism involving a mutual friend:

> If you let [V...] go and just listen and agree, you can get a lot of pleasure out of his conversation. He told me his opinion of neighbouring Ritualistic clergy, and said he could not understand why a man could not pray to God without dressing up like a Chinaman first. Once he had taken duty for another man, and they wanted him to put on a lot of fancy dress, a thing round his neck and white petticoat and a lot of coloured ribbons and an opera cloak; and he had said he worshipped God in spirit and truth and a surplice and a hood, as the early Christians did. He does not think much of the Fathers and suspects that a great many of them were Roman Catholics; at any rate they were not what he would call Church of England. He would not be surprised if they had interpolated the Prayer Book, taken an Eastward position and concealed the Manual Acts ... It is a shame to rag on about him. He is an awfully good sort really and he was very nice to me. But there is no danger in the insidious growth of sacerdotalism through [V...][98]

Clearly, although Kitty was working to support her husband's interest in Cornish, her primary concern was Catholicism. Even so, it seems she still wanted to engage in debate. Kitty's correspondence during the First World War tells us much about her personality and interests towards the end of her life. Those writing to her always address her as the familiar Kitty. As we might imagine, the Jenners maintained their support for Brittany during the conflict. A correspondent from New York – Mrs A.M. Mosher – wrote on 24 January 1917 saying how 'For the Benefit of Breton Soldiers who are prisoners of war in Germany' that she will 'give a lecture on Brittany at Mrs Grace Wood's 340 Park Avenue, on

Sunday February 4th at four o'clock' with 'Tea at five'.[99] During the war, some 250,000 Bretons perished, the highest death toll per head of population of any region in the world, many of those killed serving in the Navy.[100] Brittany and its Catholicism, art and language continued to fascinate Kitty, in the same way that it intrigued Henry. Certainly, some Anglo-Catholic mysticism is noted in Kitty by her friends, but this is tinged by what the cultural critic Edward Said has since termed fashionable 'Orientalism'.[101] A correspondent named M.U. Green, writing on 26 October 1916 from Riviere House, Phillack, explains how she imagines Kitty when she thinks of her (in so doing, bringing to mind her bardic robes):

> I always "see" you in Eastern clothes, Egyptian, I think, digging a little garden in a very sandy place in a very hot sun, with a cat and a little wooden water-mill somewhere at hand.[102]

This somewhat alternative image of Katharine's would have contrasted, we might imagine, greatly with that of standard Cornish dress of the period. This mysticism is a crucial factor in understanding Kitty's poetry, which comes to full fruition in her 1926 collection, *Songs of the Stars and the Sea*. Published during the final run-up to the first Cornish Gorsedd in 1928, and with her husband in his eighties, it is in this writer's view, Kitty's finest work. In the collection, a specific sequence is dedicated to Cornwall, falling into nine distinct parts, and in several ways covering selected phases of Cornish historical experience. This mysticism is intimately connected with Kitty Lee's Catholicism, where for her, the Cornish landscape itself is not only redolent of the mystery plays and holy wells of an idealised, fully operational Cornu-Celtic-Catholic culture, but of Catholic struggle and suffering:

> On every vale and hill
> Are holy names, which still
> Can stir men's hearts and thrill
> With love of holy deeds,
> By saints and Martyrs done,

Who won their deathless crown
For sowing in thy soil the blessed Gospel seeds.[103]

Central to Kitty Lee's poetic vision however, is a poem like 'Can Gwlasol Agan Mam-Vro/A Patriotic Song of our Motherland' which contains a very narrow vision of Cornish history, based on Arthuriana and Grail-lore ('Thine was Arthur, thine his knights,/Strong Geraint his admiral'[104]), but then shifting seamlessly into the Civil War and Saints, where the reader supposedly reflects on these glorious moments of Cornwall's past, seemingly ideal for the new patriotism promoted by the Revival:

Sons of thine with Grenville fell
For their King in Lansdown's fray;
Let the Royal Letter tell
How they failed him not that day.

Michael of the Guarded Mount,
Saints before God's Face who stand,
Keyna of the hallowed fount,
Piran of the drifting sand... [105]

But there is a curious kind of blinkered ideology at work here, which suggests that these themes are the only ones which ignite the average Cornish person's passion. If we are seeking passion, then it is perhaps surprising that it is the colour grey which forms the metaphorical basis of many of her poems. In 'On the Cliff', the Saints of Cornwall are again evoked and there is perhaps even a taste of a Betjemanesque playful marriage of the pagan and Christian, but this is deceptively covered by the 'glamour of the grey' and the 'glitter of the grey': the grey somehow the Cornish themselves.[106] This theme is continued in 'O Lone Grey Land' where the 'mystic circles on bare moors alone' collide with 'grey stones' and the 'grey land' itself.[107] A further poem, 'A Grey Day', unites these themes, where the grey romantically blends the sky, land and sea.[108] Realism is given little truck – perhaps only found in one of her finest poems 'The Boats of Sennen', where, picking up on the folk-rhyme 'The corn is in the shock/And the fish are on the rock', she develops a poem on the tragedy of loss at sea:

> The corn is in the shock,
> And the fish are on the rock,
> And the golden sun is gleaming on the Islands of the West;
> I hear the huer's cry,
> And I see the dappled sky,
> And my heart is dead with sorrow for the lad I love the best.[109]

The one poem that makes a concession to modernity is 'The Exile', a work that acknowledges that many Cornish people live and work away from the territory. In some senses, this picks up on the common theme of exile developed from the 1850s onwards in respect of Cornwall's emigrant and mobile workforce not only moving to elsewhere in Britain, but huge distances across the globe. That said, though, 'The Exile' explores a very real and modern Cornish theme, doing so in a highly sentimental and idealised way:

> On the line of purple hill against the west,
> On the falling of the land towards the sea,
> There are brakes of golden blossoms, where they rest
> Mid the crimson of the heather on the lea,
> In the land that is mine own, the land of flowery down,
> While I gaze down upon the streets of London Town.[110]

There is no doubt that *Songs of the Stars and the Sea* is an important collection of Anglo-Cornish verse, yet in the aftermath of the publication Kitty became increasingly frustrated with the reception the volume received. In various letters and notes she wonders if the volume has any chance of real success, but she is not confident about it.[111] She also wanted to read the work in London, but this never happened. Kitty felt her best attempt at promoting the work might be through the Catholic Poetry Circle, which was run out of Corpus Christi Hall, Leigh-on-Sea in Essex. The Circle was headed by Evan Morgan; other activists included Alfred Noyes (who had violently anti-Modernist views on literature),

G.K. Chesterton (whose verse celebrated the Englishness of England) and Compton Mackenzie (the author of *Whisky Galore*). Kitty had much correspondence about the Circle during this time. Its aims seemed to suit her precisely:

1. To promote an abiding interest in Catholic Poetry – in the widest and most Catholic sense of the word.
2. To make more widely known the works of Catholic poets.
3. To link together all those who are interested in Catholic poetry.[112]

A Catholic Poetry Circle leaflet of 25 August 1929 mentioned how they were 'very interested' in *Songs of the Stars and the Sea* but it seems nothing further materialised. Perhaps the Circle itself rejected both Kitty as a modern 'female' poet, and her 'Cornish' peripherality. Ironically, a day earlier, on 24 August of the same year, Kitty wrote a letter expressing her frustration to the Circle, but the letter was never sent. In it she expresses how angry she is that the Catholic papers and magazines seem so disinclined to publish verse. All this seems to have contributed to the reason why she published no more poetry.[113]

Box 10 of the Jenner Papers at the Royal Institution of Cornwall gives us insight into the aftermath of her husband's death in 1934. There are many letters and cards of sympathy (Kitty was a great horder), several from Brittany and one letter from the Penzance poet John Baragwanath King, who had been made a bard of the Cornish Gorsedd in 1930.[114] Two pieces of correspondence are of most interest to us here, however. The first comes from Melilia Hilton, a cousin of Kitty's who was an actress and played at one point the role of 'Salome' on the London stage. Melilia wrote in dire circumstances begging Kitty for money. Kitty dutifully obliged by sending her sums of two and five pounds between 1 September 1934 and 6 February 1935.[115] Robert Morton Nance, meanwhile, writes on 10 January 1935, obviously interested in Henry's archive and notes. He comments, 'I need not give you any further trouble except for the collection of the books',[116] which both suggests Nance's sensitivity to Kitty's mourning and his need to continue Jenner's work. Kitty Lee died on 21 October 1936, two years after the passing of her husband. She was aged eighty-three and was buried with her husband in the churchyard at Lelant.

Ysolt Jenner (Sister Mary Beatrix Jenner of the Order of the Visitation of Our Lady).

By permission of Mary Beazley

The Life of Ysolt

It seems Kitty Lee had a major influence on her daughter Ysolt, and her choice to join the Order of the Visitation at Harrow-on-the-Hill. This silent Order is also known as the Visitandines, and as Cross and Livingstone note, was founded by St Francis of Sales and St Jane Frances de Chantal, and designed to include women unable to bear the austerities of the older orders, devoting itself to the special cultivation of humility, gentleness, and sisterly love.[117] Over time the Order has remained primarily contemplative, perhaps the reason why there is very little information on Ysolt's life. A few events are known though. In the Autumn of 1895, the Jenners had a week in Paris in order to take Ysolt (then aged sixteen) to school at the Sacré Coeur convent at Conflans. The likely reason for this was that her parents wanted her to learn French. They both spoke French, and to complete her education in France was a natural choice for them. At this point there was never any suggestion that Ysolt wanted to join a convent. However, when she was around eighteen or nineteen years old, she realised that she had a vocation to give her life to Christ. According to Mary Beazley, Kitty Lee and Henry Jenner in particular were very concerned about her wish to become a nun. They never pressurised her to do so. She was a lively and lovely girl and her parents were worried that she was going to be bound up in religious matters at too young an age. If she had been a man, then she would have had the option of becoming a priest; as it was, however, she informed her parents that she wished to enter a convent. The Jenners contacted a local priest for advice, and it was felt that the best course of action was for her to join her mother and father on tours in both 1898 and 1900 to give her a sense of foreign travel. The idea was that this would give her the necessary life experience before she committed herself. However, she still chose to enter the Order aged just twenty-one.

In Ysolt, arguably we witness another manifestation of the Jenner family's commitment to Catholicism, and perhaps paradoxically her spurning of both her Cornishness and any familial proto-nationalism. This can uncritically even be noted in the eventual rejection of her ultra-Cornish name. In the Eighty-Fourth Annual Report of the Royal Cornwall Polytechnic Society of 1917, Henry Jenner describes his daughter as 'Cecily Katharine Ysolt, *now* [my italics] Sister Mary Beatrix Jenner of the Order of the Visitation of Our Lady',[118] whereas in the *Royal Cornwall Gazette*, a writer in 1934, refers to her as 'Miss

Isolt [*sic*] Jenner'.[119] She was aged fifty-five; the journalist keen to make the link to her father for the *Gazette*'s readers. However, in this writer's opinion such a critique is wrong-footed. Ysolt's decision was clearly a personal one and nothing to do with her parents. We must remember that the rejection of their names is something all nuns must do when they take their final vows, and are then given a name 'in Christ'. When writing to Ysolt, her family always addressed her as Sister Mary Beatrix, but called her Cousin Ysolt. This is a crucial point in understanding the life of Ysolt.

Final Meanings: The Legacy of Mr and Mrs Jenner
For some observers of both Kitty Lee and Henry Jenner, Ysolt's stepping outside of the 'Revival', not to mention her Catholic commitments in the face of a broadly Methodist Cornwall, as well as her seeming lack of interest in developing the Cornish language, is too much to bear: it seems to smack of an about face, considering how much work her mother and father achieved, but as we have seen above, her reasons were very personal and spiritual. Awareness of the achievement of the Jenners has only come with time. It was Jenner's followers, like Robert Morton Nance, and the post-war activists of language and nationalism,[120] who have elevated his status. It is only now in 2004 that Ottakar's Bookshop in Truro has a portrait of Jenner on the wall behind the counter.

For others, it merely cements the linkage of those who see the Cornish Revival of the early twentieth century as being too closely allied with a vision of a Catholic, Medieval and non-technological Cornwall.[121] Indeed, in some letters to Rawlings Jenner confesses how much he enjoyed imagining being back writing in 1500, a view that does reinforce the above critique. As we have seen, Kitty Lee was a Roman Catholic for a good many years and significantly, Jenner himself, always of High Church views, was received into the Roman Catholic Church a few months before his death, an event which closely parallels the final days of the Morwenstow-based poet Robert Stephen Hawker, another 'nationalist icon'.[122] Kitty Lee's commitment to Catholicism had come much earlier on in her life; Jenner's came shortly before his death (Mary Beazley suggests that Jenner made this conversion for his wife alone. He was after all, from a devoutly Anglo-Catholic background, and he hoped that this would stop Katharine Lee worrying). In contrast to much history and writing which has only told the story of Methodist and Nonconformist Cornwall (sometimes with its own inherent agenda of eradicating other religious 'Cornwalls'[123]), Keast offers a useful alternative perspective on the Catholic Revival in Cornwall,[124] contending that it is as much a part of the Cornish experience as Wesleyanism, Bible Christians and rituals around standing stones. He may well be right. Deacon and I, however, have argued that this general critique of the Cornish Revival (of which Kitty Lee Jenner and Henry Jenner were so much a part), may be too much of a binary opposition which is actually loaded with contemporary cultural politics, and notions of authenticity and inauthenticity, not to mention Modernism and Post-Modernism.[125]

People make decisions in a complex world filled with ideological illogicalities. We are unable to talk to Ysolt to ask her about the influences of her mother and father on her, her understanding of the Cornish language and/or its Catholic conception. In the end, Ysolt is not Henry Jenner, nor Jenner Kitty Lee. As I hope this chapter has shown, although Kitty Lee and Henry Jenner came to understand each other, and realise the possibilities of their union in marriage, she was a strong and determined woman, and given the social circumstances of her time, she contributed much not only to the Cornish Revival, but in many other areas of literary, cultural and religious life. The last few years have gladly brought about a more feminist consciousness in literary and cultural studies in Cornwall and finally we are beginning to witness a more enquiring scholarship into such matters. My hope for the moment, though, is that readers will now talk a little more appreciatively of Mrs Jenner, just as her husband did in his groundbreaking book on Cornish language and literature one hundred years ago:

> Kerra ow Holon! Beniges re vo
> Gans bennath Dew an dêdh a 'th ros dhemmo,
> Dhô whelas gerryow gwan pan dhetha vî,
> Tavas dha dassow, ha dhô 'th drovya dî.
> En cov an dêdh splan-na es pel passyes;
> En cov idn dêdh lowenek, gwin 'gan bês,
> War Garrak Loys en Côs, es en dan skês
> Askelly Myhal El, o 'gan gwithes;

En cov lîas dêdh wheg en Kernow da,
Ha ny mar younk-na whekkah vel êr-ma
Dhemmo a dhîg genev an gwella tra,
Pan dhetha vî en kerh, en ol bro-na;
Dheso mî re levar dha davas teg,
Flogh ow empinyon vî, dhô 'm kerra Gwrêg.

[*Beloved of my heart! Blessed with the blessing of God be the day that gave you to me, when I came to look for the feeble words of the language of your fathers, and to find you. In memory of that bright day which has long since passed, in memory of a happy day, how fortunate we were! On the Grey Rock in the Wood, which is under the shelter of the wings of the Archangel Michael, who was our guardian, in memory of many pleasant days in good Cornwall, when we were so young – and it's just as pleasant now – and when I came away I brought with me the best thing in all that land: to you I speak your beautiful language, my brainchild, to my dearest wife.*][126]

Acknowledgements

I am grateful to the following people in the preparation of this chapter: Mary Beazley, Paul Brewer, Audrey Randle Pool, Catherine Rachel John, Charles Thomas, Brian Coombes, Derek Williams, Angela Broome of the Courtney Library, the Royal Institution of Cornwall, Truro, Annabelle Read of the Morrab Library, Penzance and William Frame of the British Library, London.

Notes

1. The standard narrative is found in Peter Berresford Ellis (1974) *The Cornish Language and its Literature*, London and Boston: Routledge and Kegan Paul, pp.125–76. See also Hugh Miners (1978) *Gorseth Kernow: The First 50 Years*, Cornwall: Gorseth Kernow.
2. See Craig Weatherhill (1995) *Cornish Place-Names and Language*, Wilmslow: Sigma, pp.156–8 and pp.163–6.
3. Lizbeth Goodman (ed.) (1996) *Literature and Gender*, London and New York: Routledge and the Open University.
4. Alan M. Kent (1998) *Wives, Mothers and Sisters: Feminism, Literature and Women Writers of Cornwall*, Penzance: The Jamieson Library and Patten Press, pp.23–8; (ed.) (2000) *Voices from West Barbary: An Anthology of Anglo-Cornish Poetry 1549–1928*, London: Francis Boutle, pp.162–8.
5. George Clement Boase and William Prideaux Courtney (eds.) (1878) *Bibliotheca Cornubiensis*, London: Longman, Green, Reader and Dyer, Vol. 2, p.551.
6. Cornwall Record Office, P59/1/10, p.136 #1095. The spelling of Katharine or Katherine with an 'a' or an 'e' is unclear. Confusingly, Rawlings and her publishers altered the spelling throughout her career. In this chapter, I have settled on Katharine, as in her *Songs of the Stars and the Sea* (1926).

7. 1861 Census, St Erth folio, 114 schedule #95. She married 12 October 1805 at St Hilary. There were four children from the marriage: Thomas, who was christened in Marazion on 16 February 1806, became a clerk with Roberts' legal firm in Helston, and represented the Harveys in some of their disputes with the Cornwall Copper Company, Mary Ann Shorland, who married George William Gibson from Worcestershire, William John and Susanna herself.

8. Cornwall Record Office, H208/8.

9. Ibid., H217, p.19.

10. For an understanding of the Stannary system, see G. Harrison (1835) *Substance of a Report on the Laws and Jurisdiction of the Stannaries of Cornwall*, London: Longman, Rees, Orme, Brown, Green and Longman.

11. See the observations on A.J. Ellis in Martyn F. Wakelin (1975) *Language and History in Cornwall*, Leicester: Leicester University Press, p.28.

12. *Cornish Telegraph*, 21 August 1890, p.7. The article also states how 'he was an enthusiastic collector of old and rare porcelain; the splendid collection which he exhibited at the Hayle Industrial and Art Exhibition a few years since was greatly admired'.

13. Ibid. It is known that Rawlings commissioned E. and J.D. Sedding, who were best known for church architecture to design a house and garden for him. See June Fenwick 'Cornwall Gardens Trust' in *National Association of Decorative and Fine Arts Societies News*, Spring/Summer 1996, p.11.

14. Cornwall Record Office, P186/1/9, p.148 #295. There is the possibility of a family link here with Joseph Hambley Rowe – a leading figure in the Cowethas Kelto-Kernuack/Cornish Celtic Society at the turn of the twentieth century. See Hugh Miners and Treve Crago (2002) *Tolzethan: The Life and Times of Joseph Hambley Rowe*, Cornwall: Gorseth Kernow. Miners and Crago note that in 1904, Hambley Rowe sent a telegram in Cornish to Henry Jenner on Cornwall's admission to the Celtic Congress. See p.4.

15. *1861 Census*, St Erth folio, 115 schedule #106. Interestingly, 'The Downes' was later to become a convent for several years, until c.1995.

16. Cornwall Record Office, P186/1/5, p.62 #492. The name Giddy may be intentional or fashionable, since it links to another famous Cornishman of the St Erth/Hayle area, one Davies Gilbert (1767–1839), who had originally been a Giddy. See A.C. Todd (1967) *Beyond the Blaze: A Biography of Davies Gilbert*, Truro: D. Bradford Barton.

17. Cornwall Record Office, P186/1/17, p.146 #1168.

18. Ibid., P186/1/18. See also *Cornishman*, 21 August 1890, p.5. The obituary states that 'probably there has not for many years been a more largely-attended interment, every inhabitant apparently being out to witness the extraordinary long procession as it passed from Downes to Phillack church and churchyard'. It is known that Marion Hughes stayed at Downes from 7 August to 8 October 1874. Marion Hughes and Kitty Lee were friends already by October 1873.

19. For background to this period, see Derek Williams (1996) 'Henry Jenner: The Early Years' in *An Baner Kernewek/The Cornish Banner*, No. 84, pp.17–20.

20. Alan M. Kent and Tim Saunders (eds.) (2000) *Looking at the Mermaid: A Reader in Cornish Literature 900–1900*, London: Francis Boutle, pp.30–31.

21. See Ibid., p.322–23. See also Weatherhill, op.cit., pp.135–8; Brian Murdoch (1993) *Cornish Literature*, Cambridge: D.S. Brewer, pp.142–4.

22. See www.familysearch.org – *1881 Census*, Family History Library Film 1341036, PRO Reference RG11, Piece/Folio 0168/53, p.48.

23. *The Jenner Collection*, British Library.

24. Ibid., 27 August 1873.

25. Ibid., 14 October 1873. She later moved to the Slade Art School.

26. Ibid., 17 September 1873.

27. Ibid., 17 October 1873.

28. Ibid., 29 October 1873, 31 October 1873. Despite my efforts, I can neither find the surname nor background of Nellie.

29. Ibid., 13th November 1873.

30. Ibid., 3 December 1873.

31. Ibid., 5 January–6 February 1873.

32. Ibid., 20 February 1873.

33. Ibid., 9 April 1874.

34. Brian Bates (2002) *The Real Middle Earth: Magic and Mystery in the Dark Ages*, London: Sidgwick and Jackson, pp.5–6, pp.41–2 and pp.197–8.

35. Alan M. Kent 'Celtic Nirvanas: Constructions of Celtic in contemporary British youth culture' in David C. Harvey, Rhys Jones, Neil McInroy and Christine Milligan (eds.) *Celtic Geographies: Old Culture, New Times*, London and New York, pp.208–226.

36. See Henry Jenner (1904) *A Handbook of the Cornish Language, chiefly in its latest stage, with some account of its history and literature*, London: David Nutt.

37. *The Jenner Collection*, British Library, 22 June 1874.

38. Ibid., 8 July 1874.

39. Ibid., 18 July 1874. Kitty Lee did become an artist. The Beazley Archive contains a large number of watercolours. She enjoyed painting mountains and seascapes.

40. Ibid., 3 August 1874.

41. Ibid., 4 September 1874.

42. Ibid., 4 October 1874. Lach-Szyrma (1841–1915), the son of an ex-patriate Pole, was poet and vicar at Carnmenellys, near Newlyn. His centrality in the Revival of Cornish is now being realised by a number of scholars. See Kent and Saunders (ed.) (2000), p.357. Interestingly, on the 1 November 1874, Jenner notes that Lach-Szyrma has advised him to write his book on Cornish in French or Latin, because he thinks it will sell better.

43. Ibid., 7 November 1874.

44. Ibid., 18 November 1874. Two days later Jenner explains how he is going to a Philological Society meeting, and if Prince Lucien Bonaparte is there, he intends to ask him about the possibility of a Cornish Eisteddfod. The inaugural Cornish Gorsedd took place at Boscawen-Un in 1928, but the dream of its founding fathers for a national cultural festival would not be realised for a further fifty-five years when, in 1985, the first Esethvos Kernow was held in Truro.

45. Ibid., 27 November 1874. According to Mary Beazley, Henry Jenner and Kitty went rowing on the river at Hammersmith on 22 April before they were engaged. In her diaries, Kitty Lee describes Jenner in 'boating costume, he looked very well in flannel trousers and shirt and a blue cap'. Apparently they went on the river a number of times. See the Beazley Archive.

46. Ibid., 7 December 1874.

47. Ibid., 19 December 1874.

48. Postcard correspondence, 23 November 1875. I am indebted to Audrey Randle Pool for bringing this item to my attention.

49. *The Jenner Collection*, British Library, 12 October 1874. A lengthy critique of one of Rawlings' manuscripts follows the statement. It appears to complain of the 'surface-level' characterisation, though is hard for any observer to relate to the later published novels, since no names are given and neither is the manuscript's title. Kitty makes no mention of her novel-writing in either the diaries of 1873, 1874 or the period 1877–79 in the Beazley Archive.

50. Katherine Lee Jenner (1882) *A Western Wildflower*, London: Longmans. The Beazley Archive (June 1879) mentions a novelette titled 'A Wisht Old Story' but whether this is an earlier draft of the same book is unclear. In January 1880 she is writing a second serial for an unnamed weekly magazine. By July of the same

year, she had begun a new novel about John Ennis and Katherine of Hayle. By December the draft of the novel had been re-titled 'Sandhills of St Conan'.

51. Katherine Lee Jenner (1884) *In London Town*, London: Longmans, (1886) *Katherine Blythe*, London: Longmans, (1888) *An Imperfect Gentleman*, London: Longmans. The Beazley Archive has only the second and third volumes of the three volumes that make up the latter novel. A handwritten draft of *In London Town* is also in the Archive.

52. Katherine Lee Jenner (1891) *Love or Money: A Novel*, London: Bentley and Son.

53. Katherine Lee Jenner (1895) *When Fortune Frowns: Being the Life and Adventures of Gilbert Cosworth – A Gentleman of Cornwall*, London: Horace Cox. The proofs of this novel are held within the Beazley Archive.

54. Alan M. Kent (2000) *The Literature of Cornwall: Continuity, Identity, Difference 1000–2000*, Bristol: Redcliffe, p.130–1.

55. Alan M. Kent (2002) *Pulp Methodism: The Lives and Literature of Silas, Joseph and Salome Hocking*, St Austell: Cornish Hillside Publications, pp.127–39 and pp.178–88.

56. See Ella Westland 'The passionate periphery: Cornwall and romantic fiction' in Ian A. Bell (ed.) (1995) *Peripheral Visions: Images of Nationhood in Contemporary British Fiction*, Cardiff: University of Wales Press, p.154.

57. Christine Poulson (1999) *The Quest for the Grail: Arthurian Legend in British Art 1840–1920*, Manchester: Manchester University Press.

58. Jenner (1891) op.cit., p.7.

59. Ibid., p.27.

60. Ibid., p.36.

61. Ibid., p.46.

62. Ibid., Vol. 2, pp.176–7.

63. See Kent (2002) op.cit.

64. For useful background on this conflict, see Michael Hechter (1975) *Internal Colonialism: The Celtic Fringe in British National Development, 1536–1966*, London: Routledge and Kegan Paul, pp.106–9.

65. Peter Berresford Ellis (1985) *The Celtic Revolution: A Study in Anti-Imperialism*, Talybont: Y Lolfa, p.44.

66. The title of the work is apparently derived from Mackinnon's narrative *The Lyon in the Morning*: ' "Why, Morar," said the Prince, "this is very hard: you were very kind to me yester-night, and said you would find out a hiding place proof against all search of the enemy's forces, and now you say you can do nothing at all for me ... When Fortune smiled on me I found some people ready enough to serve me; but now WHEN FORTUNE FROWNS [her capitals] on me and I have no pay to give, they forsake me in my necessity." ' This quotation is found on the jacket of the book.

67. Jenner (1895) op.cit., p.i.

68. See for example Henry Jenner (1910) *Cornish Place-Names: A Lecture given at the Truro Church Institute*, 6 December. Pamphlet reprinted from the *Truro Diocesan Magazine*.

69. Jenner (1895) op.cit., p.i.

70. Ibid., pp.1–2. See 'The Cornish Catholics' in A. L. Rowse (1990 [1941]) *Tudor Cornwall*, Redruth: Dyllansow Truran, pp.342–79. For an alternative perspective on Catholics in Cornwall, see John Chynoweth (2002) *Tudor Cornwall*, Stroud: Tempus, pp.238–43.

71. Ibid., p.34.

72. Ibid., pp.54–6.

73. Ibid., p.12.

74. Ibid., pp.102–4.

75. Ibid., p.139.

76. Ibid., p.144.

77. Ibid., p.251.

78. Ibid., p.326.
79. H. A. Grueber, H.A. Dillon, H. Jenner and others (1889) *Exhibition of the Royal House of Stuart, The New Gallery, Regent Street*, London: The New Gallery; Henry Jenner (ed.) (1903) *Memoirs of the Lord Viscount Dundee, the Highland Clan and the Massacre of Glenco &c by Charles Leslie*, London: Robinson. The Beazley Archive contains several of Jenner's notebooks. One contains his investigations into his family history. It seems that one of Jenner's distant relatives had been imprisoned under the rule of William, Prince of Orange. Jenner writes 'That upon the occupation of the Crowns of these kingdoms by William, Prince of Orange in 1688, the above named Thomas Jenner was committed to the Tower of London'.
80. Kent and Saunders (eds.) (2000) op.cit., pp.224–7 and p.346.
81. Ibid., pp.232–5 and p.347.
82. Williams, op.cit., p.18.
83. Walter de Gray Birch and Henry Jenner (1879) *Early Drawings and Illuminations: An Introduction to the Study of Illustrated Manuscripts with a dictionary of subjects in the British Museum*, London: Bagster and Sons
84. Williams, op.cit., p.18.
85. (1903) *Christ in Art*, London: Methuen, (1907) *Our Lady in Art*, London: Methuen, (1910) *Christian Symbolism*, London: Methuen. The manuscript of a fourth book titled *Clergywomen* is held in the Beasley Archive. No doubt it was difficult to find a publisher for such a progressive work.
86. Jenner (1907), p.xv.
87. Peter Berresford Ellis (1993) *The Celtic Dawn: A history of Pan Celticism*, London: Constable, pp.73–86; Dillwyn Miles (1993) *The Secret of the Bards of the Isle of Britain*, Llandybie: Gwasg Dinefwr Press; Marion Löffler (2000) *A Book of Mad Celts: John Wickens and the Celtic Congress of Caernarfon 1904/John Wickens a Chyngres Geltaidd Caernarfon 1904*, Llandysul: Gomer.
88. Ibid., p.64.
89. Miners (1978) op.cit., p.20.
90. Ibid., pp.11–34; Derek Williams (1996) 'Henry Jenner: The Years of Fulfilment' in *An Baner Kernewek/The Cornish Banner*, No. 85, pp.15–18.
91 Katherine Lee Jenner (1919) *Christmas Verse*, Penzance: Beare and Son.
92. See The Jenner Papers, Courtney Library, Royal Institution of Cornwall. In the years 1972–73 a Mr Nicholls catalogued a 'rough' list of the contents of each box, as they arrived in Truro from the British Museum. Approximately 24 boxes arrived, but these have since been much amalgamated and altered. Nicholls' rough list is very useful however. Box 10 holds most of Kitty Lee Jenner's correspondence. Much of this collection's contents are ephemera, but there are some interesting documents.
93. Ibid. Box 1, Bundle 1. Bernard Rawlings eventually became an Admiral during the Second World War. He was buried at sea.
94. Ibid. Box 1.
95. Ibid.
96. See Bernard Walke (1935) *Twenty Years at St Hilary*, London: Methuen. For a wider picture, see John Hurst '"The Long Friendship": Painters and Writers in Newlyn' in *Journal of the Royal Institution of Cornwall* (2000), pp.168–85.
97. *The Jenner Papers*, Box 1, Bundle 1.
98. Ibid. For detail on Adrian Fortescue (1874–1923), see John G. Vance and J.W. Fortescue (1924) *Adrian Fortescue: A Memoir*, London: Burns, Oates and Washbourne Ltd.
99. Ibid.
100. Statistics from Lindsay Hunt (1999) *Brittany*, Windsor: AA Publishing, p.42.
101. Edward W. Said (1979) *Orientalism*, New York: Vintage.
102. Op.cit., Box 1.
103. Katharine Lee Jenner (1926) *Songs of the Stars and the Sea*, London: Erskine MacDonald, p.16.

104. Ibid., p.19.
105. Ibid., p.20.
106. Ibid.
107. Ibid., p.21.
108. Ibid., p.23.
109. Ibid., p.24.
110. Ibid., p.25.
111. *Jenner Papers*, Box 2.
112. Ibid.
113. Ibid. I can find no further examples of Kitty Lee's poetry in either the Jenner Papers at the Royal Institution of Cornwall or the Jenner Collection at the British Library.
114. See Kent (ed.), op.cit., p.215. For a useful obituary of Henry Jenner, see *Western Morning News*, 9 May 1934, p.8.
115. Jenner Collection, Box 10, Bundle 2.
116. Ibid., Bundle 3.
117. F.L. Cross and E.A. Livingstone (eds.) (1974) *The Oxford Dictionary of the Christian Church*, Oxford: Oxford University Press, p.1446.
118. *The Eighty-Fourth Annual Report of the Royal Cornwall Polytechnic Society*, Vol.3 1917, p.168. Ysolt had an early and advanced interested in Christianity. A small book of religious questions written while she was still a small girl remains in the Beazley Archive.
119. *Royal Cornwall Gazette* 9 May1934
120. Weatherhill, op.cit., p.163–5; Kent (2000) op.cit., p.199.
121. Philip Payton 'Identity, Ideology and Language in modern Cornwall' in Hildegard L.C. Tristram (ed.) *The Celtic Englishes*, Heidelberg: Universitätsverlag C. Winter, pp.100–122.
122. Piers Brendon (1975) *Hawker of Morwenstow*, London: Jonathan Cape.
123. See for example, Peter Isaac (2000) *A History of Evangelical Christianity in Cornwall*, Cornwall: Peter Isaac.
124. Horace Keast (n.d.) *The Catholic Revival in Cornwall 1833–1983*, Helston: Catholic Advisory Council for Cornwall.
125. Kent (2000), op.cit., p.262; Bernard Deacon 'Language Revival and Language Debate: Modernity and Postmodernity' in Philip Payton (ed.) (1996) *Cornish Studies Four*, Exeter: University of Exeter, pp.88–106.
126. Jenner (1904) op.cit., p.v; Tim Saunders (ed.) *The Wheel: An Anthology of Modern Poetry in Cornish 1850–1980*, London: Francis Boutle, pp.40–1. The Handbook contains this dedicatory poem to his Katharine Lee Jenner: 'Dho'm Gwreg Gernuak/To my Cornish wife'. The reference to the Grey Rock in the Wood is to the old Cornish phrasing for St Michael's Mount (before it was flooded by the sea) – 'Garrek Loys en Côs'.

Two poems by Katharine Lee Jenner

The Boats of Sennen
(Cornish Fisher-girl's Song)

The corn is in the shock,
And the fish are on the rock,
And the merry boats go dancing out of Whitesand Bay,
I hear the huer's cry,
And I see the dappled sky,
And it minds me of the days that are long gone away.

The corn was in the shock,
And the fish were on the rock,
And the sea was all alive from the Wolf to Castle Treen,
But the fog came down by night,
And it hid the Longships light,
And the men that went a-fishing never more were seen.

The corn was in the shock,
And the fish were on the rock,
When the boats went out from Sennen with the pilchard seine;
But the morning broke so fair,
And not a boat was there,
And the lad I loved was with them and he came not back again.

The corn is in the shock,
And the fish are on the rock,
And the golden sun is gleaming on the Islands of the West;
I hear the huer's cry,
And I see the dappled sky,
And my heart is dead with sorrow for the lad I love the best.

The Old Names

The half-forgotten music of old names
    Clings to the rocks and hills,
And an intangible human fragrance gives
    To senseless earth, and fills
With glamour half divine all the wild places,
    Recalling the old days,
When man on earth believed that the Divine
    Encompassed all his ways.

Out of the vast void of oblivion
    Rings the wild melody
Of those old words, whose only resting-place
    Is the vague memory
Of man, the creature so prone to forget,
    Yet who forgetting clings,
Subconsciously remembering their sense,
    To the old names and things.

The music of the old names is worn thin
    By busy lips of men;
Yet they are eloquent of ancient dreams
    Of knightly valour, when
The hills were purpled and the valleys stained
    With battles and sore strife,

And of the deeds, achievements, hopes, and fears,
        Of long-forgotten life.

Come to Carn Brea, beside Trevorian Down,
        And hear the Gwynver call[1]
From Vellandreath, Carn Bargas, and Carn Ky,
        While evening shadows fall
On Tregonebris and Boscawen-Oon,
        And over Crows-an-Wra,
And on Bartinny and Caer Brane there shines
        The light of dying day.

Away beyond Rospannel and Boscarn
        And Buryan tower above,
The southern sea is gleaming through the gap,
        That marks Lamorna Cove,
And all about St Levan and Penberth
        On to Pedn-Men-an-Mere
The sunset shines upon a land whose names
        Are music everywhere.

These names of our dead speech are music still
        In our dear living land,
Which never can be void or desolate
        While here on every hand
Is still the record of our fathers' lives,
        Though their old hopes and fears
Have passed away like sunlight on the hills
        Down through the path of years.

---

1. The 'calling of the Gwynver' is the sound of the sea breaking upon Gwynver Sands by Sennen. The story is
    that it is the sea moaning for the loss of Guinevere who escaped from it when Lyonnesse was submerged.
    Sometimes it can be heard as far off as Penzance, and it betokens evil fortune.

From *Songs of the Stars and the Sea*, London: Erskine Macdonald, 1926

'Gathering the fragments…': Henry Jenner, the Old Cornwall Societies and Gorseth Kernow

Brian Coombes

Introduction: The Lineage

Gorseth Kernow – the Gorsedd of Cornwall[1] – has become the most distinctive public manifestation of the revival of Celtic national awareness in Cornwall and the Old Cornwall Societies are a uniquely Cornish concept. These two institutions are closely linked, not least because Henry Jenner was not only the first Grand Bard of the Gorsedd, but also the founding President of both the first Old Cornwall Society and the Federation of Old Cornwall Societies.

Although the cultural life of Cornwall prior to the Anglo-Saxon incursions of the ninth century must have been reasonably similar to that in Wales, Jenner himself acknowledged that any documentary evidence for the existing Cornish bardic system is non-existent. It is therefore to Wales that we must look for the existence of what Hugh Miners calls 'a thin, tenuous but unbroken line of bards'[2] through to our own time. Specifically, it was Edward Williams (Iolo Morganwg) who 'revived' the Gorsedd of Bards in 1792, with three orders: Druids, Bards and Ovates. This and such symbolism as the three ways of the 'awen' (the Welsh 'Nod Cyfrin' or mystic mark), though based often on mis-readings of prehistory and classical writers – 'fakes', perhaps – do, in accordance with the best contemporary scholarship, contain the essence of a genuine idea of how things must have been. After 1858, the ceremonies devised by Iolo for his Gorsedd became an integral part of the Eisteddfod. Towards the end of the nineteenth century the adoption of the white, blue and green robes and regalia – vaguely Bronze Age! – designed largely by the artist Hubert Herkomer made what was by then the Welsh National Eisteddfod a striking and memorable festival. It has been pointed out by Ellis that 'although, on a scholastic level, one can criticise Iolo Morganwg, as Professor Piggott has done ... his inventions have now been given two hundred years of tradition ... [and the Gorsedd] has taken on a serious and respected life of its own'.[3] It should also be noted that local eisteddfodau, consisting essentially of music and poetry competitions, are a feature of cultural life in Wales.[4]

'The great Celtic-Cornish project'

At the beginning of the twentieth century the Celtic Association, with the Anglo-Irish peer Lord Castletown as President, was active in promoting games, folklore, language and costume.[5] *Goursez Breizh* was publicly recognised in 1901 after several Breton delegates were made bards at Cardiff two years earlier, but the Gaelic-speaking nations did not follow Wales and Brittany down the Gorsedd path, preferring instead to let national competitive festivals such as the *Mòd* (Scotland) and the *Oireachtas* (Ireland) express their Celtic pride. In the meantime, J. Hobson Matthews, the historian of St Ives, and Reginald Reynolds, a Cardiff architect, and his wife were admitted to the Welsh Gorsedd at Cardiff in 1899. It seems as though they were among the representatives preparing for the 1900 Celtic Congress.[6] In 1901 the *Cowethas Kelto-Kernuak* (Celtic Cornish Society) was formed under the presidency of Sir W.L. Salisbury-Trelawny, with Henry Jenner as the Vice-President responsible for the language.[7] One of its main aims was '[t]o revive the Cornish Language as a spoken tongue, by publishing a Grammar and Dictionary of the Language' – an aim that was realised with the publication of Jenner's *Handbook*. Another priority was 're-establishing the Cornish Gorsedh of the Bards at Boscawen-Un'.[8] Its secretary, L.C. Duncombe Jewell, even designed a Cornish national costume, which Jenner himself is said to have worn at the Welsh National Eisteddfod on more than one occasion.[9] *The Outfitter* for 30 August 1902 describes the full costume thus:

The dress itself is to consist of a kilt of homespun dyed woad-blue. A short tunic of the same, blue hose for those who are courageous, and blue "tights" for those who are not. The head-covering of the same blue will be somewhat conical in shape, and much like the low "bassinet" of the crusader. To it may be brooched the badge of the Cornish "An bannal", the broom-plant. But yellow – saffron yellow – is the real colour of Cornwall found not only in the broom-blossom, but in the bezants of its arms; and therefore yellow may be employed to relieve the monotony of woad-blue.[10]

Duncombe Jewell was made a member of the Welsh Gorsedd at Bangor in 1902, taking the name *Bardd Glas* (Blue Bard).[11] Two or three years later ill-health forced him to retire as the organisation's secretary and its decline thereafter was fairly swift, in all probability because its London base was too remote. In 1903 Jenner gave a speech to the Congress of the *Union Régionaliste Bretonne* before having a Bardic degree conferred on him by the Breton Gorsedd at Plounéour-Trez and taking the name *Gwaz Mikael* (Servant of Michael).[12] It appears, too, that shortly afterwards he corresponded with the then Welsh Archdruid and others in the Welsh Gorsedd about the possibility of a Cornish Gorsedd. 'They were all vaguely sympathetic,' wrote Jenner years later, 'but the time was not ripe and nothing came of it then. There were not enough Cornish people who were sufficiently interested to make it possible.'[13] The story of Jenner's pivotal role at the Caernarfon Celtic Congress of 1904 is well documented, and related elsewhere in this volume. He went on to represent Cornwall at the Edinburgh Congress three years later and at the London Eisteddfod of 1909, where he was a representative of the Royal Institution of Cornwall.[14]

Such was the mix of 'nationalist' activities and those with a more cultural or linguistic slant that was characteristic of what Hale calls 'the great Celtic-Cornish project'[15] during the first decade of the twentieth century. Although by 1907, Jenner had translated parts of the Welsh Gorsedd ceremony into Cornish 'just in case the time should come',[16] they would not be needed just yet. It was rather as a local historian and scholar that he would initially carve out a niche for himself when he retired to Cornwall in 1909, working closely with such well-established bodies as the Royal Institution of Cornwall, the Royal Cornwall

Polytechnic Society and the Penzance Library.

In 1917 Jenner sent an address to the Celtic Congress at Birkenhead in which he showed considerable pessimism about any possible new use of the Cornish language and any literature in it. '[T]hey have no position,' he wrote, 'except in the grave, and no prospects of any joyful resurrection.'[17] Instead, his survey of Cornish scholarship was largely concerned with place-names and antiquities. Interestingly, he expressed the view that he was not at all sure that a society that would confine its attention wholly to the Celtic aspect of Cornwall would be either desirable or useful. 'I really think we can get on very well with the societies that we have got,' he continued.[18] At the 1918 Neath Eisteddfod Jenner met D. Rhys Phillips (*Y Beili Glas*), a Welsh Bard and secretary of the Celtic Congress, who was keen for a Gorsedd to be established in Cornwall.[19] The meeting was to prove highly significant, for ten years later Phillips was to be the crucial link between the Welsh Gorsedd and those in Cornwall who had been working towards the establishment of a Cornish Gorsedd. In due course, then, Phillips' correspondence with Jenner and later with Robert Morton Nance would bear fruit, but for the time being, both men were content to gather up those fragments of Cornish history and culture that remained and move forward from there. For after the Great War, the idea of a more widespread Cornish Revival again appeared feasible and Nance and Jenner jointly took centre-stage in the effort to 'rouse Cornish people from their indifference to their own past'[20] and 'to inculcate [the] consciousness [of their Cornishness] in the people of Cornwall'.[21]

Cuntelleugh an Brewyon us Gesys...

Nance had started learning Cornish in 1904. Until moving to St Ives in 1914, he lived at Nancledra where he wrote *The Cledry Plays* in dialect for production by the villagers. After serving in the war, he put on a production of one entitled *Duffy* at St Ives in 1919, partly in aid of war charities. His sister, Mrs Morton Raymont, thought that the 'club for young and old of both sexes', the founding of which was the object of another of her brother's plays, must have been the Old Cornwall Society[22] There is no proof of this, but in his Preface to the 1956 edition of the plays, Nance wrote, 'It was a performance of "Duffy" in St Ives that led to the formation there in 1920 of the first Old Cornwall Society and so in time to the Federation of Old Cornwall Societies and to the Cornish Gorsedd.'[23] In September 1920 Henry Jenner gave a Presidential address to the Royal Cornwall Polytechnic Society in Falmouth, which 'for want of a better title I have called ... "The Renaissance of Merry England" ... counting Cornwall, for this occasion only, as if it were part of England.' Having dealt with libraries, music, dancing, folklore and others topics, he mentions the St Ives Old Cornwall Society – 'chiefly organised by Mr Nance' – as an example for 'studying, collecting and preserving ... language, dialect, manners, customs, folk-lore...' and continues, 'Why not have Old Cornwall Societies all over the County? ... they might be on lines similar to ... those excellent things ... the Women's Institutes.'[24] It is interesting to see how closely these subjects mirror those set out by the Celtic Cornish Society in its prospectus two decades earlier. The 1920s was a period of progress for cultural activities both locally and beyond the Tamar. Women's Institutes (the Cornwall Federation dates from 1918), folk dancing, music festivals (Jenner himself had been President of the 1917 Cornwall Music Competition[25]), ramblers' groups, the National Trust – all these activities and groups flourished alongside and sometimes also in sympathy with the Celtic revival in both Cornwall and in other lands.

The St Ives Old Cornwall Society, then, grew out of Nance's *Cledry Plays* and the community's interest in the Cornish dialect. Following a meeting in the council chamber on 21 January 1920, the Mayor presided over a public meeting in the Public Hall three weeks later at which Jenner gave 'a most interesting and informative address, cursorily tracing the history of the county from the stone age ... to the present time'. After Jenner had referred to the enthusiastic support given to his scheme for the collection of Cornish folklore by the County Education Committee and promised to do all he could to assist in making the newly formed St Ives Old Cornwall Society successful, Nance 'presented quite an ambitious programme for [its] future working...'[26] Jenner became the first President of the new society, which held Cornish Language classes in addition to running a full lecture programme, and normally addressed its annual meetings. Although he did not always attend committee meetings, he was as frequent a lecturer at St Ives as he was at other societies. With the preservation from extinction of all that was peculiarly Cornish and all that was Celtic in Cornwall, especially the language, as its core aims, the society proved so popular that new branches were set up to meet the demand. Truro and Redruth Old Cornwall Societies were formed in 1922, followed by Hayle, with Jenner as founder-president, on 10 February the following year.[27]

By 1924 there were enough societies to form a Federation, with Jenner a natural choice for permanent president. A biannual journal, with Nance as editor, was launched the following year. As well as carrying news of the various societies in its 'Federation Report', *Old Cornwall* acted as a means of preserving in print some of the more important papers and notes contributed to society meetings on subjects such as Cornwall's history, folklore and language.[28] The first issue in April 1925 led with an article by Robert Morton Nance entitled 'What We Stand For', much of which underlined the importance of recording Cornwall's traditions, customs, dialect and language and thus living up to the Federation's motto, '*Cuntelleugh an Brewyon us Gesys, Na Vo Kellys Travyth*' – 'Gather up the fragments that remain, that nothing be lost'. However, such fragments were to be gathered 'not as dead stuff to be learnedly discussed nor as merely amusing trifles', but in order that those building a 'New Cornwall' would be equipped with the right tools, namely 'the Living Tradition of the Cornish People'. For Nance, at least, it was 'the beginning of a National Movement'.[29] In contrast, the essay by Jenner, which followed Nance's wake-up call, was entitled 'The Preservation of Ancient Monuments in Cornwall'. Since 1913 he had been chairman of the committee that had been charged with safeguarding Cornwall's ancient monuments and his suggestion here was that it would be appropriate for each Old Cornwall Society to take informal charge of those monuments in its district, make lists of them, inspect them periodically, and report on them to the Federation.[30]

Over the next six years Jenner was fortunate enough to enjoy the services of a distinguished team to back him in his twilight years as Federation President nominally in charge of guiding seventeen societies. Canon Sims Carah of Camborne was Vice President, A.K. Hamilton Jenkin, an authority on mining and social history, was Secretary and Nance doubled as Recorder and editor of *Old Cornwall*. Although it is clear from Hayle Old Cornwall Society minutes that ill health had begun to curtail his involvement in its day-to-day affairs, he continued to play as full a part as possible. On 23 June 1931, for instance, he climbed Trencrom to light the annual mid-summer bonfire that the Federation had revived 'from Chapel Carn Brea to Kit Hill' two years earlier. And the following season he adapted his address to the 1932 Celtic Congress – 'The Awakening of Celtic Cornwall' – for both Hayle and St Ives Old Cornwall Societies.[31]

Charles Henderson, the historian whose death at an early age in 1933, was such a loss to Cornwall, began his period with the extra-mural department of the then University College of the South West at Exeter in 1924. Three years later Henry Jenner's appointment there as honorary St Petrock Lecturer in Celtic Studies reflected the growing status of Cornwall's language and culture beyond the Tamar. While the Workers' Educational Association and the older 'County' societies undoubtedly played their part in this recognition, it was the Old Cornwall Societies that provided a base from which the actual foundation of the Cornish Revival could spread. Indeed, in Jenner's view it was their unqualified success that made a Cornish Gorsedd possible. '[T]here is no doubt,' he wrote in 'Bards, Druids and The Gorsedd', 'that to the Old Cornwall Societies belongs the credit of making it [a Cornish Gorsedd] an accomplished fact'.[32] What he did not say was that his own local and wider prestige and his towering personality were likewise vital ingredients.[33]

Revisiting the circle: Boscawen-Un

In the meantime the campaign to 'revive' the Gorsedd in Cornwall had continued, mostly behind the scenes. *Y Beili Glas* had kept up a correspondence with Nance, with Jenner surely being appraised of the situation.[34] On 25 June 1927, resplendent in the white head-dress and robes of the Breton Gorsedd, he read a paper to a pilgrimage of the Federation of Old Cornwall Societies to Boscawen-Un stone circle in the parish of St Buryan, near Penzance. In it he spoke of the meaning of the Gorsedd for the Celtic nations, discussing the significance of the site as 'Beisgawen', one of the three *'Prif-orsedd Beirdd Ynys Prydain* ... principal Session-places of the Bards of the Island of Britain...', in an early Medieval Welsh Triad. He explained the significance of the three Orders or Bardic degrees – 'an important part of a gorsedd' – and commented that the Old Cornwall Societies were already doing on a modest scale what the competitions devised by the Welsh and Breton *gorseddau* were doing for their countries. Finally, without giving a sign that he knew of any other moves that were afoot, he stated, 'I should like to throw it out as a hint that we really ought some day to have a Cornish Gorsedd ... The Welsh or Breton Gorseddau would, I know, encourage us ... and I beg of you to let that idea sink into your minds.'[35] In August the main 'players' met at the Inter-Celtic Festival at Riec-sur-Bélon in Brittany. Notice of this event had been given in *Old Cornwall* that April and the October issue carried a report that included part of a letter from *Y Beili Glas*, who was also secretary of the Welsh Delegation, that had appeared in the October *Consortium Breton:*

> The Welsh Gorsedd members have in view the holding of a Gorsedd ceremony in Cornwall in September 1928 or 1929, for the purpose of bringing the ancient Land of Cornwall into more immediate association with Wales ... By doing so we shall be happily answering the appeal which Cornwall's most distinguished scholar, Mr Henry Jenner, has continued to urge upon us for many years past.[36]

The correspondence between *Y Beili Glas* and Nance – or at least, the former's side of it – is explored by Hugh Miners in *Gorseth Kernow: the first 50 years*. The main proposals, with the aim of realising 'Dr [*sic*] Jenner's time-honoured desire for a Gorsedd meeting while he yet lives', included the reception at Treorchy during the first week of August 1928 of three or four – later five – Cornish scholars who, with the Reynolds and Jenner, would give Cornwall the nucleus of a mid-September Gorsedd celebration in which Jenner would be the first 'Derwydd Mawr'. In this correspondence there is more than a hint that the latter's vitality was beginning to falter – he was seventy-nine, after all – with phrases such as 'this to be done while Jenner is with us to help' and 'that will ensure your carrying on after his [Jenner's] time' being used. A letter dated March 1928 suggests that 'if Dr Jenner is able to move about, make him head for a year or two'.[37] Such statements dovetail quite nicely with Jenner's own view that his share of the proceedings at Boscawen-Un on 21 September 1928 was 'chiefly confined to putting on pretty clothes and trying to look the part'[38] and underline the essentially ceremonial nature of his involvement. Behind-the-scenes discussions, with Jenner undoubtedly being briefed on any progress, continued until 11 February 1928 when, at its Conference, the Federation of Old Cornwall Societies decided, at the suggestion of *Y Beili Glas*, to invite officials of the Welsh Gorsedd to hold a ceremony in Cornwall, in the hope that this exchange would lead to the formation of a Cornish Gorsedd.[39] Arrangements for Boscawen-Un were set in motion, with the Federation being in overall charge. Nance convinced *Y Beili Glas* that no distinction should be made between possible candidates, with all being admitted to the Order of Bards, which would itself be headed by a 'Grand Bard'. This became the rule 'until the Council [of the Gorsedd] shall determine otherwise'. Nance wrote many years later that such rules were devised 'so as to follow our watchword of 'One and All' and ... avoid the accusations of ... reviving Druidism...' Although there have since been moves to change this, majority opinion has always been for a 'blue gorsedd' with everyone on a 'flat rate'.[40]

Events moved fairly swiftly following the Federation's invitation. That July, after the Welsh Gorsedd Proclamation Ceremony in Liverpool, the following telegram was received, 'Cornish Gorsedd sanctioned – Archdruid Pedrog', thus nicely balancing Hambley Rowe's telegram to Jenner at Caernarfon twenty-four years earlier.[41] A month later, on 7 August, Archdruid Pedrog initiated eight Cornish men and women as bards of Wales at Treorchy. They included Robert Morton Nance, Canon Gilbert Doble, the leading authority on the Celtic Saints, Canon J.S. Carah and Dr Hambley Rowe. One of the new bards, W.D. Watson, spoke in Cornish and, according to the *Western Mail*, in 'fairly good Welsh'.[42] Later that same day this nucleus of a Cornish Gorsedd met in Cox's Café, Cardiff to discuss what should be done next. Among the decisions made were that they and Mrs Jenner should constitute the Council of Gorseth Kernow, that Jenner should be Grand Bard with Nance as his deputy, and that a number of other Cornish men and women would be initiated at Boscawen-Un.[43] Three weeks later the first meeting in Cornwall of some of those who had been accepted as members of the Breton and Welsh *gorseddau*, and Edgar Rees, the Secretary of Penzance Old Cornwall Society, was held at 'Bospowes', Hayle.[44] In a statement to the Cornish press, which may or may not pre-date this meeting, Jenner, Nance and Rees outlined the background to the coming event which 'ought to be of great interest to Cornwall ... [and] a very full and marked recognition of Cornwall as a sister Celtic nation by a body well qualified to act in the name of Wales [the Gorsedd of the Bards] ...' The organising triumvirate then stressed the hugely beneficial effects – 'literary, educational and otherwise' – of

Boscawen-Un Gorsedd, 21 September 1928, with Henry Jenner and Archdruid
Gorseth Kernow Archive

the immensely popular Welsh Gorsedd with 'its encouragement of intelligent local patriotism' – Jenner's pet phrase![45]

That the Gorsedd ceremony held at Boscawen-Un stone circle, near St Buryan on 21 September 1928 was a splendid affair, blessed with perfect weather, is clear from the personal reminiscences of those present, Jenner's included, and contemporary press coverage, not least a fifteen-page souvenir produced by *The Cornishman*. All the arrangements were ably co-ordinated by Edgar Rees, one of the new initiates who, it may be recalled, died during the installation of E.G. Retallack Hooper as Grand Bard at Callington in 1959. 'May I be allowed to say,' said Jenner following Rees' initiation, 'that we owe a great deal to Mr Rees for the arrangement of this Gorsedd. He has taken the whole work upon him; he worked tremendously hard, and, as far as we have gone, worked extremely successfully ... He did not want to be a Bard, but he had to be.'[46]

Gwas Myghal

It is Jenner's installation as Grand Bard that concerns us most here, of course, and it was this ceremony, performed by Archdruid *Pedrog* (Rev J.O. Williams), that preceded the initiation of the twelve new bards who included historians A. K. Hamilton Jenkin and Charles Henderson, W.B. Tregoning Hooper of the Cornish Wrestling Association and the doyen of Cornish writers, Sir Arthur Quiller-Couch, Professor of English Literature at Cambridge. '[T]his is a head worthy of putting a crown on,' said the Archdruid as he placed a laurel wreath on Jenner's brow. 'They tell me,' he continued, 'that the word translated glory in our Bible was 'heaviness', but it developed into a better meaning, and that was 'importance' – weightiness. My friends, your Grand Bard fills both meanings – he is both heavy and important.'[47] Although Jenner wore his white Breton Druid's robes at Boscawen-Un, in a painting of the 1933 Roche Gorsedd by Herbert Trueman which is now in the Royal Cornwall Museum, he is dressed in blue robes and a hood with adornments.

Speeches on the history and functions of the Gorsedd by ex-Archdruid *Elfed* (Rev Elvet Lewis) and the Rev Principal J. Maurice Jones, were later described by Jenner as 'a standard to which we must try to attain'.[48] Offering Cornwall's welcome to the Gorsedd, first in Welsh and then in English, he remarked, 'I cannot speak Welsh well enough to make a speech in it,[49] but I feel I must try and say one word in your language – a word which comes from the heart of all Cornwall: "welcome – the best of welcomes – to the Bards of Wales".' Having thanked the Archdruid and the Druids for their presence and support, he continued, 'It is beyond doubt a formal and a very marked recognition of Cornwall as a sister Celtic nation. People did not recognise that a little time ago, and I only wish that Cornwall recognised it more now.' Underlining the great power in Wales of the Gorsedd as a connecting link between academic scholarship and popular culture, Jenner hoped that it would do the same in Cornwall, supplementing the work that had been done in a quiet and modest way for some years by the Old Cornwall Societies. The Cornish motto was 'One and All' and this was what the Gorsedd stood for.[50]

It is clear from Jenner's open letter of thanks to *The Cornishman* after the events of 21 September that the Welsh contingent had on that memorable day a pretty full schedule. In the morning they were taken to Paul Church because of its associations with the late stages of the Cornish language, the Merry Maidens stone circle and Land's End. Thankfully, the perfect weather played its own part in the event's success. 'Surely the Cornish Saints – and they are many – must have been on special duty that day,' wrote Jenner, 'and saw to it, so we will thank them at a venture.' He concluded his letter with a spirited rallying cry to the faithful and perhaps also to the 2,000 or so people who witnessed the events at Boscawen-Un:

> The Gorsedd is now a real thing and it remains to be seen what will come of it. The organisation and general arrangements have yet to be settled and you will hear more of it before long, but the reception of the event, and that not only by those who were present, showed a striking and sudden re-awakening of Cornwall to its Celtic character, and we do not mean to let it go to sleep again if we can help it.[51]

Another feature of Cornwall's first Gorsedd that was reported at great length by the press and one which continues to play a part is the civic element. Indeed, present at a reception that was given later that day at Penzance, were the mayors and mayoresses of no less than eight Cornish towns, namely Helston, Penryn, St Ives, Falmouth, Truro, Bodmin, Liskeard and, of course, Penzance. In his remarks, the Mayor of Penzance, Alderman Howell Mabbott, said that

Henry Jenner's hope that Cornwall would have a Gorsedd of its own had been realised and at last the nationality of Cornwall had been established. A thousand years had elapsed since the Bards had visited Cornwall, and Cornwall extended to them the greatest possible welcome.[52]

However 'wobbly' the detail of both these remarks and headlines such as 'Thousand Years' Old Ceremony Re-enacted', they do catch the spirit of the event and its significance in Cornish history. Bringing a crowd of upwards of 2,000 onside was no mean achievement, for as Jenner himself acknowledged, 'a very little would have got a laugh in the wrong place ... [and] would have made it a failure...'[53] There is no doubt, either, that Jenner's personal prestige, stature and bearing added to its success, as they did to the choice and acceptance of the new Bards. 'In controversial matters he was courteous in his diction,' wrote Hambley Rowe and Nance on his death, '[and] being wise enough not to neglect the press, he became a power ... amongst people who came not into contact with him in academical matters.'[54] His installation as the first Grand Bard of Cornwall and the reception of the twelve initiates on that September day in 1928 marked the culmination for *Gwas Myghal* of years of campaigning on behalf of his native land. Although, as we have seen, much of the work involved in setting up and organising this and subsequent *gorseddau* fell to Nance, Jenner's guiding hand was, nevertheless, crucial and he continued to chair both the Annual Meetings of the Gorsedd itself and its council meetings until July 1933. Equally important was the support that he received from his wife Kitty who was present at both the pre-Boscawen-Un meeting at 'Bospowes' and at that which took place in the mayor's parlour, Penzance, on the very evening of that historic occasion when an executive of fourteen bards was appointed for one year in order to carry out the aims and objectives of the Gorsedd. Her last recorded attendance was at the Annual Meeting at St John's Hall, Penzance on 4 September 1931.[55]

In 1930 Jenner was invited to preside over the International Arthurian Congress in Truro, to which delegates came from the Continent and the United States as well as from all over the United Kingdom. Though 'courteous in his diction', Jenner invariably spoke his mind and on this occasion aroused considerable controversy by declaring that, in his opinion, the castle at Tintagel had no connection with King Arthur![56] It is possible to see the influence of Jenner's

interest in Arthurian matters in the closing stages of the Cornish Gorsedd ceremony where bards swear loyalty on the sword of King Arthur – 'Arta ef a dhe!
He shall come again!'[57] Whilst the symbolic language contains an emotional
truth, in his writings Jenner showed another type of truth, that of sound scholarship.[58] It is noteworthy, too, that in the badge of the Federation of Old
Cornwall Societies is the legend 'Nyns yu marrow Myghtern Arthur' (King
Arthur is not dead), so perhaps theirs was, initially at least, a more consciously
'revivalist' agenda than is sometimes supposed.

Two years later Jenner presided over the first Celtic Congress to be held in
Cornwall, again in Truro. Delegates from Brittany, Wales, Ireland, the Isle of
Man and, of course, Cornwall heard short addresses in Cornish from eight
Cornish bards, and were entertained by the performance of Nance's one-act
play in Unified Cornish, *An Balores* (The Chough). In his presidential address
entitled 'The awakening of Celtic Cornwall' Jenner put forward the view that
the Cornish language should be an optional subject in the schools of Cornwall.[59]
His ceremonial role at both these congresses, as well as the events themselves,
would have hastened the acceptance of the infant Gorsedd and added to its
prestige. Indeed, having in 1931 expressed the view that the days of the language were probably numbered and that it was surely destined to fade away for
ever, the Welsh cleric and historian G. Hartwell Jones revised his prediction
after attending the Truro Congress a year later and hearing the speeches and
papers in Cornish. In a speech of his own that he delivered at the Dinard
Congress in 1933 he praised 'the influence and inspiration of scholars' who had
helped Cornish arise from the dust, and the band of young Cornishmen who
had 'thrown themselves with ardour into the scientific study of the language
and the remnants of its literature'.[60] At Truro in both 1930 and 1932, some of the
delegates were made honorary bards, including on the latter occasion the Irish
scholar and folklorist Douglas Hyde, who was later to be the first President of
Ireland.[61]

There is no doubt that Henry Jenner was fortunate in having such men as
Robert Morton Nance, Hambley Rowe, W.D. Watson and A.K. Hamilton Jenkin
as co-workers in the Cornish Revival. His own achievements, though, were substantial and he fully deserved the reverence and cult status that were his
towards the end of his life. Ernest Morton Nance, *Mordon*'s nephew, remem-

bered him as 'the mighty patriarch'; for Susan Hosking (*Dynsak Porthya*), an early Cornish Language student, he looked 'like Moses'.[62] Brian Sullivan of Hayle Old Cornwall Society records that, during the early decades of the twentieth century, '[t]he ultimate honour, short only of being elected a Bard, would be an invitation to tea at Bospowes'.[63] George Pawley White (*Gunwyn*), Grand Bard 1965–71, recalls being sent to the Jenners' house as a junior bank clerk. To his amazement, ' "Moses" appeared at the door and I was absolutely struck dumb ... I didn't know what to say – because this was the man I had read so much about and had admired so much...'[64] Certainly, as Miners has written, 'he led his people to the Promised Land he saw for them – acceptance of them as Celtic by the Welsh and other Celtic peoples.'[65]

Jenner's legacy

It has been argued that the early Cornish Celtic revival in general and the Gorsedd in particular represented an idea of 'Medieval Celtic Catholic Cornwall' and that a strong element of Anglo-Catholicism was ingrained in the leading figures of both.[66] This is a valuable insight, but it is not the whole story and does not seem to have been apparent to many of the participants in the Cornish Revival of the period.[67] It is important, too, not to over emphasise any breaks in Cornwall's character; tin, fishing and scattered chapels, together with a certain nonconformity – 'bloody-mindedness', if you like – were already representative of Cornwall in the Middle Ages. Jenner's leadership ensured that *all facets* of Cornish life were embraced by the Gorsedd: the Cornish language, dialect, Methodism, maritime prowess, literature, art, radicalism, the Royalist tradition, various Anglican and Nonconformist traditions, the memory of the Saints and of the Tudor martyrs alike, the Cornish Diaspora and much besides. Jenner, himself, always stayed in touch with his native land, with Cornish life in all its diversity. He had been a founder of the short-lived Cornish Manuscripts Society in 1876, had chaired a County Council committee and held posts in a number of Cornish learned societies and at the Penzance Library. His wife's family, too, were from the heart of the mining area that was centred on Hayle. On the wider stage, he was honoured by the Society of Antiquaries, being made a Fellow in 1883, awarded an honorary M.A. by the University of Wales in 1919 and, towards the end of his life, was appointed honorary St Petrock Lecturer in Celtic Studies at Exeter, a move which Nance thought might in the future result in the establishment there of a Celtic chair. [68]

The idea of a Cornish Eisteddfod was, like its Welsh counterpart, invariably linked to the Gorsedd, indeed, had preceded it. Nance and Henderson had thought it a natural next step, but Jenner was worried about 'upsetting the admirable work being done by the [Cornwall] Music Festival',[69] which was, of course, founded by Lady Mary Trefusis, a much-loved figure in Cornwall, in 1910 before the idea of a widespread Cornish Revival had seemed possible. Virtually all the Festival was, and still is, conducted in English and there would have been immense logistical problems in moving out of Truro. As early as 1932, much of the discussions at the Annual General Meeting of the Gorsedd centred on the idea that its activities should be expanded to encourage music and poetry. A proposal in favour of a Cornish Eisteddfod put forward by Walter Barnes (*Pen Ylow*) was referred to the Gorsedd Council.[70] The idea resurfaced regularly in the intervening years until finally, in 1983, *Esethvos Kernow* emerged as a triennial event, with the Truro-based Annual Music Festival at its core, but in tandem with a programme of plays, concerts and lectures at venues throughout Cornwall. Although very different from both its Welsh sister and from what was once envisaged in Cornwall, it too is part of Henry Jenner's legacy, coming jointly under the auspices of the Gorsedd and the Music Festival, with the support of the Old Cornwall Societies. It should be remembered that the Gorsedd itself organises a large number of annual competitions involving writing and composition rather than performance and that these, together with the Festival and the triennial Esethvos, constitute a form of Eisteddfod which addresses the fears that Jenner expressed.[71] Indeed, it is just the compromise posited by Jenner himself when he put forward his vision of a future where 'one might ... see someday a Cornish Eisteddfod Association which, with the Gorsedd in its centre, might include the Cornwall Music Competitions, the Folk-dancing Festival, the Band Competitions, the Wrestling Tournaments and last, but by no means least, the various activities of the Old Cornwall Societies...'[72]

Gorseth Kernow – the Gorsedd of Cornwall – and the Federation of Old Cornwall Societies owe their existence and their ethos to Henry Jenner. Indeed, writing in 1952, Nance considered that 'the Cornish Gorsedd began as a tribute to its venerable and beloved Grand Bard, and as part of the Old Cornwall Movement'.[73] Eighteen years later, on the occasion of the Golden Jubilee of the first Old Cornwall Society, Grand Bard G. Pawley White (*Gunwyn*) sent a letter of congratulations in which he stated categorically that Gorseth Kernow owed its origins to the Old Cornwall Movement. 'The College of Bards,' he continued, 'remembers that its first two Grand Bards, Henry Jenner and Robert Morton Nance, were also the founders of the Old Cornwall Movement ... That the past half-century has seen a transformation in the attitude of Cornish people to their own separate identity is largely due to the spirit which the Old Cornwall Societies have engendered.'[74] The two organisations depend on each other to achieve their aims and, although they have been joined by many other cultural, political, social and linguistic bodies, it remains true that they stand at the heart of the Cornish Revival and that they are largely the legacy of Henry Jenner.

Notes

1. 'Gorsedd', meaning a Bardic Assembly', is a Welsh word which has been absorbed into the English language. 'Gorseth' is its Cornish equivalent.
2. Den Toll (Hugh Miners) (1978) *Gorseth Kernow: the first 50 years*, Penzance: Gorseth Kernow, p. 10.
3. P. Berresford Ellis (1994) *The Druids*, London: Constable, p. 270.
4. See Dillwyn Miles (1992) *The Secret of the Bards of the Isle of Britain*, Llandybie: Gwasg Dinefwr; Alistair Moffat (2001) *The Sea Kingdoms: the story of Celtic Britain and Ireland*, London: HarperCollins; Prys Morgan 'From Death to a View: the Hunt for the Welsh Past in the Romantic Period' in E. Hobsbawm (ed.) (1983) *The Invention of Tradition*, Cambridge: Cambridge University Press.
5. See Marion Löffler (2000) *A Book of Mad Celts: John Wickens and the Celtic Congress of Caernarfon 1904*, Llandysul: Gomer.
6. Miners (1978), p. 54; Miles (1992), pp. 220–225.
7. See Amy Hale 'Rethinking Celtic Cornwall: an Ethnographic Approach' and 'The Genesis of the Celto-Cornish Revival? L. C. Duncombe-Jewell and the Cowethas Celto-Kernuak' in Philip Payton (ed.) (1997) *Cornish Studies Five*, new series, Exeter: University of Exeter Press.
8. *Celtia* vol. 2, no. 5, May 1902, p. 79. See also P. Berresford Ellis (1974) *The Cornish Language and its Literature*, London: Routledge and Kegan Paul, pp. 150–162.
9. Löffler (2000), p. 64.
10. *Celtia* vol. 2, no. 9, September 1902, p. 134.
11. Ibid. p.144; Miles (1992) gives 1904 as the year that Jewell was made a member of the Welsh Gorsedd, as do Peter Laws (1978) *Gorseth Byrth Kernow: Bards of the Gorsedd of Cornwall 1928–1982*, Penzance: Gorseth Kernow, and Miners (1978). In Zonia a Geraint Bowen (1991) *Hanes Gorsedd y Beirdd*, Felindre, Abertawe: Cyhoeddiadau Barddas, Zonia Bowen's chapter on the Cornish Gorsedd follows these sources and gives 1904, while Geraint Bowen correctly uses 1902, the year that appears in the official Welsh Gorsedd report for that year.
12. Henry Jenner (1905) 'Cornwall: A Celtic Nation' in *The Celtic Review*, 16 January, p. 245.

13. Henry Jenner (c. 1929) 'Bards, Druids and the Gorsedd' [a paper delivered to ? Old Cornwall Society?], ms in Box 3 of the Robert Morton Nance Collection, Courtney Library, Truro. Extracts are reproduced in this volume.

14. Henry Jenner 'The Present Position and Prospects of Celtic-Cornish Studies in Cornwall' in D. Rhys Phillips (ed.) (1917) *The Celtic Conference 1917: Report of the Meetings held at Birkenhead, September 3 – 5,* Perth: Milne, Tannehill and Methuen, p. 114.

15. Hale (1997) 'Genesis...' p. 109.

16. Miners (1978), p. 13

17. Jenner (1918), p. 96.

18. Ibid. pp. 100–101.

19. There is conflicting information about the date of the Neath Eisteddfod. Miles (1992) states that Jenner met D. Rhys Phillips at Neath in 1917 to discuss forming a Cornish Gorsedd. However, in the same book he talks of the 1918 Neath Eisteddfod and of the many Celtic delegates who were present following their success the previous week in re-establishing the Celtic Congress. That Birkenhead was the location for the Celtic Congress in 1917 and Neath for the Eisteddfod the following year in reinforced by Geraint and Zonia Bowen (1991) who state that Jenner met Phillips at the 1918 Neath Eisteddfod.

20. R. Morton Nance (1934) '"Gwas Myghal" and the Cornish Revival' in *Old Cornwall*, vol. 2, no. 8, Winter 1934, p. 5.

21. *The Cornishman* and *Cornish Telegraph* 9 May 1934.

22. Mrs C. Morton Raymont (1962) *The Early Life of Robert Morton Nance*, Cornwall: New Cornwall, p. 32.

23. R. Morton Nance (1956) *The Cledry Plays*, [St Ives]: Federation of Old Cornwall Societies, [p. 3].

24. Henry Jenner (1920) 'The Renaissance of Merry England' in *Royal Cornwall Polytechnic Society Annual Report, 1921–22*, pp. 59–60.

25. J[oseph] H[ambley R[owe] and R[obert] M[orton] N[ance] (1934) 'Henry Jenner, M.A., F. S. A.' in *Royal Cornwall Polytechnic Society 101st Annual Report*, new series, vol. 8, p. 59.

26. St Ives Old Cornwall Society Minutes; *St Ives Times* 13 February 1920.

27. *Old Cornwall* no. 1, April 1925, pp. 40–41; Brian Sullivan (1984) 'Hayle Old Cornwall Society and Henry Jenner' in *Old Cornwall*, vol. 9, no. 11, Autumn 1984, pp. 522–525. According to the first issue of the Federation's journal, Camborne Old Cornwall Society had in 1925 'been in existence for about two years' and the current secretary confirms 1923 as the year of its foundation. In mistakenly dating this to 1921, A.K. Hamilton Jenkin is possibly remembering a one-off lecture. See 'How it Started' in *Old Cornwall*, vol. 7, no. 7, Autumn 1970, p. 291.

28. R. Morton Nance (1927) '"Old Cornwall" Movement' in *Cornwall Education Week Handbook...*, Truro: Cornwall County Council Education Committee, p. 93.

29. R. Morton Nance (1925) 'Old Cornwall Societies' in *Old Cornwall*, no. 2, October 1925, p. 41.

30. *Old Cornwall* no. 1, April 1925, p. 7. Up to 1973, committees could co-opt non-councillors.

31. Sullivan (1984), p. 523; *Old Cornwall*, vol. 2, no. 6, Winter 1933, pp. 39 and 42.

32. Jenner (c. 1929); See also Henry Jenner (c. 1928) *Who are the Celts and what has Cornwall to do with them?* St Ives: Federation of Old Cornwall Societies, p. 11.

33. See Federation Reports in *Old Cornwall* 1925–

34. Miners (1978), p. 16

35. Jenner (1928), p. 5. The paper is reproduced in full in this volume. See also R. Morton Nance (1928) 'Cornwall and the Gorsedd' in Trelawny Roberts and Charles Henderson (eds.) *Tre, Pol and Pen: The Cornish Annual 1928*, London: Dodsworth, pp. 97–99.

36. Miners (1978), p. 16; Federation Report in *Old Cornwall*, no. 5, April 1927, p. 31; Federation Report in *Old Cornwall*, no. 6, October 1927, p. 29.

37. Miners (1978), pp. 16–17.

38. Jenner (c. 1929)

39. Federation Report in *Old Cornwall*, no. 7, April 1928, p. 34.

40. Miners (1978), p. 20; R. Morton Nance (1951) 'The Cornish Gorsedd' in Denys Val Baker (ed.) *Cornish Review* no. 7, Spring 1951, p. 27; Miles (1992), p. 227.

41. Miners (1978), p. 19.

42. Cornish Gorsedd Minutes. See also The Gorsedd Kernow Archive Survey (n.d.) *A Summary of the Minutes of the Cornish Gorsedd* (August 1928 – September 1939), p. 1.

43. Miners (1978), p. 19

44. Gorsedd Kernow Archive Survey, p. 2.

45. Henry Jenner, R. Morton Nance and E. A. Rees (1928) 'The Cornish Gorsedd', letter to unidentified Cornish newspaper, [August} 1928.

46. *The Cornish Gorsedd at Boscawen-Un Stone Circle ... September 21st, 1928* Penzance: The Cornishman, p. 12.

47. Ibid.

48. Jenner (c. 1929).

49. Jenner was perhaps being rather modest here, for in his lecture 'Bards, Druids and the Gorsedd' (c. 1929) he put a rather different slant on his abilities as a Welsh speaker: 'I don't mind admitting that I was rather pleased with my success in firing off a long bit of Welsh so that the Welshmen understood it – at least they said they did ... It was the first time I had ever tried such a thing, though I know Welsh fairly well on paper.'

50. *The Cornish Gorsedd at Boscawen-Un...* (1928), p. 13.

51. Ibid. p. 10.

52. Ibid. p. 14.

53. Jenner (c. 1929).

54. J. H. R. and R. M. N. (1934), p. 62.

55. Gorsedd Kernow Archive Survey, passim.

56. *Royal Cornwall Gazette* 9 May 1934.

57. *Ceremonies of the Gorsedd of the Bards of Cornwall*, [Gorseth Kernow], [n.d.], pp. 4–5.

58. Henry Jenner (1921) 'Castle-an-Dinas and King Arthur' in *Royal Cornwall Polytechnic Society Annual Report*, 1921–22, pp. 81–101. See also Henry Jenner (1927) 'Tintagel Castle in History and Romance' in *Journal of the Royal Institution of Cornwall*, vol. 22, pt. 2.

59. Ellis (1974), p. 162.

60. G. Hartwell Jones (1931) 'The Celtic Renaissance and how to forward it' in *Y Cymmrodor* vol. 42, p. 126; G. Hartwell Jones (1935) 'Breiz ha Kemri' in *Y Cymmrodor* vol. 44, p. 105.

61. Gorsedd Kernow Archive Survey, passim.

62. Miners (1978), p. 26.

63. Sullivan (1984), p. 522.

64. Film interview with Ted Chapman in Gorsedd Archive; personal reminiscence. See also Cornwall Audio-Visual Archive interview with Treve Crago 25 January 2000.

65. Miners (1978), p. 26.

66. See Philip Payton (2002) *A Vision of Cornwall*, Fowey: Alexander Associates, pp. 136–139; Philip Payton (1996) *Cornwall*, Fowey: Alexander Associates, pp. 269–273; Philip Payton [1993] *The Making of Modern Cornwall*, Redruth: Truran, pp. 132–134; Garry Tregidga (1997) 'The Politics of the Cornish Revival, 1886–1930' in Philip Payton (ed.) *Cornish Studies Five*, new series, Exeter: University of Exeter Press. See also Philip Payton (1997) 'Paralysis and Revival: The Reconstruction of Celtic-Catholic Cornwall, 1890–1945' in Ella Westland (ed) *Cornwall: The Cultural Construction of Place*, Penzance: Patten Press.

67. G. Pawley White (1975) *A Half-Century of Cornish Methodism 1925–1975: a local preacher's experience*, Redruth: Cornish Methodist Historical Association/Institute of Cornish Studies, especially pp. 16–18 'The Cornish Revival'. Feeling confirmed by personal interview in 2003. Hugh Miners had not heard of the idea.

68. J. H. R. and R. M. N. (1934), p. 60; University of Wales *Minutes of the Annual Collegiate Meeting of the University Court and of the Congregation of the University... July 15th, 1920*, p. 199; F. R. Rayner, F. L. Harris and Philip Payton (1997) 'Cornwall Education Week: Seventy Years On' in Philip Payton (ed.) *Cornish Studies Five*, new series, Exeter: University of Exeter Press, p. 184.
69. Miners (1978), p. 52.
70. Gorsedd Kernow Archive Survey, p. 9.
71. See Cornwall Music Festival and Gorsedd Annual Reports and Esethvos Triennial Reports.
72. Jenner (c. 1929).
73. Nance (1951), p. 27.
74. 'Greetings from Gunwyn' in *Old Cornwall*, vol. 7, no. 7, Autumn 1970, p. 327.

Acknowledgements

Many Bards, Old Cornwall Society members and others have given me help, including some who remember Henry Jenner or spoke with those who knew him. I have known all the Grand Bards and most of the leading officers of the Gorsedd in the last fifty years, though I did not know Nance well, being in 'exile' during his time. I have talked about the Gorsedd with many of them and with others, and much of my knowledge and perception of its history is based on this personal contact. In particular I am grateful to the late Grand Bards *Talek* (E.G.Retallack Hooper) and *Map Dyvroeth* (R.G.Jenkin) and to past Grand Bards *Gunwyn* (G.Pawley White) and *Den Toll* (Hugh Miners). I also thank Geraint Bowen for the clarification of discrepancies concerning the early Cornish Bards, Eva Bowen for information about the Neath Eisteddfod of 1918 and Audrey Randle Pool, Derek Williams and Treve Crago for their help and for their kindness. There are various Cornish institutions which hold material. These include the Courtney Library, Royal Institution of Cornwall, Truro (especially the Jenner and Nance bequests), the Morrab Library, Penzance, Bodmin Library, the Cornish Studies Library at the Cornwall Centre, Redruth and the Cornwall Record Office, Truro (for Gorsedd Minutes). I thank the staff of all of them. Amongst Old Cornwall Society officers who provided access to minutes and were willing to enter into discussions, I especially thank Brian Stevens and Wyn Cothey (St Ives), Roy Kelynack (Camborne), Cedric Appleby and Brian Sullivan (Hayle), Ron Opie (Redruth) and Arthur Lyne (Truro). All the interpretations of the facts are my own as are any errors and omissions, for which I can only apologise.

Further reading

In addition to those cited, there are other relevant works that may be consulted. These include:

Henry Jenner and R. Morton Nance (2003 reprint of 1930s publication) *Old Cornwall Societies: what they are doing.*

William Morris (1974) *The Gorsedd and its Bards in Britain*, Penzance: Gorseth Kernow.

R. G. Jenkin 'Gorseth Kernow' in *Cornish Studies for Schools* (1989), [Hayle: Ann Jenkin].

E. G. Retallack Hooper 'Recollections of Henry Jenner' in *An Baner Kernewek/The Cornish Banner 34*, November 1883, pp. 13–14.

Two recent Gorseth Kernow booklets:

Tolzethan: the Life and Times of Joseph Hambley Rowe (2002) by Hugh Miners and Treve Crago and *Map Kenwyn: the Life and Times of Cecil Beer* (2000) by Garry Tregidga and Treve Crago give a flavour of the times during which the Gorsedd was founded.

The Importance of Being Cornish and *The Importance of Being Cornish in Cornwall*, Professor Charles Thomas's Inaugural Lectures for the Institute of Cornish Studies in 1973, give a good overview of the Cornish Revival as does 'An Dasserghyans Kernewek', his 1963 Presidential Address to the Cornish Branch of the Celtic Congress (*Old Cornwall* vol. 6, no. 5, Autumn 1963).

The Cornish weekly newspapers and *The Western Morning News* (Plymouth) are always relevant, as are such journals as *Old Cornwall*, *Cornish Studies* and *An Baner Kernwek/The Cornish Banner*.

Finally, the *Royal Cornwall Polytechnic Society's Annual Reports* and the annual *Journal of The Royal Institution of Cornwall* also contain much relevant information.

The Gorsedd of Boscawen-Un

[A paper read at the meeting of the Federation of Old Cornwall Societies at Boscawen-Un on 25 June 1927]

Henry Jenner

The circle of Boscawen-Un is the most noteworthy stone circle in Cornwall, but before I tell you why I must explain one thing. It was the practice of the Welsh bards in quite early times to tabulate their wise (or otherwise) sayings, whether of philosophy, theology, history, literature or any other subject, in the form of what were called *Triads* (Welsh *Trioedd*) or sets of three, and there are literally many hundreds of such Triads. The practice is only traceable by any real documentary evidence back to about the 14th century, but in many of the existing Triads there are indications of much greater antiquity, and even in some of the vague accounts of the Druids and Bards of Gaul and Britain in the classical writers, such as Strabo, Diodorus Siculus, Julius Caesar, Pliny and others, there are slight indications of a tendency to group things into threes. Diogenes Laertius, a Greek writer, who composed a large treatise on the lives of philosophers, and died in A. D. 222, has some allusions to the Druids, whom he equates with the Greek philosophers, the Persian Magi, the Indian Gymnosophistae (or what we should now call "Yogis" or "Fakeers") and the Chaldaeans. He gives one set of maxims in Triad form, which resembles very closely an actually existing Welsh Triad, but I have no copy of his works to refer to, and am not sure whether he really attributes it to the Druids. It has even been said that when St

Patrick came to preach Christianity in Ireland, where Druids, almost invariably called "Magi" in the Latin lives of Irish saints, just as the Magi of St Matthew's gospel are called "Druidhean" Druids, in the Gaelic New Testament, were in great power, he found that the existing familiarity with the idea of Triads helped him in inducing the people to accept the doctrine of the Trinity. But I should like more evidence for that last statement, including evidence that the Irish Druids, of whom a good deal is known, used Triads at all. Be this as it may, there is one Welsh Triad which should interest us here today. I will give it in the original:

"Tair Prif-orsedd Beirdd Ynys Prydain, Gorsedd Moel Meriw, Gorsedd Beisgawen, Gorsedd Bryn Gwyddon."

[*Three principal Session-places of the Bards of the Island of Britain, the Session-place of the Hill of Meriw, the Session-place of Beisgawen, the Session-place of the Hill of Gwyddon.*]

There are at least three other variants of this Triad. One of these substitutes "Moel Efwr" for "Moel Meriw", the others being the same. Another says that Bryn Gwyddon is in Caerleon on Usk, and a third, which is perhaps the best, gives the three as: Beisgawen in Dyfnwal, that is, Damnonia – the old kingdom, which included Cornwall, – Caer Caradog in Lloegr, that is to say, Salisbury in England, meaning either Old Sarum, or possibly Stonehenge, and Bryn Gwyddon in Cymru, that is, in Wales. I cannot identify "Moel Meriw" or "Moel Efwr", but I think they must be alternative names for "Caer Caradog", as the other two are always the same, and the intention seems to be to locate one in each of the principal divisions of Britain, Dyfnwal or Damnonia, Cymru or Wales, and Lloegr, the Logria of the Arthurian romances, which is the Welsh for England. The Hill of Gwyddon, who is probably Gwyddon Ganhebon, described in another Triad as one of the three "deifnogion cerdd a cheudawd," inventors of song and imaginative works, of the Island of Britain, a legendary character of uncertain date, may possibly be discovered by the excavations that are now being made at Caerleon, or it may be the great amphitheatre there, which has already been dug out. Caer Caradog, Moel Efwr or Moel Meriw, may be either the great mound of Old Sarum, once a British hill-fort and later a

Henry Jenner at Boscawen-Un, 25 June 1927. Gorseth Kernow Archive

Roman, Saxon and Norman city, whence the present city of Salisbury was removed in the 13th century, or it may be Stonehenge, both of which are well known. From the word "moel," the Welsh equivalent of the "mul" in "Mulfra," a bald or round-topped hill, being used, I am inclined to think that Old Sarum has the best claim. As for "Beisgawen yn Nyfnwal," Boscawen in Damnonia, we are in it now.

What is a Gorsedd? is the next question. The word means a place of session. "Gor" as a prefix is an augmentative. The root is "sedd," a seat, the same word as "sedes" in Latin and "seat" in English, so a Gorsedd is a great or important seat. We find in another Triad "Tair gorsedd freiniawg, gorsedd brenhin, gorsedd esgob, gorsedd abad," three privileged thrones or tribunals, those of a king, a bishop and an abbot. But the Gorsedd of the Bards of Britain means the place of assembly or session at which the Bards met and went through various ceremonies and held contests in song and poetry. It is impossible to tell how old any form of the existing Bardic system of Wales and Brittany may be, or whether there is any continuity, however slight, with the ancient Druidical institutions described by Strabo and others; but in some form or other it and the Eisteddfod are traceable well back into the Middle Ages. The matter has been complicated by the imaginative character of so many Welsh writers, and notably of an important one, Edward Williams, better known by his bardic name "Iolo Morganwg," Ned of Glamorgan, who died just a century ago. He might be described in Triad form as one of the Three Champion Liars of the Island of Britain, and he mixes up truth and imaginative fiction to such an extent that it is impossible to disentangle them. He had a vast knowledge of Welsh literature, and was one of the editors of that very valuable collection the "Myvryrian Archaiology of Wales." But, unluckily, when he could not find an authority for what he wanted he usually invented one, and very cleverly, too, so that unless one can find something to corroborate his statements, one must not believe them too much. He is largely answerable for the modern form of the Welsh Gorsedd, though the general principles of it are much older, and in his vast reading he did get hold of some real things, which he "improved," not to say "faked," freely.

The system of Bardic degrees or orders – an important part of a gorsedd – is founded on Strabo and Diodorus Siculus, but chiefly on the former. Strabo says that there were three others, "Bardoi, Ouateis kai Druidai." The Bards were singers and poets, the "Ouateis" were, as *he* says, sacrificers and students of nature ("phusiologoi"), but Diodorus calls them "manteis", prophets or sooth-sayers, and says that they practised augury; and the Druids, besides being students of nature, practised ethical philosophy. At present the three orders are (1) Druids, who in Wales are usually clergymen, with an arch-druid as their chief. They wear white robes, and the apparel of the arch-druid is very gorgeous, (2) Bards, who wear blue robes, and (3) what are called "Ovates," which is a curious misreading of Strabo's "Ouateis," which is really the Latin, "vates," prophets, translated into Greek, with *ou* to represent the *w* sound which the Romans gave to *v*. These last wear green robes. When a Gorsedd is held the Archdruid takes the chair, so to speak, that is to say he stands on or at a large stone in the middle of the circle of stones. Proceedings are opened by an official holding up a sheathed sword and shouting the question "A oes heddwch?" Is there peace? And, if "the answer is in the affirmative," as they say at question time in Parliament, all make reply "Heddwch!" Peace! I was present at a Gorsedd at Neath in August, 1918, when for obvious reasons there was no answer. Indeed I do not think the question was even asked. Then follows the Prayer of the Gorsedd, which is in its way rather a fine one, and when the archdruid is a good reciter sounds well. It is:

> "Dyro Dhuw dy Nawdd,
>   Ag yn Nawdd, Nerth,
>   Ag yn Nerth, Deall,
>   Ag yn Neall, Gwybod,
>   Ag yngwybod, Gwybod y Cyfiawn,
>   Ag yngwybod y Cyfiawn, ei garu,
>   Ag o garu, caru pob Hanfod,
>   Ag ymhob Hanfod, caru Duw,
>   Duw a phob Daioni."

> *"Grant, O God Thy protection,*
>   *And in protection, strength,*
>   *And in strength, understanding,*

And in understanding, knowledge,
And in knowledge, the knowledge of that which is just,
And in the knowledge of that which is just, the love of it,
And from love, the love of all that exists,
And in all that exists, the love of God,
  God and all goodness."

Then comes, so to speak, the business of the Gorsedd, the conferring of bardic degrees, the recitation of prize "englynion" or epigrams and other pieces of verse, and the singing of "penillion" or extemporised verses, often topical, to a set tune. Degrees of Ovate, Bard or Druid, are conferred on those who have passed qualifying examinations, fairly stiff ones too, "honoris causa" on distinguished persons of all sorts, including Royal personages, and sometimes as a recognition of valuable work. The Breton Gorsedd in 1903 was good enough to think that my work on the Cornish language was worthy of the degree of Bard. Each new graduate has a "bardic name" conferred on him. Mine is "Gwas Myhal," which signifies "The Servant of St Michael," the patron-saint of Cornwall. Perhaps it was rather presumptuous of me to nobble the patron of all Cornwall for myself, but I was, I believe, actually the first native of Cornwall to be made a bard, so I may be excused. I think it would be a good idea for Cornish people who get bardic degrees in future to put themselves under the patronage of Cornish saints in the same way. We might have "Gwas Piran," "Gwas Petrock," "Gwas Ia," and plenty more. There are quite enough Celtic saints to go round. The proceedings with regard to "englynion" recitation and "penillion" singing are often very interesting, and the whole thing is worked out to encourage Welsh or Breton nationality, patriotism, language and literature, to do indeed, on a large and special scale in their larger countries what we of the Old Cornwall Societies are doing in our little Motherland. I should like to throw it out as a hint that we really ought some day to have a Cornish Gorsedd that should hold its meetings sometimes in our own "Priforsedd" of "Beisgawen yn Nyfnwal." The Welsh or Breton Gorseddau would, I know, encourage us, and then the concert of the three Brythonic nations would be complete. I beg of you to let that idea sink into your minds.

I do not know when a Gorsedd was last held in this place, or what sort of an affair it was; but the circle was probably not originally built for such a purpose, though it has not yet been decided by antiquaries why such circles were constructed. There are too many theories to discuss now, but the most probable seems to be that they were temples with a special orientation, which might indicate the seasons through the rising of certain stars. The lines of menhirion which are directed from them, as may be seen here and at the Dawns Meyn, which we shall see later, seem to point to some such purpose being in the minds of the constructors, but one must beware of carrying that argument too far, for we know perfectly well that Christian churches, which commonly point to the east, were not built to teach astronomy or to tell us where the sun rises, but for quite different purposes. One thing, however, appears to be fairly certain, that these circles and their attendant menhirion belong to the Neolithic or New Stone Age, which was succeeded by the Bronze age in Britain perhaps about 1800 B.C. If, as many people now think, Druidism was originally not a Celtic or Aryan religion, but pre-Celtic, these circles may possibly have been connected with it. But of that at present we know next to nothing, so it is not much use making guesses. Certain it is that whatever Bardism may have existed in Cornwall must have sunk very low by the 12th century, when the Cornish vocabulary defined "Barth" as "mimus vel scurra," a comic actor or buffoon, not as "poeta."

There is one other point to mention about this place – its name. There are three places called Boscawen in Buryan parish, Boscawen-Un, or Boscawen-noon, as it is sometimes written, which means Boscawen-en-Ûn, Boscawen on the Down; Boscawen-Rose, which is Boscawen on the Heath, and is the original seat of Lord Falmouth's family; and Boscawen-vean or little Boscawen. It has been commonly held that "Boscawen" means "The Dwelling of the Elder-tree (scawen)." I think this a mistake. The epithet in names beginning with "bos," dwelling, is almost invariably a personal name, and finding in the Welsh Triad the form "Beisgawen" with a *g*, not a *c*, and the same or a similar form being found in early documents, I am more inclined to interpret it as "The Dwelling of (some one called) Gawain." Whether it is called after the Sir Gawain, Arthur's nephew, of the mediaeval romances, or after some one of the same name, we of course cannot say, but close to Boscawen-rose there is "Rosemodres," which can only mean "The Heath of Modred," bringing in the name of another nephew of Arthur, and there is a definite tradition of a battle of Arthur on Vellandruchar Downs, on the river of Kemyel, which flows into Lamorna Cove. If Kemyel is Camlan, where Arthur and Modred killed each other, Gawain having died not long before the battle, we have some apparent reason for these names, and there are several other places in Paul and Buryan which have what seem to be Arthurian names. But all this may be only a passing fancy, and though I think that Boscawen was the dwelling of some Gawain, we will leave it at that until more evidence turns up.

Gwas Myhal

Bards, Druids and The Gorsedd

Henry Jenner

Possibly some of those who are here now were present at the memorable inauguration of the Cornish Gorsedd at Boscawen-Un on September 21st 1928 and I think those will agree with me that it was a great success. The idea of having a Cornish Gorsedd is not a new one. As long ago as 1903, when I attended the Breton Gorsedd at Plounéour-Trez and had a Bardic degree conferred on me, the idea had occurred to me, and not very long afterwards I had some correspondence with the then Welsh Archdruid and others of the Welsh Gorsedd about it. They were all vaguely sympathetic, but the time was not ripe and nothing came of it then. There were not enough Cornish people who were sufficiently interested to make it possible. Long after that the Old Cornwall movement began with the establishment of the St Ives Old Cornwall Society in 1920, and that movement has been an unqualified success. It was that success which made a Cornish Gorsedd possible, and there is no doubt that to the Old Cornwall Societies belongs the credit of making it an accomplished fact. We really ought to be pleased with ourselves.

The Gorsedd had, I am told, a fine spectacular effect. I cannot vouch for the truth of that statement. Lookers-on see most of any game, and I was not a looker on, but so much in the middle of it that, as the German proverb has it, 'I couldn't see the wood for the trees', but I felt that it was going all right and was able to agree with the Archdruid Pedrog when, as we left the lane leading from the circle, he turned to me and said. 'It has gone without a single hitch, which is more than we can always say in Wales.' Much praise is due to the organisers, to

Gorsedd at Roche Rock, 1933. © *Royal Cornwall Museum MOTRUH01*

Mr Morton Nance, who conducted the rather difficult preliminary negotiations with Mr Rhys Phillips and others of the Welshmen, and was, indeed, the prime mover in them; to Mr Edgar Rees, the most valuable organising secretary, a born organiser, if ever there was one, and to others of the committee. I can praise these workers with a clear conscience, since my own share in the proceedings was chiefly confined to putting on pretty clothes and trying to look the part on the day itself. Great praise is due to the crowd of upwards of 2000 spectators, whose sympathetic, reverend and orderly behaviour was wonderful. It would have been no small feat to manage such a crowd, but we didn't – they manage[d] themselves. I must confess that I was a little bit anxious about how the crowd would take it. A very little would have got a laugh in the wrong place; but they took it in the right way, and the ceremonies, however quaint and strange, never became ridiculous to them. The quite unrehearsed effect of the procession over the down seems to have appealed to most people more than anything else. It was astonishing how well it went! A very little would have made it a failure, especially in the difficult manoeuvre of turning the procession inside out as it reached the round field where the circle of stones, and of course the Welshmen who are used to this sort of things, did their part very well.

The programme of the proceedings at the circle was modelled on the usual Welsh programme. Some people have asked me whether it was meant to be a religious service. Perhaps the use of the word 'Druid', the name of the Pagan priesthood of the ancient Celts, was the cause of such a question, and I may as well make it clear that there is no idea of Paganism in it at all. The Archdruid is a Congregationalist minister, the ex-Archdruid Elfed is also some sort of nonconformist clergyman and Canon Maurice Jones, another of our Welsh guests, is Principal of St David's College, Lampeter, the training college for the clergy of the Welsh Church. All of these are, I have no doubt, excellent Christians, who would be horrified at the idea of professing any sort of Paganism. It is well to explain this because the objection has been made, not only in Wales but also in Brittany where, though many of the members of the Gorsedd are quite good Catholics, the clergy do not altogether like it, because of the title 'Druid'. It is not because of any suspicion of real Paganism at the back of it, but because of possible misunderstandings. Considering that Gorseddau of Bards probably went on all through the Middle Ages, then the Welsh were every bit as good

Gorsedd at Carn Brea, 1929. Gorseth KernowArchive/Ann Trevenen Jenkin

Christians as any other nation, and that Druidism as a religious system, ceased to exist by the sixth century at the latest, there is not likely to be any idea of reviving its tenets, even if we quite knew what they all were – which we don't…

It is true that after four blasts of the trumpet to the four quarters of heaven, the Gorsedd opens with the fine Gorsedd Prayer, which was printed in Cornish, Welsh and English on the programmes. But that does not make it into a religious service any more than a dinner party becomes a religious service because one asks the Vicar to say grace. At any rate it ensures it's not being irreligious – which is something to its credit. The question 'Is there Peace?' and the response 'Peace' is symbolical and of obvious meaning. The arts patronised by the Gorsedd, literature etc. are emphatically arts of peace. The presentation of a bouquet symbolising the fruits of the earth, which on the late occasion, Mrs Mabbott, the Mayoress of Penzance, performed so gracefully does not require explanation. The inauguration of the Cornish Gorsedd and the appointment of the Grand Bard was, of course, a specific item for this occasion. The Archdruid performed his part of the ceremony with great dignity and with an ease which argued an intimate acquaintance with the ritual. Indeed there was something rather pleasing about the unaffected way in which all the Welshmen did their part. They looked as if they were thoroughly accustomed to the ceremony, as they probably were, and not as if they thought everybody was looking at them, though that was also the case. The initiation of the 'aelodau newydd', the new Cornish Bards [literally 'new members'], was an interesting sight. The selection was not an easy matter. We limited the number and did not want to scatter Bardic degrees broadcast, and we made the best selection that we could, representatives of literature, archaeology, journalism, linguistics, and other matters, not forgetting the distinctively Cornish institutions of wrestling, but of course there were others on whom degrees might have been conferred, and those will be left for another occasion. The Welshmen, who during the excursion for which we took them in the morning and the luncheon which followed it had had opportunities of making the acquaintance of some of the new bards, were good enough to express themselves as highly pleased with the very promising material for a Gorsedd that Cornwall could show. I don't know what they expected to find there, but we have got to live up to their estimate of us now. The discourses by the ex-Archdruid Elved and Canon Maurice Jones on the

Gorsedd and its effects on Wales were intensely interesting and gave us a standard to which we must try to attain. These discourses were a little out of the usual run of Welsh Gorsedd proceedings but, like scripture, were 'written for *our* learning' and gave us many valuable hints. The welcome from Cornwall to the Welsh visitors, which I was told off to make, was, so to speak, another 'extra'. I don't mind admitting that I was rather pleased with my success in firing off a long bit of Welsh so that the Welshmen understood it – at least they said they did. I hope they spoke the truth and it was not only their politeness. It was the first time I had ever tried such a thing, though I know Welsh fairly well on paper. The songs and recitations which followed are part of the usual programme of a Gorsedd, and it was a pleasing feature to get a real Breton boy to sing a verse in his own language. There was one disappointment. Mr Rhys Phillips, the Herald Bard, was to have sung some 'penillion', as they are called, original stanzas theoretically extemporised but in practice usually got up beforehand, to a harp accompaniment, a very prominent feature at Gorseddau, but unluckily he had so bad a cold that that item had to be cut. However, Mr Crwys Williams made up for it with his delightful little extemporised poem in Welsh and English on Dolly Pentreath, certainly composed since our visit to Paul Church at about 11 o'clock that morning. There are light elements as well as serious ones in Gorsedd proceedings. Finally there was one most satisfactory detail for which the organisers cannot claim credit. The absolutely perfect weather…

It [the Welsh Gorsedd] is now a great institution, and the now annual Eisteddfod is attended by many thousands. As the ex-Archdruid Elfed said, the Gorsedd has become the medium between academic scholarship and popular culture. Some might be found to ridicule the ceremonies. If one were so inclined, it would be easy to find something to laugh at in any ceremonies, even in those of that most solemn of all national functions, the coronation of a King or Queen – as indeed the author of the *Ingoldsby Legends* did in 1838 – but the ritual and pageant are not the only things about the Gorsedd, though they do catch the popular imagination. Its real use is the spread of culture, not for its value in any sort of business, trade, commerce or money-making, but for its own sake, it brings that culture – and Celtic culture at that – into the lives of thousands of Welshmen, who would otherwise be without it, and it fosters the valuable sentiment of nationality in its best form. In Cornwall we have only the memory of the national language and the scanty remains of its literature, but we have, I know, the sentiment of Cornish nationality and that, with many details of culture which are not especially nationalistic, is what the Cornish Gorsedd is out to encourage. Exactly what form it will have it is too early to say, but if one were given to visions of the future one might seem to see someday a Cornish Eisteddfod Association which, with the Gorsedd in its centre, might include the Cornwall Music Competitions, the Folk-dancing Festival, the Band Competitions, the Wrestling Tournaments and last, but by no means least, the various activities of the Old Cornwall Societies – everything, in fact, that makes Cornwall Cornwall.

These extracts from Jenner's manuscript in Box 3 of the R. M. Nance Collection are reproduced with the permission of The Royal Institution of Cornwall – Courtney Library

The Poetry of Henry Jenner

Donald R. Rawe

If he had not been a Cornish language scholar, indeed the father of the Kernewek revival, Henry Jenner might well have made his mark as a respected minor Victorian and Edwardian poet. At work in the British Museum during the 1870s and '80s, he could have published his personal poems with the help of various literary friends and, along with a host of second-rank – if not second-rate – poets, could have had a career with some impact on the English literary scene. Here is one example of his work, dated 1893:

> When first we met, just twenty years ago,
> We would be friends, not lovers, so we said,
> And follow friendship only where it led;
> But whither that would be we could not know.
> It led us on by ways of Joy and Woe,
> By handclasps, kisses, leaning of a head
> Upon a breast, to Love; and we were wed.
> This was our fate, for God had willed it so.
>
> In the dark dawning of our brighter life,
> Lovers and friends as youth and maid were we,
> And now that twenty years have passed away,
> Lovers and friends we are as man and wife;
> For God's great gift of love to me and thee
> Hath kept us married lovers to this day.

I sent thee sonnets on a Christmas Day
Long years ago, and called thee then my friend,
And so thou art; our friendship hath no end;
What I said then today again I say –
God bless and keep my darling love alway;
And every Christmas blessing to thee send,
His ear of pity to thy pleadings bend,
When as before his Altar thou dost pray.

Hope was our chief thought in those days gone by –
Now thankfulness and hope are both in one; –
Good hope of what the future will bestow
(So that we are together, thou and I)
And thankfulness for what God's love hath done
In giving us each other long ago.

This was written on Christmas morning, between 2am and 3am, as an anniversary present to his wife Katharine. It amply illustrates Jenner's grounding in strict prosody, in the tradition of most Victorian poets such as Tennyson, Arnold, Meredith and so many others; also the Victorian ideal of marriage, realised in love and devotion to God, who must be thanked for this great bounty. It is pleasing to remember that the hope and prayer of the last stanza were in fact answered, both Henry and Katharine living together into their eighties, until Jenner's death in 1934.

Thus Jenner might have continued with his verses; but instead, seduced by the sheer romantic fascination of rediscovering his own native language, he chose to devote most of his spare time to deducing the workings of Kernewek – or Cornuack, as he would then have written – from the various publications and manuscripts that came his way.

In 1858 Edwin Norris' *The Ancient Cornish Drama* (i.e. The *Ordinalia*) had been published, with Norris' own English translation and grammatical notes; Whitley Stokes published *Pascon Agan Arluth*, the Passion Poem, in 1861, and *Gwryans an Bys* with English translation in 1864. Robert Williams had produced his comprehensive *Cornish Dictionary* in 1865; Whitley Stokes followed with *A Cornish Glossary* and then *Bewnans Meryasek* in 1872. Seven years later W. C. Borlase produced *Nebez Gerriau dro tho Cornuak* and in 1887 Dr F. W. P. Jago brought out his *English-Cornish Dictionary*. The stage was thus set for a revival of interest in the language, if not actually of spoken Kernewek. Jenner himself discovered in the British Museum the Charter fragment, part of a lost Cornish play, on the back of a medieval charter document. He therefore had the tools to hand wherewith to realise Cornish once more as a written language, and even to write and compose poetry in it, which he proceeded to do.

He was not the first scholar to attempt this. Georg Sauerwein, the north German linguist, had written two poems, one to Edwin Norris and another entitled 'Cowyth Ker, dhe Dhen Claf' (Dear Friend, to a Sick Man), basing his grammar and spelling on the work of Edward Lhuyd, Dr William Pryce and Norris himself. His poems are remarkably competent, with an excellent grasp of grammar and verb tenses. Against this background Jenner's Cornish was naturally that of the later period, as we have it from Lhuyd, Nicholas Boson, John Keigwin, William Bodinar and others – i.e. Late or 'Modern' Cornish.

What Jenner's first attempt at verse in Cornish was, and exactly when it was written, must remain open to doubt. There are several short pieces dated 1874, and these appear to be the first he considered worth preserving: 'To LLR', 'Ave Maris Stella', and 'O Salutaris Hostia', which are all among his papers in the Courtney Library, Royal Institution of Cornwall, Truro. He continued practising and developing over the years, his work culminating in his Cornish versions of the Welsh 'Land of My Fathers' (composed by the James brothers) – 'Bro Goth Agan Tasow', which is sung lustily every year at Gorseth Kernow and spontaneously at other events, such as the St Piran's Day celebrations.

With a growing sense that the realisation and spread of the Cornish revival depended principally upon himself, Jenner's verse projects were mainly directed towards supplying Cornish words for songs and anthems for use on public occasions. We have relatively few personal and intimate poems from him in Cornish. The best is to be found as a dedication for his seminal *Handbook of the Cornish Language* of 1904 – 'Dho'm Gwreg Gernuak' (To My Cornish Wife). This is a highly wrought and finished sonnet, exact and perfect in its rhythmic and rhyming scheme: proof that Jenner had mastered completely the idioms and had become fluent, after studying deeply Celtic prosody and verse.

Later he saw it as his duty to produce modern Cornish versions of 'God Save the King', 'Trelawny' ('Song of the Western Men') and patriotic verses such as 'An Pemthek Pell' and 'Can Gwlascor Agan Mamvro'. He was, without doubt, a convinced royalist; in fact, he was, as much of his correspondence in the Courtney Library attests, a Jacobite and an enthusiastic member of the Legitimist Society. He must have been somewhat jolted to find among Lhuyd's papers a poem in Cornish lamenting the death of William of Orange (William III) in 1702. But as late as 1905, his Stuart sympathies were still coming to the fore in 'Can Contellyans an Kernewyon/Gathering Song of the Cornishmen … in 1715', his contribution that year to *The Royalist*, which he helped to edit and to which he contributed over the years.

Jenner's verse output may conveniently be divided into three sections: early verse, 1874–1904; miscellaneous verses to 1934; and patriotic and ceremonial verse from 1900 onwards.

The three earliest dated poems are the following from 1874, which are to be found in the Nance papers in the Courtney Library. I have not been able to discover who L.L.R. was or the circumstances which prompted the verse. It would appear not to be an epitaph, but a farewell blessing:

To L.L.R.

Dew ha'n Eleth byth genes
Ynno le tennya hedre an bys
Y vennath war'n bythans
Nos ha deth hedre vewnans
Dre bop amser forth gorwythys Mam Cryst whek
Dy vones ha dy dewelles.

[*God and the Angels be with you,*
by His hand drawn through the world;
His blessing on your journey be,
night and day throughout life,
along all dangerous roads protected by Christ's Mother,
to go and to return.]

Ave Maris Stella

Heyle dhys, Varya steren a'n mor
Heyle dhys, Vam Dew an whecca
Heyle a Vagteth dek ha vor:
Porth a'n nev an lowenha.

[*Hail Star of the Sea. Hail to thee, Mary, star of the sea.*
Hail to thee sweetest Mother of God:
Hail O Maiden great and beautiful,
bear us to heaven's greatest joy.]

O Salutaris Hostia

A perth sylwy an nev ygerys
Porthow nef dho dignes dor.
Adro yskerans den dha cas
Drew gwer thynny ha pallwid mor.

Thys, Dew an Tri hag an Unan
Bythen a lowen heb diwidh,
Neb thynny bewnans dha ha splan
Yn agen g'low benery reth.

[*Bearing salvation, (you) who opened*
The gates of heaven to lowly earth:
All around us (are) enemies warring;
Bring help to us and great, far-reaching protection.

To thee, God of the Three and One
Be joy without end
Who to us life good and bright
(Gives), in our light forever.]

These appear to be in the nature of student verses, through which Jenner was feeling his way to expressing his deepest thoughts. No accurate translation is possible for us, and he did not bequeath us one of his own, as he usually did for later verse. His spelling tends to vary since, apart from Lhuyd and Pryce, there was no glossary or dictionary for him to follow. *Pallwid* for instance is not to be found in any of our modern dictionaries, or in Jago; but consulting Lhuyd, who gives *wid* as the late Cornish form of *gwyth* in its meanings 'work' and 'bushy vegetation', we may fairly assume that the sense of *gwyth* as 'care' or 'guardianship' is here intended, prefixed by *pall* (Middle Cornish and Unified *pell*), thus meaning 'far-reaching protection'. Jenner may possibly have had in mind *pal* as 'mantle' or 'cover', but this is not so poetic a conception.

Few of the existing verses in the Nance papers are dated, the next being 'Dho'm Gwreg Kernuak' of 1904. There are, however, some interesting devotional verses and translations into Cornish, including his 'Hymn to Sen Pethrik' (St Petroc):

> Den deu skientek[1] era 'gan Sen Pethrik,
> Cosel ha deskes. Dhe y bregoth a wolsow
> Constantyn Matern. Dhodho de an bestes
> Tennes a'y dhader.
>
> Ple a gemesk an Mor ha'n Heyl 'ga dowrow,
> Pres hy ow triga, gonas ev an Awayl
> Ha dhort Bosmanagh dhe Dhew
> Ev a dremenas.

> [*A learned man of God was our St Petroc,*
> *Quiet and wise. To his preaching listened*
> *King Constantine. To him came the animals*
> *Drawn by his goodness.*
>
> *Where mingles the sea and the estuary their waves*
> *Long there he lived, sowed the Gospel*

Henry Jenner in retirement. By permission of Mary Beazley

And from Bodmin to God
Was he translated.]

Constantine was a prince or petty king of north Cornwall who, in the *Vita Petroci*, was prevented from hunting a fawn by Petroc at his hermitage and, having been converted by him, spent the rest of his days in prayer at Constantine Bay, where his little ruined church may still be seen on the golf course.

At some time in the 1890s or early 1900s Jenner composed a moving epitaph for the young son of Dr E. Hambley Rowe (Bard *Tolzethan*). Hambley Rowe – himself an avid student of Cornish – was a polymath and antiquarian who, despite living in Bradford, was deeply involved in Cornish affairs. He it was who sent the congratulatory telegram in Cornish to Jenner at Caernarfon in 1904, when Kernow was admitted to the Celtic Congress. Later he was Mordon's Deputy Grand Bard, installing him at the 1934 Gorsedd. Jenner's epitaph for young Hambley Rowe reads as follows:

> Wherow ha gwag yu ol agan dagrow
> Ragos do kens dhe dermen es marow
> Dhe'th gerhas arta; mes gans Dew a vedh
> Golow dhesdi ha powes heb dewedh.

> [*Bitter and vain are all our tears*
> *For thee who art dead before thy time:*
> *But with God there shall be*
> *Light to thee and rest without end.*]

Jenner's high churchmanship – indeed, Anglo-Catholicism; he converted to Rome shortly before his death – resulted in a number of devotional poems and translations. Among them we find 'Sqyth yth osta?' (Art Thou Weary?):

> Squyth yth osta, lean awander?
>   Es ponvotter dhes?
> Yn un dos dhemmo, 'meth Onen
>   Kyf powes.
> Es coron 'vel matern dhodho,

Settyes war y ben?
Nyns yu coron yn dyogel
    Saw a dhreyn.

[*Art thou weary, art thou languid,*
    is distress with you?
Come to me, saith One,
    and find rest.
Has he a king's crown
    set upon his head?
No crown, surely,
    except (one) of thorns.]

Jenner's Cornish version of the medieval Latin hymn 'Adoro Te Devote' should be considered here:

Mi a'th wordh en dhewesek, a Dheses kidhes,
Es dan an firvow-ma en wir gorheres.
Dredhos ol ow halon a wra omhivla,
Dreven ow predery warnas dho falla.

[*I worship Thee devotedly, O hidden Godhead,*
Who art covered beneath these forms;
Through Thee my heart humbles itself,
Because my thoughts on Thee fall.]

....

War an grows a gidhas en ednak Dewses:
Omma worherer enwedh an Denses.
An deu mi ow cresy, ow fidhva an deu.
Avel ladron eddrak, mi a bes dho Dhew.

[*On the cross there suffered the only Godhead;*
Here let be worshipped also the Manhood.

In both I believe, having faith in the two:
ike the repentant thief, I pray God.]

....

Pelican a drewath, Jesu, Arledh vi,
Mostes ov, gwra'm glanhe en dha sans woys di
Anodho un banna selwans lor a vo
Ol an bes dhe wolhy dhort e behassow.

Jesu, breman goyles, warnas mi a vir:
Pesav, gwra disehy ow sehas en wir.
Dha fas di may helle gweles diwolves
En wolok dha wordhans dho vos beniges.

[*Merciful Redeemer, Jesu, my Lord,*
Foul I am; clean me in thy blood:
One drop of salvation enough will be,
All the world to wash from its sins.

Jesus, now wounded, on you I gaze
I pray, quench my thirst truly.
May I see your face unwounded,
In sight of your glory to be blessed.]

Note the word *firvow*, here translated as 'forms'; the Unified *furf*, respelled from Old Cornish, would appear to be related to the word firmament, i.e. creation, as in the verb *formya*, which was probably Jenner's meaning by association. The use of the word Pelican, for Redeemer or Saviour, is an interesting medievalism; in the Middle Ages the church often represented Christ as a pelican, a fabulous bird said to feed its young with its own blood, as the wine of the Eucharist, the Blood of Christ, is said to feed the faithful. Jenner was sufficiently enamoured of this idea to use it in his own epitaph.

In 1900 he wrote in English, to a tune by the Jenners' only child, Ysolt, the following poem entitled *Stella Maris* (Star of the Sea). Ysolt followed her parents in becoming religious, so much so that she entered a sisterhood as a young woman and remained there for the rest of her life:

> Slowly the sunshine fades on the wall
> Over the meadows black shadows fall.
> Hushed is the songbird, closed is the flower,
> Softly the Angelus sounds from the tower.
>   Mist on the mountain, gloom on the strand:
>   Spirits of darkness abroad in the land.
>   Where shall we turn for a succouring hand?
> Ave Maria! Mother of might,
> Grant us and shield us all through the night.
>
> Over the ocean darkness is spread.
> Only the starlight gleams overhead;
> Sweetly the Angelus floats on the wind,
> Calling the mariners safety to find.
>   Clouds of the murk gather over the sky,
>   Stars blotted out when the tempest is nigh.
>   Where shall we turn and to whom shall we cry?
> Gratia plena! Star of the Sea,
> Shine like a beacon to guide us to thee.

In 1901 Jenner produced the following, in English only, which appears to be a poem to congratulate a friend or acquaintance on reaching the age of seventy. The title is unexplained, in that there seems to be no clue as to the term *Anglica*, although he may have wanted to distinguish this version from a Latin original:

> *Ad Multos Annos!*
> *Congratulatis Anglica.*

> Thou needst not grieve, although the Psalmist say:
> The life of man is threescore years and ten,

And if by strength they come to fourscore, then
Labour alone with sorrow hath its day,
Until the weary spirit pass away.
Nor shalt thou dread the unseen future, when
Some, like his son, the wisest King of men,
In life's vain shadow find no cheering ray.

Ad multos annos! Health and wealth be thine,
Joy and repose for many another year,
When life and love shall give thee of their best.
On thee and thine God make his face to shine
To keep thee safe from sorrow, pain and fear,
Until He bring thee to His endless rest.

An emendation to the third line of the second stanza reads, 'Whom art and song have given thee of their best,' prompting the speculation that the addressee of these lines was a musician.

Returning to verse in Cornish, in 1904 Jenner produced one of his most ambitious and successful poems, entitled 'Halan Gwav: Prederyans rag Mis Du, es Mis an Enevow Sans en Purgator/All Souls' Day: Reflections on November, month of the Holy Souls in Purgatory'. It is well worth quoting in its entirety:

'Dhort an Downder mi re gryas dhes di, Arledh: Arledh, clew ow lev' (Psalm cxxix)

A glewsta lev Mor mer? War an garrek ton a der,
En ogo faborden bras, War an dreth en idn hanas,
     A glewesta lev Mor mer?

A glewsta lev an Cos? En nans cosel dre an nos,
Son an gwins en gwedh ewhel, Hanas edom drist ha lel,
     A glewsta lev an Cos?

A glewsta lev an Bal, Es ow tos a'n whel isel,
Avel clownans bannow dour, Son dagrow ow cotha lur:
    A glewsta lev an Bal?

Ti a glew an Enevow; Ol adro yu'n dis verow.
En agan mesk carhares, Yu'n speressow tremens:
    Ty a glew an enevow.

Asken aga garm dho Nev, Garm enevow en peyn grev,
En hanas mor, bal ha cos, En lev colom dre an nos,
    Aga garm a dhe dho Nev.

Dhort an downder y a gry, 'Gwra tregereth warnen ny!'
Mam Maria, sens a ban, Greugh golsowas aga han!
    Dhort an downder y a gry.

A glewsta can an sens? Son pibannow, lev gyttrens,
Can crowd, ha'y warak tennes, Menestrouthy beniges:
    A glewsta can an sens?

Halan gwav dre ver-borthow Nev dho garhar speressow
Miras sens, len a bite, Dres an downder a dhe:
    Halan gwav dre ver borthow.

Halan gwav an sens a gan Rag enevow es en tan.
Pur dhevry an burthen yu 'Gweres an enevow, Dhew!'
    Halan gwav an sens a gan.

A glewsta'n offeryas Ow cana en Eglos vas,
Ow cana an offeren Rag enevow an anken?
    A glewsta'n offeryas?

Halan gwav an dis a bes Ancow Crist yu disquidhes,
Ancow Crist es bewnans tis En plas rial Paradis.
        Halan gwav a dis abes.

Gwren ny pesy gensans y Rag cardoryon, ha'gan cry,
Powes bithol ro dhodhans 'Golow dho'n Enevow sans!'
        Grwen ny pesy gensans y.

'Powes bithol ro dhodhans Golon bisquedhek warnans
Gans dhe sans es en Nev tek, Rag a bosta triwathek
        Powes bithol ro dhodhans.'

Re vo clewes Lev an Crist. Dres an downder mer ha trist,
'Deugh why, beniges ow Thas, Dho lowender en ow gwlas,'
        Re vo clewes Lev an Crist.

Re vo gordhyans a'n Drenses, An Tas, an Mab, ha'n Speres,
Genen ny gans Sens a eugh, Hag Enevow kerm geneugh.
        Re vo gordhyans an Drenses.

Jenner appends a note which sets the poem in context:

An gwers-na yu trelyans an can es Lenwes en Latenek, 'Communio en offeren an Re Varow. Requiem aeternam dona eis, Domine et lux perpetua lucat eis, cum sanctis tuis in aeternum, quia pius es.'

[*Mass or Communion for the Dead. 'Rest eternal give them, Lord, and light perpetual shine on them, with your holiness in eternity, who are faithful.'*]

Although not a Roman Catholic at the time that this was written, Jenner evidently subscribed wholeheartedly to the doctrine of Purgatory, something avoided or even suppressed by the Anglican and dissenting churches. The following translation does not claim to be literal, but is an approximation of Jenner's meaning:

'Out of the depth I have called to thee, Lord: Lord, hear my voice.'
(*Psalm 129*)

Dost thou hear the voice of the great sea? On the rocks waves break,
In the caves with a great bass voice, on the strand with a sigh –
    Dost hear the voice of the great sea?

Dost hear the voice of the wood? In a quiet valley through the night
The sound of the wind in the high trees Whispers desire, sad and true:
    Dost hear the voice of the woods?

Dost hear the voice of the mine? It is coming from the workings below
Like the sound of high water, A sound of tears falling to earth:
    Dost hear the voice of the mine?

Thou hearest the spirits: all around are the dead.
In our midst are friends: they are spirits passed over:
    Thou hearest the spirits.

Their cries fly up to heaven: a cry of souls in grievous pain,
In the sigh of the sea, mine and woods, In the heartfelt voice through the
                    night

    Their cry comes to heaven.

From the depth they cry, 'Grant mercy to us!'
Mother Mary, Saints above, hear their song!
    From the depths they cry.

Dost thou hear the song of the Saints? A sound of pipes, voice of the lute,
The song of the viol with its stretched bow, blessed minstrelsy.
    Dost hear the song of the Saints?

Winter month through Heaven's great gate, at the prison
of spirits Saints gaze, full of pity Across the looming abyss,
    Winter month, through great gates.

Winter month of the singing Saints For souls who are on fire.
Verily the chorus is 'Help the spirits, God.'
    Winter month of the singing Saints.

Dost thou hear the Mass, sung in the great church,
Sounding the Offertory For souls in distress?
    Dost thou hear the Mass?

Winter month of men who pray Death of Christ is shown:
Death of Christ is life to men In the royal palace of heaven.
    Winter month of men who pray.

Let us pray with them For loved ones, and our plea:
Give eternal rest to all, 'Light to the holy souls!'
    Let us pray with them.

'Give eternal rest to all: May light shine upon them
With the Saints in fair Heaven At the victorious Feast
    Give eternal rest to all.'

May the voice of Christ be heard Through the great sad depths;
'Bring Thou, blessed father, Joy to our land.'
    May the voice of Christ be heard.

May there be glory to the Godhead, the Father, Son and Spirit,
With us and the Saints on high, and the souls dear to us.
    May there be glory to the Godhead.

At the end of 1901 Jenner produced his 'Kan Nadelik' (A Christmas Song), subtitled 'En Tavaz Kernuak an Sethdegvas Cans vledhan' (in the Cornish Language of the 17th century). It was published in *Celtia* the following June, with a translation by L. C. Duncombe Jewell, Secretary of the Celtic Cornish Society, and an eager student of Cornish as Jenner was then presenting it.

En pedn an vledhan, pan gwav o gwyn,
Be gennes Map Dew a Varya wyn,
Rag sawya dhort pehas an bys-ma,
Ha bownans rag dry dh'an pople da.

'Rig kana an El dh'an bugely en gwêl,
Hedna o kan pur lawenek dho whêl:
"Gorryans dho Dew ez en Nef braz,
Cres war an tir dho deez vodh vaz!"

A vez an dhuyran war degl an Stûl,
A dheth teez fyr, o Maternow ul,
Ha'n gy 'rig dos aberth an bow-gy,
Hag ubba 'rig gorria 'gan Arleth ny.

Ha ny vedn mos dho worria genzyns,
Teez fyr, ha bugely ha chattol ul myns.
En termen Offeren ny vedn e gwellas,
Pan ef 'ra dyskynnya rag dh'agan whellas.

Dew reffa sawya coth Gernow whêg,
Dhort Pedn an Wollas bys Tamar teg,
Ha gwitha y bisqueth en carenja ef,
Dho worria Map Dew ha Maternes Nef.

Bennath Nadelik gena why re bo
Dhort an Tas Dew ny, ha dhort e Hloh,
Ha dhort Dama Dew, an Vahteth 'lan: –
Hedna yw duath dho ul ow han.

[*At the end of the year, when the winter was white,*
Was born the Son of God of Mary Blessed,
For to save the world from sin,
And life for to bring to good people.

The Angel did sing to the shepherds in the field,
That was a song very joyful to man:
"Glory to God in the heavens high,
Peace upon Earth to men of good will!"

From out of the East on the Epiphany,
Came the wise men – they were kings all –
And they did come into the stable,
And there did homage to our Lord.

And we will go for to worship with them,
The wise men, and the shepherds, and cattle all.
At Mass-time Him shall we see,
When He shall descend to seek us.

God save old Cornwall dear,
From Land's End to Tamar fair,
And keep it ever in His love,
To the glory of God and of the Queen of Heaven.

A Christmas blessing with you be
From God the Father, and from His Son,
And from the Mother of God, the Virgin pure
This is the end of all my song.]

This carol was actually set to music by a rising composer of the time, Philip Heseltine, who wrote under the name of Peter Warlock. Warlock's work, particularly his 'medieval' Capriol Suite, has often been performed by leading orchestras, and it is to be hoped that we can rescue the music of Jenner's carol so that it can again be performed in Cornwall. How far Warlock understood Cornish is open to doubt, but he is said to have boasted that he 'had his own private language'. Was he being serious, or merely provocative? Jenner's use of Late or 'Modern' Cornish here is interesting to the language student. Note the late intrusive consonants in *pedn* (*pen*), *hedna* (*henna*), etc. *Ubba* in stanza three seems to be a Late version of *omma*, 'here', though translated as 'there'. *Hloh* in the last stanza uses a mutation, now defunct, of F to H; we should now write *y Flogh* (son). Jenner was here still using the form *dho* for *dhe*; both would be pronounced 'dhuh' with a neutral, indeterminate vowel.

Jenner was now well into his stride. About this time he produced a rhyming translation of his wife's poem 'The Boats of Sennen', later set to music by Ralph Dunstan for his *Cornish Song Book* of 1929. As a combination of sound, sense, rhythm and rhyme, it is an ingenious rendering, and no small achievement. Here are Jenner's first and fourth stanzas, with literal English equivalents:

'Berh an manal yu an is
Worth an garrek hern a mis
Ema scathow strik ow lemmel adheworth Gwindreath a les;
Mi a glew huer e lev,
Mi a wel mar vrith an nev,
Ha dhemmo mi a cov an termen neb yu passyes sol-a-bres.

'Berh an manal yu an is
Worth an garrek hern a mis
War Guesons an Howlsedhas ma howl owrek ow splanna;
Mi a glew huer e lev,
Mi a wel mar vrith an nev:
Mes ow holon vi yu marow gans anken ow herra.

[*Stacked in sheaves is the corn*
On the rock the pilchards swim,
And nimble boats leap out from Gwindreath away;
I hear the huer's voice
I see the dappled sky
And to me come memories of a time gone past.

Stacked in sheaves is the corn,
On the rock the pilchards swim,
On Islands of the West the golden sun now shines;

I hear the huer's voice
I see the dappled sky;
But my heart is dead with sorrow for my most beloved.]

Note the use of the word *berh* for *bern* (Unified) meaning 'rick' or 'stack' (verb *bern*, to pile up or stack. *Mar vrith: bryth*, 'speckled' or 'mottled'. *Guersow* for 'islands' is obscure, but to use *enesow* would, of course, have spoiled the rhythm.

Also of this period was Jenner's rendering of the British national anthem into Cornish – another example of his ability to find a strictly rhythmic scheme, consonant with the original:

Dew saw 'gan Matern fir;
Yeghes ha bewnans hir
         Dh'agan Matern!
Danvon e bidhek dhen,
En gordhyans ha lowen,
Pell dho roulya warnen;
         Dew, saw'n Matern!

A'n gwella a'th arhow
Wornodho skull roow;
         Re roulo pell.
Re witho 'gan lahes
May rollo cas beppres
En grev dho gana dhes,
         Dew, saw'n Matern!

Sav aman, Arledh Dew,
Scat e skerens e vew,
         Dho'n lur toul y.
Dyswra 'ga drog doulow,
Ha'n hager oberow:
Warnos 'gan trest re bo;
         Dew, son oll ny.

Jenner's own literal translation of the third verse is:

> *Rise up, O Lord God,*
> *Smite the enemies of his life,*
> > *To the ground cast them.*
> *Frustrate their evil tricks*
> *And their ugly works;*
> *On Thee may our trust be –*
> > *God save us all.*

This would appear to be a response in honour of the new king, Edward VII, at his coronation.

'Gwaynten yn Kernow', one of Jenner's most attractive sonnets, was written about 1903 or 1904, and gives us the heartfelt thoughts of an exiled Cornishman working in London. It was published at that time in *Celtia*, but a Unified version appeared in *Old Cornwall* in 1956. Although Jenner is identified there as the author, it is likely that Robert Morton Nance was responsible for the new spelling. The original reads as follows:

> Gwaynten en Kernow! 'Ma Miz-Me ow tos;
> > Floures agor, edhyn bian agan,
> > Gwerdh yu an gwedh, ridhek en blejyow glan
> Avalow yu an jarnow, war peb ros
> Savor an eithin melen ol an nos
> > A-lenw an ayr, warlergh houlsedhas splan,
> > A wrig golowa'n don las avel tan;
> Ha son an mor a wortheb lef an cos.
> Re wrellen bos en Kernow! Lowenek
> > Clewav lef ton, ha gwainten devedhes,
> Gwelav gun las Mor Havren, gwils ha whek,
> > Gwelav blejyow, 'vel henros beniges
> Govi! ni dhre dhemmo 'gan gwainten tek,
> > Divres a'm bro, neb whekter en Loundres.

Jenner's own translation reads as follows:

> *Spring in Cornwall! The month of May is coming,*
> *Flowers are opening, little birds are singing,*
> *Green are the trees, reddening in the pure blossoms*
> *Of apples are the orchards, on every heath*
> *The scent of the yellow furze all the night*
> *Fills the air, after the sunset*
> *Which has lighted up the blue wave like fire,*
> *And the sound of the sea answers the voice of the wood.*
> *Oh that I were in Cornwall! Gladly*
> *I hear the voice of the wave, spring being come,*
> *I see the blue plain of the Severn Sea, wild and sweet,*
> *I see flowers, like a blessed dream –*
> *Ah me! Our fair spring brings not to me,*
> *An exile from my country, any sweetness in London.*

A footnote to the poem explains that he has 'followed the strict rules of the Italian sonnet, as to the arrangement of the quatrains and tercets and rhymes … it shows that one can apply Cornish to various purposes'. He also pays tribute to Duncombe Jewell for having written, some time previously, the first sonnet in the language, which had also appeared in *Celtia*.

'Can an Pescador Kernuak', The Cornish Fisherman's Hymn, was originally written at Easter 1905 and published by Jenner as a Christmas card later that year. A version in Unified Cornish ('Can an Pescajor Kernewek) appeared in Dunstan's *Cornish Song Book* and is still occasionally performed by male voice choirs and school choirs. Here are the first two and the last two verses of the eight-verse hymn, together with Jenner's translation:

> 1. Adro'n Lethowsow, 'ma an mor ow-crya,
>   Rag corfow tus Carak an Bleith a-wol;
>   Gwren mos yn rag, dre weres Mab Marya,
>   Dhe beryl mor ha carak heb own ol.
> *Burdhen:* Cryst, Mab Marya, Steren an Mor,
>   Golsow ha gortheb pesadow pescajor.

2. Cryst, ty 'elwas pescajoryon a'n kensa
    War dreth Mor Galylea dhe'th holya;
Ol agan gweyth haneth rag dha garensa
    Dheso yn len offrynny ny a-wra.
Burdhen:

7. Yn dha dheula ny a-gemmyn an lester;
    Ro gwynsow mas hag awel deg dhen-ny,
Myghal an Argh-El, marghak agan Mester,
    Danvon dhen-ny rag agan hembrenky.
Burdhen:

8. Gwren mos yn rag, ow-trestya yn dha weres:
    Yn dha dhorn-sy yu bewnans hag ancow.
Gordhyans re-bo dhe Das ha Mab ha Speres,
    Try yn Onen, Gwythyas 'gan enevow.
Burdhen:

[1. All round the Longships mighty waves are crying,
    For lives of men the howling Wolf doth call;
Forth let us fare, on Mary's Son relying,
    Fearless of rock and flood, whate'er befall.
Chorus*: Christ, Son of Mary, Star of the Sea,*
    Listen and answer a fisher's cry to Thee.

2. Fishers were they whom first Thy Name confessing
    Thou calledst by the Sea of Galilee;
For Thy dear sake, and mindful of Thy blessing,
    This our night's toil we dedicate to Thee.
Chorus:

7. Into thy hands our vessel now commending,
    Grant us, we pray Thee, wind and weather fair;

Michael, Thy Knight, Thine own Archangel, sending
*   To be our guide and guardian everywhere.*
Chorus:

8. *Let us go forward, trusting in Thy merit;*
*   Both life and death Thy loving hand controls.*
Worship be done to Father, Son, and Spirit,
*   God Three in One, the Keeper of our souls.*
Chorus:]

Given that the English version should rhyme and scan as the Cornish does –
the suggested tune is 'Pilgrims of the Night' by Henry Smart – the translation is
remarkably close. Jenner does not appear here to have embraced fully Nance's
new Unified spelling, so we have *dhen-ny* instead of *dhyn-ny*, *ol* instead of *oll*
(all), *gweyth* for *gwyth* (work, toil) and *pesad*ow for *pysad*ow (prayers). The name
of the Wolf Rock would now be written *Carrek an Blyth*, not *Carak an Bleith*.

One of the most significant pieces Jenner ever wrote was the dedicatory
poem, 'Dho'm Gwreg Gernuak' (To My Cornish Wife), which he used as a preface to his *Handbook* of 1904. This well-planned sonnet is not simply a love poem
to his wife Kitty, but a proclamation of his love for and devotion to Kernow and
its language:

Kerra ow Holon! Beniges re vo
Gans bennath Dew an dêdh a 'th ros dhemmo,
Dhô whelas gerryow gwan pan dhetha vî,
Tavas dha dassow, ha dhô 'th drovya dî.
En cov an dêdh splan-na es pel passyes;
En cov idn dêdh lowenek, gwin 'gan bês,
War Garrack Loys en Côs, es en dan skês
Askelly Myhal El, o 'gan gwithes,
En cov lîas dêdh wheg en Kernow da
Ha ny mar younk-na whekkah vel êr-ma
Dhemmo a dhîg genew an gwella tra,
Pan dhetha vî en kerh, en ol bro-na;

Dheso mî re levar dha davas teg,
Flogh ow empinyon vî, dhô 'm kerra Gwrêg.

[*Beloved of my heart! Blessed may be*
With the blessing of God the day that gave
You to me, when I came to look for the faint words
Of the tongue of your fathers, and to find you.
In memory of that bright day now long past,
In memory of one happy day, splendid our world!
On the Grey Rock in the Wood, under the shelter of the wings
Of Michael, Archangel, who was our protector;
In memory of many delightful days in good Cornwall,
When we were so young – no sweeter than the present –
With me I brought away the best thing of all
When I left, in all that land:
To you I have spoken your beautiful tongue
Child of my mind, my dearest wife.]

From this time onwards Jenner's verse was almost entirely directed outward
to public and patriotic themes. He had undoubtedly attained such stature
among his Cornish countrymen that they accepted him, at this stage, as their
great, if unofficial, Bard. Familiar with his many achievements, including his
membership of the Breton Gorsedd, they had come to expect him to make significant public pronouncements in their resurrected language. One of the most
interesting, perhaps, is his Cornish version of the First World War marching
song, 'It's a long way to Tipperary', which followed the numerous other versions
in the various languages of the British Empire that were published in the *Daily
Mirror* in 1916. Again, with simplicity and feeling, Jenner produced a singable
text:

Pel yu fordh Tipperary,
Hir yu'n gerdh dhodho.
Pel yu fordh Tipperary,
Dho'n voren es kerra dhemmo.
Bennath Dew dhes, Piccadilly,

Plas Carleryon, dhes di.
Pel yu fordh Tipperary,
Mes enno yu ow halon vi.

Typically he found a Celtic name for Leicester – Carleryon. This contribution to the war effort was followed by his Cornish language version of Hawker's 'Song of the Western Men' (Trelawny), which had been gathering popular acclaim across Cornwall and among Cornish exiles, being often sung at dinners and celebrations by some of the leading singers since the 1860s or 1870s – in particular by the tenor N. B. Bullen of Truro. There have been other versions in Kernewek, but none to outshine Jenner's:

'Ma lel an lef, 'ma'n cledh a mas,
'Ma'n golon lowen, gwyr!
Tus Myghtern James 'wra convedhes
Pandr' allo Kernow, sur!
(*Burdhen*):   'Verow Trelawny bras? 'Verow Trelawny bras?
Mes ugans myl a dus Kernow
A woffyth ol an cas.

Yu ornes le ha prys ancow?
'Verow Trelawny bras?
Mes ugans myl a dus Kernow
A woffyth ol an cas.
(*Burdhen*):

'Meth aga Hapten cref ha drus,
Gwas lowen ef a ve,
"Mar pe Tour Loundres Carak Lus,
Ny a-n-kergh mes an le."
(*Burdhen*):

"Ny a dres Tamar, tyr dhe dyr,
A pe 'vel Havren doun,

Onen hag ol dhe'n den es fur
Dhe 'gan lettya vyth own."

(*Burdhen*):

"Pan wrellen dos dhe Fos Loundres,
Dhe wel a blek dhen-ny:
"Ownegyon ol, gwreugh dos yn mes
Dhe dus es gwell es' why!"

(*Burdhen*):

"Yn carghar kelmys rag ancow
Myreugh Trelawny bras!
Mes ugans myl a dus Kernow
A-woffyth ol an cas."

(*Burdhen*):

Only in the fourth stanza does Jenner depart from the strict sense of the original. The last line of the chorus (*burdhen*) must have presented some difficulty, as there is no literal Cornish version of 'the reason why' which would have fitted the rhythm. *Ol an cas* (all the cause) was a brilliant solution to the problem. *Carghar*, 'fetter' or 'shackle', is perhaps something of an overstatement; one can hardly imagine the Bishop actually in chains, but it is an effective image. The foregoing is the Unified version supplied by Jenner for Ralph Dunstan's *Cornish Song Book*.

'An Pemthek Pell' (The Fifteen Bezants) well illustrates Jenner's medieval researches and their effect on his interpretation of Cornish history. It is itself a remarkable interpretation of the shield of Cornwall and its devices. It seems unsatisfactory that we have no recorded Cornish language term for 'bezant' – the gold coin reputedly from Byzantium or the Byzantine Empire – other than *pel*, which can be used for any sort of round object, sphere or ball. However, the scheme of the poem takes us from the figure of the Archangel Michael, who was recognised as the Patron Saint of Cornwall, at least by the Norman earls, to an examination of his shield on which the bezants appear.

War e scouth yu costan hir,
Costan Kernow, dour ha gwir;
En tewolgow an bes deu
Golow owr a dhe a Dhew.
         Gorwyth Kernow, 'Gostan Hir!

En owr splan an Pemthak Pell,
Arvow Kernow lel, es gwel
Ages arvow ol an bes,
Mysteryow an Vaternes:
         Onen hag ol, 'Bemthak Pell!

[*On his shoulder is a long shield,*
The Shield of Cornwall, bold and true:
In the darkness of the black world
Golden light comes from God.
         Guard Cornwall, Long Shield!

In the bright gold of the Fifteen Bezants
The Arms of loyal Cornwall, better
than all the arms of the world:
Mysteries of the Virgin:
         One and All: Fifteen Bezants!]

We are then given the meaning of these golden symbols:

Thera dinerhyans² deuweth;
Sans era'n Genesegeth;
Deuweth 'berh an Eglos Dek
Be Jesu, gans E Vam whek:
         Otta Pemp es Lowenek.

Whes a Woys agan Matern,
Scorjans: Coronyans gans Spern;

Pren a Grows dho vos deges,
Wher an Ancow rag an bes:
　　Otta Pemp es Morethek!

De Zil Pask ha'n Askenyans;
Ha Sil-Gwidn an Speres Sans;
Ha Ewhellyans Dama Dew;
Ha'y Horanyans gans Jesu:
　　Otta Pemp es a Wordhyans.

Gans an Pemthak Pell yu gwres
Garlons agan Arledhes;
Crist, Maria, Myghal El,
Gwitheugh Gwlas an Pemthak Pell,
　　Kernow ker, Onen hag ol!

[There was a rejoicing twice;
Holy was the Nativity;
Twice within the Fair Church
Was Jesus, with his sweet Mother;
　　Behold five which are Joyful.

The bloody sweat of our King
His scourging; the crowning with thorns;
The timber cross to be carried,
The Agony of Death for the world:
　　Behold five which are Sorrowful.

Easter Sunday and the Ascension;
And the Pentecost of the Holy Spirit;
And the Assumption of the Mother of God,
And her crowning by Jesus:
　　Behold five which are Glorious.

From the fifteen bezants are made
the Garlands of our Lady;
Christ, Mary, Archangel Michael,
Guard the land of the Fifteen Bezants:
Dear Cornwall, One and All!]

All this is a far cry from the popular tales of the bezants being Cornwall's contribution to the ransom of Richard the Lionheart, imprisoned in Austria during the period of the Crusades. As Jenner was no doubt aware, arrangements of bezants on or around the shields of various Cornish kings and Earls of Cornwall predate the Crusades by several centuries.[3]

By way of a Christmas greeting from Kitty and himself in 1906, Jenner composed a nativity carol in Cornish and English entitled 'Devedhyans an Matern' (The Coming of the King):

Sav aman, Dinas Dew, devedhes yu
　　Dha Wolow, an roul coth yu tremenes,
Fethes an Escar, taw an Tuller deu,
　　An Matern gwir a dhe wostewedh dhes.

[*City of God, arise, thy Light is come,*
　　Now is the ancient usurpation past,
Vanquished the Foe, the Dark Deceiver dumb,
　　Thy true King cometh to His own at last.]

After a celebration of the stable scene, with the Queen (Mary) holding the Christ-child and shepherds and the three Kings worshipping, we move on to a prevision of Christ the King who will eventually rule over all.

'Wren E gorona lemmen? Nyns yu gwres
　　E ober; tanow yu E servisy.
En dadn E dreys pan vedh pebtra settyes,
　　Coron adro dhoy dal y whorrans y.

'Wren E gorona gans owr? Nyns yu'n êr;
Garlons a dhevnedh aral rag E ben,
Pan wel tîs ol an bes en gordhyans mêr
Agan Matern ow roulya a'n Grows-Pren.

[*Shall we crown Him now? His work is not complete;*
Only a few His subjects now.
When He shall put all things beneath His feet,
There shall be set a crown upon His brow.

Crown Him with gold? It is not time:
Of other ware His diadem shall be,
When all the nations of the earth behold
The King of Glory reigning from the Tree.][4]

Between 1890 and 1905 Jenner helped to produce *The Royalist*, which was an unashamed Jacobite organ. Nowhere does his own attitude to royalty come more to the fore than in 'Can Contellyans an Kernewyon En Mis Hedre en Vledhan 1715/The Gathering Song of the Cornishmen in October 1715', a remarkable anthem that he contributed in April 1905 to what was probably the penultimate number of the journal.

Jenner was convinced that, at the time of the 1715 Rebellion, most Cornish people – which in effect meant the gentry, their servants and their tenants – were at heart strongly sympathetic to the Jacobite cause. After all, had they not, in the main, supported Charles I during the Civil War? Were not many of them, especially the Arundels, the Vyvyans and families around St Columb, his birth-place, actually still Catholics? And not only the gentry: in 1717 a woman called Wilmot Mitchel was publicly whipped at Launceston, then the 'county' or Assize town, for proclaiming, 'Good news from Dover – they are all acoming over: we'll bring him in and crown him King, and send the cuckold back to Hanover.'

However, the attempted proclamation of James III was abortive. James Paynter of Trelissick in St Erth, a Catholic married to Elizabeth Rawe of Trevithick, did come to St Columb on market day to read it, but found the yeoman farmers of the parish more interested in the price of cattle and sheep. The government of George I was evidently paranoid about a possible rising to re-establish the Stuarts and the Catholic faith. The Old Pretender's first intention had been to land in South Devon and rally both Cornwall and its neighbour, but while at St Malo, James heard that one of his agents had informed, and so switched his landing place to Scotland. A letter from one of Paynter's associates was intercepted and a number of his accomplices were arrested, with Sir Richard Vyvyan of Trelowarren being sent to the Tower.

'Can Contellyans an Kernewyon...' is, then, Jenner's rallying song, in the mode of R. S. Hawker's 'Gate Song of Stowe', which commemorates another lost cause – that of Sir Beville Grenville. However, in an address given to the Royal Institution of Cornwall in 1917 and published in the society's journal that year, Jenner admitted that by the time of the 1745 Rebellion, there remained little if any support for Jacobitism in Cornwall.

To compare Jenner's 'Gathering Song...' with Hawker's 'Gate Song...' is interesting. Both men supported the Stuarts, both wrote of failed uprisings. Jenner mentions Godolphin (Francis, second earl), whose father, Sidney, had been Queen Anne's chief minister – hardly a likely supporter of the Pretender. However, the Song invokes the son of Arundel of Trerice – 'John for the King' – who at the age of seventy had held Pendennis Castle for Charles I, and also John Trevanion of Caerhayes, Vyvyan, and St Aubyn of Clowance. It is all very reminiscent of Hawker's

> Trevanion is up, and Godolphin is nigh,
> And Harris of Hayne's o'er the river;
> From Lundy to Looe, 'One and all!' is the cry,
> And the King and Sir Beville for ever!

The comparison makes it quite clear that both Jenner and Hawker supported the Stuarts and that both wrote of failed ventures in songs that are inspiring, arousing and ingenious. (Hawker's 'The Song of the Western Men' is, of course, yet another example, although Bishop Trelawny was actually in little danger, and no march to Exeter or London resulted from his imprisonment.)

Improvements in the mining industry and the abundance of pilchards and good harvests appear to have persuaded the Cornish between 1715 and 1745 that Georgian prosperity was hardly worth opposing, and Jacobitism had died a natural death by the time the Seven Years' War and the Napoleonic Wars were fought. Yet, as late as 1743 John Wesley was accused of Jacobitism in turning the Cornish people against the established church. From Gwennap to Altarnun it was rumoured that he had actually brought the Young Pretender to Cornwall, disguised as one of his preachers.

As Jenner makes clear in an explanatory note, the language of the song is late seventeenth century and early eighteenth century Cornish, and the metres 'heptasyllabic lines in six-lined stanzas rhyming a a b c c b, one of the commonest metres in the Cornish and other mediaeval dramas'.

Can Contellyans an Kernewyon, En Mîs Hedre en Vledhan 1715

Scrîfes en Kernûak gans Gwas Myhal, Bardh a Worsedh Breton-Isal

Pobel Kernow, contelleugh,
Hag en agas milyow deugh,
    Dreugh genough agas cledhyow,
Rag dhô gerhas dres Mor Hîr
Jago agan Matern gwîr;
    Contelleugh, a Dîs Kernow!

Mîreugh, dres Mor an Dehow
Agan Matern caradow
    Divres yu en gwlascor bel,
'Mesk an Vrethon, 'gan kerans,
Ow cortos en esperans
    Ragough why, Kernewyon lêl.

Ha dheugh why ev a wra dos,
E dîs lêl a garn ha ros,

Tîs an whêl ha tîs an ton.
Dres pub tra es en e wlas
Ev a drest e Gernow mas;
 Contelleugh, a Gernewyon!

Mab Jûan Rag an Matern,
Dên Trerys, deugh, ha Lanhern,
 Deugh, Vyvyan ha Kellygrê,
Deugh, Sentaubyn ha Borlâs,
Deugh, Godolhan ha Carhâs,
 Dhô gerhas an Matern dre.

Stenoryon en garrak dheu,
Pescadoryon war mor bew,
 Gareugh palow ha rusow;
Why a gows an hen davas,
An fêdh goth why re withas;
 Contelleugh, a Dîs Kernow!

'Gas tassow a omladhas
Rag e sîra widn en fas,
 Matern Gwidn ha Merther Sans;
Deugh, omladheugh why mar grev,
Ha rag e garensa ev
 Festineugh dho'n Contellyans.

Golsoweugh; dhô Gontell vras
Dhô Bleu-Golom[5] en marhas
 Gans cledhyow deugh ol hedhyu.
Dên Trelissek why a wel
An Baner ow terevel,
 Baner Kernow our ha deu.

Govî, Dew, ro dhen idn êr,
Pan an Grenvîl y wheler!
Gew dho Lansdon, tebel vrês!
Tir an Houlsedhas, divîn!
Sav aman dheworth dha hîn,
Del ve Arthur devethes!

Gwren degelmy an Baner,
Pempthak Pell a'n costan mer,
Costan Myhal an Arhel;
"Onen hag Ol!" ow crya,
Rag Matern gwren omladha,
Ha rag Dew ha Kernow lêl.

The Gathering Song of the Cornishmen, In the month of October, in the year 1715

Written in Cornish by Gwas Myhal, a Bard of the Gorsedd of Brittany, and literally translated by H. J.

People of Cornwall, gather,
And in your thousands come,
Bring with you your swords,
To bring back across the Long Sea
James, our rightful King;
Gather, O Folk of Cornwall!

Look, across the Sea of the South,
Our beloved King
Is an exile in a distant land,
Among the Bretons, our kinsfolk,
Awaiting in hope
For you, loyal Cornishmen.

And to you he will come,
His loyal folk of rock and heath,
    Folk of the mine and of the wave.
Above everything that is in his kingdom,
He trusts his good Cornwall;
    Gather, O Cornishmen!

Son of 'John for the King,'
Man of Trerice, come, and Lanherne,
    Come, Vyvyan and Killigrew,
Come, St Aubyn and Borlase,
Come, Godolphin and Carhayes,
    To bring the King home.

Tinners in the black rock,
Fishers on the living sea,
    Leave spades and nets;
Ye speak the ancient tongue,
The old faith ye have kept;
    Gather, O Folk of Cornwall!

Your fathers fought
For his grandsire well,
    The White King and Holy Martyr;
Come, fight ye as strongly,
And for his own sake
    Hasten to the gathering.

Hearken; to a great trysting
At St Columb in the market
    With swords come all to-day.
The Man of Trelissick ye shall see
The Banner uplifting,
    The Banner of Cornwall, gold and black.

Alas, God, give us one hour,
When the Granville may be seen!
   Woe to Lansdowne, evil judgment!
Land of the Sunset, awake!
Rise up from out of thy sleep,
   As though Arthur were come!

Let us unfurl the Banner,
The Fifteen Balls of the Great Shield,
   The Shield of Michael the Archangel;
'One and All!' crying out,
For the King let us fight,
   And for God and loyal Cornwall.

The close relationship between Henry and Katharine Jenner appears nowhere so evident as in the two versions of 'Can Gwlasol Agan Mamvro' (Patriotic Song of our Motherland). It does, however, raise certain fascinating speculations as to exactly how much input into this joint venture came from each partner.

Katharine's English version was published in 1926 in her verse collection Songs of the Stars and the Sea, and it may be significant that here, for the first and only time, she used a Cornish language title, though subtitling it in English. Given that Henry had written his Cornish version some years before, it seems possible that, working from a literal English translation which he provided, she produced this inspired and polished version. After all, considering such pieces as 'O Mystic Land', 'The Old Names' and 'The Boats of Sennen', it would not be astounding that Henry's Cornish had moved her to do so. She stays very faithful to his Kernewek in sentiment, rhythm and rhyme, although there are a few lines where the versions do not exactly coincide: Katharine's line in the first stanza, 'Scattered over all the earth', does not appear in Henry's version, and neither does her reference to St Petrock in the last.

It is likely that there was close collaboration on the subject matter, which is totally consistent with Henry's view of Cornish history: the Grail, the Cornish who fell at the Battle of Lansdown fighting for Charles I, and St Michael, whose name he had taken on being made a Bard. But then, Katharine was herself Catholic and doubtless wholeheartedly subscribed to those sentiments.

Jenner identifies Lansdown with Badon Hill, the site of Arthur's last and most complete victory. Many Arthurian scholars would dispute this interpretation, with Liddington Castle near Swindon in Wiltshire, Badbury Rings in Dorset, and many other sites being suggested instead. But at least one eminent modern historian, Dr John Morris, partly supports Jenner, arguing that a careful study of the local topography suggests Solsbury Hill near Batheaston. It evidently suited Jenner to identify Badon with Lansdown.

The reference to the Royal Letter is to Charles I's letter of thanks to his loyal Cornish army, written at Sudeley Castle, and reproduced on large notice boards in many Cornish churches.

All in all, 'Can Gwlasol Agan Mamvro' is not so much a rallying cry as an elegy, full of haunting Celtic nostalgia and pride in past achievements. The last two lines of Katharine's poem, which is reproduced below after Henry's Cornish version from *The Wheel*, points the way to preserving Cornwall's great heritage: as long as the people remember and value their traditions, the heart of Kernow will be in safe hands, despite the incursions and commercialisation of the modern age.

Can Wlascar Agan Mamvro

'Sedhys war Vor Gorlewen,
Caslan a nerthow garow,
Mamvro sans ragos canyn
Ny, dha fleghes, 'gan canow.
Agan colon ny a's trel
Dhe'n wlas may fuen-ny genys
Ragos gans pysadow lel.

War dhyfyth an mor ha'n don,
Yn tewolgow an bal du,
Ple pynag 'vo dha vebyon
Dhyso-jy yn prederow

Taran mor, gun redenek,
Dhyso-jy yn covathow
Dha gaswer mar golonnek.

Arthur gans marghogyon vas,
Gerrans cref, an amyral,
Lanslot, cans cas a borthas,
Trystan, Gawen, Perseval,
Y res eth yn arvos splan
Dhe whylas kelegel sans
Dre gosow, dre dhowr ha tan,
Mystry agan crysyans.

Yn tewolgow dha dus vas
A vue lel dhe'n wyr grysyans;
Tanow, gwan, y a verwys
Yn un vresel hep sperans.
War Un Badon y codhas
Dha fleghes rag an Ruy
Y lyther del dhysquedhas
Na wrussons y dyfygy.

Myghal a'n Garrek Wythys,
Dherag Dew agan Sansow,
Ken a'n venten venygys,
Peran, Sans an tewennow,
Ruan an morrep dyghow,
Ya, Brueg, ha cans erel –
Gwreugh gorwytha agan pow!

Can Gwlasol Agan Mam-vro
(Anglice, a Patriotic Song of our Motherland)

[*Throned above the western sea,*
    Battleground of forces grim,
Holy Motherland, for thee
    We thy children raise our hymn;
Scattered over all the earth
    Loving hearts we turn alway
To the land that gave us birth,
    And for thee our voices pray.

On the billows wild and free,
    In the darkness of the mine,
Wheresoe'er thy children be
    Evermore they shall be thine;
Thine in thoughts of sounding seas,
    Downs with heath and furze aglow,
Thine in glorious memories
    Of thy heroes long ago.

Thine was Arthur, thine his knights,
    Strong Geraint his admiral,
Lancelot of a hundred fights,
    Tristan, Gawain, Percival.
Thine were they in shining mail
    Through thy forest ways who trod,
Seeking for the Holy Grail,
    Mystery of the Faith of God.

To that Faith thy sons were true
    In its hour of darkest night,
Dared to die, a faithful few,
    Worsted in that hopeless fight.

Sons of thine with Grenville fell
  For their King in Lansdown's fray;
Let the Royal Letter tell
  How they failed him not that day.

Michael of the Guarded Mount,
  Saints before God's Face who stand,
Keyna of the hallowed fount,
  Piran of the drifting sand,
Petrock of the iron shore,
  Ruan of the southern strand,
Ia, Breage – a hundred more,
  Watch and ward our native land!
  One and all, on you we call;
  Pray for Cornwall, One and All!]

If one considers what is required of a national anthem, especially today, one would surely put forward first and foremost an expression of love for and loyalty to the homeland; secondly, a celebration of the peculiar beauties and attractions of its landscape; and thirdly, an acknowledgement of its past heroes and great traditions. Such attributes may be found in most popular modern anthems: 'La Marseillaise' celebrates freedom brought by the French Revolution and 'The Star Spangled Banner' forever celebrates the American ideal of freedom. Even small nations such as Finland have found their true native voice in the celebration of their homeland. Only the English – and now, by extension, the British – appear to stand against the all-embracing tide, and for sentimental or conservative reasons continue to glorify their monarch, with some of the trappings of the Divine Right of Kings attached. (Australia would have none of this, and voted for 'Advance Australia Fair' some twenty years ago.)

But what should be Cornwall's anthem? A number of notable songs have been written and popularised over the years. From the pen of Robert Morton Nance we have at least two, 'Can Kerth Tus Kernow Goth', (the Old Cornwall March), and 'A Gernow Whek' (O Cornwall Rare), which is vigorously sung at the Gorsedd each year. Bernard Moore produced his 'Song of Cornwall' and his

'Cornish Hymn' in the 1920s, and reprinted in Dunstan's *Cornish Song Book* is 'One and All', with words by Dr E. H. Moore of Truro, music by Charles Oliver. This song was made popular by the tenor N. B. Bullen, who sang it between 1883 and the 1920s in Cornwall, London and elsewhere. Another contender is Kenneth Pelmear's fine 'Song of the Homeland' and, of course, we have the Jenners' 'Can Gwlasol Agan Mamvro', which has not yet been set to music.

Nothing, however, caught on, nothing stuck immovably in Cornish minds except Hawker's 'Song of the Western Men' which, brilliantly wedding music to the words, is certainly the most popular Cornish song, and is often referred to as the unofficial Cornish national anthem. The only real objection, as Jenner himself was well aware, is that it is historically inaccurate. Writing it in his youth, Hawker had made 'bad shot' at the setting or the song, as Jenner noted in *The Royalist* in April 1905: the wrong King James, the wrong Trelawny. It was actually the Bishop's grandfather, Sir John Trelawny, one of the leaders of the King's party in parliament who, in 1628, was imprisoned in the Tower of London for contempt of the House of Commons. The famous refrain 'Here's twenty thousand Cornishmen...' dates from that time.

At Caernarfon in 1904, the year of Cornwall's second application to join the Celtic Congress, Jenner produced his first Cornish version of 'Hen Wlad Fy Nhadau' (Land of My Fathers) to be sung to the music of James James of Pontypridd. He was well aware of the song's importance as an inter-Celtic anthem, acknowledging that he had composed his version in Kernewek from the Welsh of Evan James and the Breton of Taldir-Jaffrenou. There are several versions of 'Bro Goth Agan Tasow' among Jenner's and Nance's papers in the Courtney Library at the Royal Institution of Cornwall, each one refining the grammar down to simpler constructions. It should not be necessary here to compare these versions in detail, although any fairly advanced student of Cornish will find it instructive to seek them out.

Jenner's first (Caernarfon) version quite properly included an inter-Celtic stanza, now apparently superseded, though surely it ought to be sung at Celtic Congress gatherings:

> Nynsyu Kernow marow, na reys dho skillya
> 'Gas dagrow, i whiredh, na reys dho wola;

Lysaw, Kembra, Wordhen, Manaw hag Alban,
Gweleugh hy dho sevel aman.

[*Cornwall is not dead; scatter not
Your tears, in truth, nor lament;
Brittany, Wales, Ireland, Man and Scotland,
Behold her rise up again.*]

Likewise the fourth stanza:

Ken na wrig an Sowson dha fethy en cas,
An Sowsnak a fethas in pres dha davas;
Mes colon pur Geltek en dha vron a lam,
Ha scon a tiviny, 'gan Mam.

[*Though the Saxon did not defeat you in battle
The English in time conquered your language;
But a pure Celtic heart beats in your breast
And soon shall our Mother revive.*]

As if perhaps to compensate for some of his anti-English sentiments, he added the following verse in honour of the Duke of Cornwall for the version that was published in the *Cornish Song Book* in 1929:

Dew re-wrello sona 'gan Duk a Gernow,
Es Mab agan Myghtern hag Arluth an Vro;
Dew roy dhodho yeghes ha bewnans pur-hyr,
Ha dhen-ny prest dhodho bos gwyr.

[*May God bless our Duke of Cornwall,
Who is the son of our King and Lord of the Land;
God grant to him health and long life,
And to us ever to be loyal to him.*]

Alternatively, perhaps this was a nod in the direction of the author's own Royalist sympathies.

Jenner's various emendations and improvements resulted in the anthem, which is sung annually at Gorseth Kernow. It is succinct, singable, strict in rhyme and rhythm, and presents a view of Kernow which strikes a deep chord in all Cornish patriots. Even when regarded as simply a translation or version of the original Welsh, it is as heartfelt and effective an anthem as any we have. Whether we accept it as an impossible dream, or a deep reality existing under the dross and inanities of modern life, it is a fitting capstone to Henry Jenner's poetic achievement:

> Bro goth agan Tasow, dha fleghes a-th-car,
> Gwlas ger an Houlsedhas, pan vro yu dha bar?
> War ol an nor-vys 'th-on-ny sculyes ales,
>   Mes oll 'gan kerensa yu dhys.
> *Burdhen*:
>   Kernow! Kernow! Ny 'gar Kernow!
>   Hedra vyth mor glan 'vel fos yn dha dro,
>   'Th-on "Onen hag Oll" rag Kernow!
>
> Gwlascor Myghtern Arthur, an Sansow, ha'n Gral,
> Moy keres genen nyns-yu tyreth aral.
> Ynnos-sy pup carrek, nans, meneth ha chy
> A-berth cof 'gan tavas coth-ny.
> *Burdhen*.
>
> Yn tewlder an bal ha war donow an mor,
> Pan eson ow-quandra dre dyryow tramor,
> Yn pup le pynak hag yn kenyver bro
>   Re-dreylyen colonnow dhyso.
> *Burdhen*.
>
> [*Old Land of our Fathers, thy children love thee,*
> *Dear realm of the Sunset, what land is thy peer?*

Over all the world we are scattered abroad,
 But all our love is to thee.
Chorus:
 Cornwall! Cornwall! We love Cornwall!
 As long as the fair sea shall be like a wall around thee
 We are "One and All" for Cornwall!

Country of King Arthur, the Saints, and the Grail,
 More loved by us is no other land,
 In thee every rock, valley, hill and house
 Bears the memory of our old tongue.
Chorus.

In the darkness of the mine and on the waves of the sea,
 When we are wandering through lands beyond the sea,
 In every place whatever and in every country
 May we turn hearts to thee
Chorus.][6]

Notes

1. Compare Unified *skyansek*, derived from science, scientific.
2. Greeting or welcoming, from *dynerghy*, to welcome.
3. With one manuscript version of this poem, which doubles as an exploration of the fifteen mysteries of the rosary, is a letter – dated 19 August 1921 – to a Mr Balling from Surgeon Captain W. G. K. Barnes who describes his friend Jenner's poem as having been 'written by him for a lady, although he knew the arms ante-dated the 15 mysteries'. (National Library of Wales ms. B257)
4. A full version of this poem can be found in Tim Saunders (ed.) (1999) *The Wheel: An Anthology of Modern Poetry in Cornish 1850–1980*, London: Francis Boutle, pp. 38–41.
5. Plu-Colum, the parish of St Columb.
6. This, with the addition of the fourth verse quoted above, is the version that appears in Dunstan's *Cornish Song Book*. For comparison, the two verses now sung at Gorseth Kernow are as follows:

   Bro goth agan Tasow, dha fleghes a'th car
   Gwlas ker an Howlsedhas, pan vro yu dha bar?
   War oll an norvys 'th on-ny scullyes ales,
   Mes agan kerensa yu dhys.
   Kescan:
    Kernow! Kernow! Y keryn Kernow;
    An mor hedra vo yn fos dhys adro
    'Th on "Onen hag Oll" rag Kernow.

Gwlascor Myghtern Arthur, an Syns kens, ha'n Gral
Moy kerys genen nyns yu tyreth aral,
Ynnos-sy pup carn, nans, meneth ha chy
A gows yn Kernewek dhyn-ny.
Kescan.

[*Old country of our fathers thy children love thee,*
Dear land of the west, what country is thy equal?
Over all the world we are scattered abroad,
But all our love is thine.
Chorus*:*

    Cornwall! Cornwall! we love Cornwall;
    While the sea is around thee like a wall
    We are one and all for Cornwall!

Kingdom of King Arthur, the Saints and the Grail
More loved by us is no other land
In thee every carn, valley, hill and house
Speaks in Cornish to us.
Chorus.]

Henry Jenner and the Anglo-Catholic Movement

David Everett

Introduction: Beliefs and Practices

In July 1913, the Royal Cornwall Polytechnic Society made its Summer excursion to St Michael's Mount, where a paper entitled *The Alabaster Carvings in the Chapel of St Michael's Mount*[1] was read by Henry Jenner. He began by stating:

> In the reredos of the chapel of St Michael's Mount there are nine alabaster reliefs of small size in a row. They do not belong to the original building, but have been placed in their present position in quite recent times. There does not seem to be any record of how they came into the possession of the St Aubyn family. The three of larger size, one of which is immediately over the middle of the Altar, and of the other two one is at each end of the row, are of English workmanship, and are probably of the early 15th century. The six little tablets along the top of the Altar are of Italian workmanship and are of the 16th century.

He then listed the subjects of the nine alabaster panels, from north to south, as follows:

1. Large tablet on the north side. A Pope, probably Gregory the Great (590–604 A.D.), celebrating Mass.

2. Small tablet. The Story of Susanna and the Elders (found in the Apocrypha).
3. Small tablet. The Adoration of the Magi.
4. Small tablet. Our Lord giving Holy Communion to the Apostles after the Last Supper, with Judas kneeling before Jesus.
5. Large tablet. St John the Baptist's head on a charger.
6. Small tablet. Our Lord washing St Peter's feet.
7. Small tablet. The Adoration of the Magi.
8. Small tablet. The Sacrifice of Isaac.
9. Large tablet on the south side. Christ before Pilate. Pilate washing his hands.

Jenner commented: 'With the exception of the tablet representing the Communion of Judas (no.4) there is nothing especially noteworthy in the six smaller tablets. They present the usual conventional treatment of the subjects in the religious art of the 16th Century. The selection of the subjects is so devoid of all sequence, that there seems little doubt that five of them are all that remain of a very much larger series ... The duplicate of the Magi probably belonged to another set.' He did not comment in any further detail on the smaller panels. Instead he concentrated on the subject of the large central panel, explaining that the subject of the Head of John the Baptist was a popular topic in medieval art and literature, and was interpreted as a type or symbol of the Lord's Supper. He also compared it with the story of the Holy Grail. According to Jenner, the central panel and the two outside larger panels are earlier than the smaller panels and are of English origin, 'once very common in England, of which a fair number still remain. I have seen a large number of them myself ... they are made of alabaster from the quarries of Chellaston, near Derby, by craftsmen of Nottingham and ... they are all connected with the great York Guild of Corpus Christi, a medieval Confraternity of the Blessed Sacrament.' In 1913, such a talk could only have been given by a High Churchman familiar with Anglo-Catholic beliefs and practices, as it brought together a knowledge of the Bible, church history – especially of the Middle Ages –, ritual and liturgy, and Christian art and architecture. Henry Jenner showed that he was proficient in all these areas.

From Tractarians to Anglo-Catholics

The start of the Anglo-Catholic Movement is usually dated to 1833, when John Keble preached his Assize sermon on 'National Apostasy' in Oxford. This was prompted by Government legislation decreeing the suppression of Irish bishoprics, which in turn raised the question of the reform of the church in general, and the authority of the state in these matters. The Anglo-Catholic movement was preceded by the Catholic Emancipation legislation of 1828 and by John Keble's book of poems *The Christian Year* of the previous year. The first outcome of the Assize sermon was a series of tracts called *Tracts for the Times*. Between 1833 and 1841, there were ninety tracts, the last one being on the Thirty-Nine Articles, one of the foundation documents of the Church of England. The movement was thus also called the Tractarian Movement or the Oxford Movement, and its adherents the Tractarians or the Oxford Apostles.[2] Some of the Anglicans who were attracted to Roman Catholic doctrine were, like Newman in 1845, received into the Roman Catholic Church, while others stayed in the Church of England. The unofficial leadership of the Tractarians, the Oxford Movement or the Anglo-Catholics passed to Dr Pusey, Regius Professor of Hebrew at Oxford.

Writing in 1864 in defence of the position he had taken, Newman outlined the main points as follows :[3] 'First was the principle of dogma: my battle was with liberalism; by liberalism I meant the anti-dogmatic principle and its developments.' He contrasted dogma with sentiment, which he called a dream and a mockery. 'Secondly,' he says, 'I was confident in the truth of a certain definite religious teaching, based upon this foundation of dogma; viz. that there was a visible Church with sacraments and rites which are the channels of invisible grace. But now, as to the third point on which I stood in 1833, and which I have utterly renounced and trampled upon since – my then view of the Church of Rome – I will speak about it as exactly as I can.' Newman had previously been against the Church of Rome, but over the years his views changed and by 1845 he was ready to join the Roman Catholic Church.

Later developments centred on the growth of ritual practices in Church of England worship and piety, and the possibility of a compromise between the Anglican and Roman Catholic Churches. So the Anglo-Catholic Movement became the dominant description of such movements for change and reform in

Katharine and Henry Jenner, with their daughter Ysolt
(Sister Mary Beatrix Jenner of the Order of the Visitation of Our Lady)
By permission of Mary Beazley

the Victorian Church. The Oxford Movement was accompanied by a parallel movement in Cambridge which centred on church design and architecture and was called the Cambridge Camden Society. It was founded in 1839 and known from 1845 as the Ecclesiological Society. The founders, John Mason Neale and Benjamin Webb, were clearly young men deeply impressed by the tracts which followed the start of the Oxford Movement. As John Pearce put it: 'They saw a need not only for an erudite appeal from the sister university, by scholars to scholars, but they felt that this should be complemented by an aesthetic witness. So they studied gothic architecture and ecclesiology.'[4]

A Spiritual Upbringing

Henry Jenner had been born in St Columb Major in 1848 where his father, the Revd. Henry Lascelles Jenner, was curate. Jenner senior was the son of Judge Jenner-Fust, but dropped the Fust surname, as he probably did not want to be identified with the person who gave the judgement against stone altars.[5] He joined the Cambridge Camden Society as an ordinary member when he was a student at Trinity Hall and when, in 1845, it was reformed and changed its name to the Ecclesiological Society, he contributed his own expertise in the area of church music, having a fine tenor voice himself. After serving in parishes in Chevening, near Sevenoaks, Kent, St Columb Major and Maryfield in Cornwall, Leigh-on-Sea, near Southend, and Brasted near Sevenoaks, Kent, eventually, in 1852, he applied for a minor canon's post at Canterbury and was successful. Two years later he moved to Preston-next-Wingham near Canterbury, the parish that went with the appointment. He was consecrated the first Bishop of Dunedin, New Zealand in 1866, and although he visited his diocese between November 1868 and July 1869, controversy over his appointment meant that he was never enthroned. He resigned any claims to his see in June 1871.[6]

Meanwhile, amidst all this moving around, his son attended St Mary's, Harlow (later Harlow College), a boarding school founded on Anglo-Catholic principles in the 1850s for the sons of the leaders of the movement. Originally called St Mary's after the nearby church in Old Harlow, it proved popular and later moved to another site in new premises which were, in fact, never finished. In the school journal, *The Harlovian*, for 1933, there was a piece about the

Oxford Movement and Harlow College, which included a section by Henry Jenner on the life of G.K.Fortescue:

> Provost Fortescue's Anglican position was the cause that he sent two of his sons to Harlow College, which had been started in the fifties as a school for sons of the extremer members of the Catholic party in the Church of England. It was encouraged by the leaders of that section, and for a while appeared to flourish, so that in 1861 a new building on a fairly large scale was needed, and the foundation stone was laid amid great pomp and hopefulness by the Hon. Colin Lindsay, the first President of the English Church Union, who backed his opinions by sending one of his own sons there. Eucharistic vestments were worn, incense was used, fast days were kept ... I think that the religion was presented in a manner which has caused very few, however they may have drifted away from the form of it, to look back upon it with repugnance or dislike; and even those who are not religious now, look back with a certain kindly feeling to the beautiful ideals, never alas to be realised, of the extremists of that day, a feeling which the said debacle of our old school could not do away with.[7]

The *Harlovian* adds: 'The last words of the quotation refer to an unfortunate scandal which brought the School to an untimely end after twelve years. It was never revived on its original lines. It was re-opened after an interval by the Rev Earle, who carried it on till his death.'[8] Another edition of the journal also mentions the contents of Henry Jenner's piece and adds, 'The founder, the Rev Charles Jonathan Goulden, a man of Jewish extraction, was a very mixed character; the discipline was fitful and irregular, the scholarship inaccurate; and everything more or less ramshackle in its ways.'[9]

Jenner left St Mary's in 1865 and then worked first as a teacher at a school in Brighton and then at H.M.Court of Probate in London. In 1870 he was appointed to the British Museum, having been helped by a letter of support from the Archbishop of Canterbury, the person who had appointed his father to be Bishop of Dunedin. The Archbishop's secretary wrote from Addington Park, Croydon on 18 April 1870 to Bishop Jenner about his son's appointment:

> In reply to your letter, the Archbishop of Canterbury desires me to say

that he will put your son's name down for a nomination for the MSS department of the British Museum, but he cannot promise a nomination at once, and he advises that your son should call upon Mr Wynter Jones, Secretary of the Museum, who will give him any information. The Archbishop and Mrs Tait join in kind regards to you.[10]

Jenner started work at the British Museum in 1870 and remained there until he retired in 1909. He later repaid his debt to the Archbishop of Canterbury for his letter of support by drawing the attention of the Society of Antiquaries to the threatened destruction of the old palace of the archbishops at Croydon.[11] During his thirty-nine years at the British Museum, Jenner was engaged, not with Anglo-Catholic activities, but with various London societies such as the Society of Antiquaries and the Philological Society. However, his expertise in the field of liturgiology and ecclesiology was well known and in a letter dated 17 July 1900, G.K.Fortescue, the Keeper of Printed Books, wrote a reference for him, in which he stated:

Mr Jenner's special knowledge of liturgiology and ecclesiology has been of great assistance to the successive keepers of the Principal Book Department both in the purchase of books and in the compilation of the catalogue, notably in the recently published liturgies.[12]

After he returned from New Zealand to his parish of Preston-next-Wingham, Bishop Jenner campaigned for the beliefs and practices of the Anglo-Catholic Movement. However, the announcement of Papal Infallibility in 1870 proved too much for him to swallow and, like so many Anglo-Catholics, he stayed in the Church of England. In 1876 he became involved in the Hatcham dispute in South-East London where a local vicar, the Revd. Arthur Tooth, was summoned to appear before an ecclesiastical court on a charge of using ritualistic practices. When he failed to do so, he was suspended from performing divine service for three months. If he disobeyed the court order, the vicar was likely to be imprisoned and the church, St James's, Hatcham, closed. Following further disturbances and his reluctance to abandon certain ritualistic practices, Fr. Tooth was committed to prison early in 1877. Among his visitors was Bishop Jenner whom the churchwardens had invited to lead the services in his absence, at St Stephen's, Lewisham, a mile or so down the road.[13]

A Cornish Blessing

In 1903 Henry Jenner was made a Bard of the Breton Gorsedd. The following year, at the Pan-Celtic Congress at Caernarfon, he spoke warmly of Breton Catholicism as 'the most beautiful of religions'.[14] One of the means he used for practising the use of the Cornish language was seasonal cards. For example, in 1905 at Easter and Christmas, he sent a card to his friends, with the text of 'Can An Pescador Kernuak, The Cornish Fisherman's Hymn', in Cornish and English. Each of the six verses had the refrain:

Christ, Son of Mary, Star of the Sea,   *Crîst, Mab Marîa, Steren an Mor,*
Listen and answer a fisher's cry to Thee.   *Golsow ha gortheb pesadow pescador.*

A similar verse appeared in the journal *Celtia* in December 1907 following the Third Pan Celtic Congress that had taken place in Edinburgh in September:

Benneth Gernûak	A Cornish Blessing
Crist, Myhal, ha Maria,	Christ, Michael and Mary,
Re wrellens dha venigya;	May they bless thee;
Bledhan Nowedh lowenek	A Happy New Year
Rens y dhes, ha Nadelek	May they give thee, and a Christmas
Fest en lowen maga ta	Right merry as well[15]

After he retired to Cornwall in 1909, Jenner wrote regularly for the *Journal of the Royal Institution of Cornwall*. For example, he gave his presidential address at the Spring Meeting on 23 May 1923 on the subject of the Bodmin Gospels. In this talk, he was able to demonstrate his knowledge and understanding of Christian antiquities, just as he had at St Michael's Mount ten years earlier. In 'The Bodmin Gospels', he stated:

In Western Christendom we are accustomed in these days to have all our church services in a small compass. The Church of England has them all in two books, the Book of Common Prayer and the Bible, and the Latin Church includes everything of liturgical use in four books, the Missal for the Mass, the Breviary for the Divine Office, the Ritual for occasional services, except those which require a bishop, which are in the Pontifical.[16]

In the Western Church before the eleventh century, and very frequently for a long time afterwards, four books were used for the celebration of the Eucharist. These were:

1. The Sacramentary, containing the Canon of the Mass, the Collects, Secrets, Prefaces and Post-Communions; in fact all that was said by the Priest.
2. The Gradual, or Antiphoner, containing the Introits, Graduals, Offertories, and other things sung by the choir, with or without the music.
3. The Lectionary or Epistle Book.
4. The Gospel Book.[17]

With recently completed work on the different western liturgies no doubt fresh in his mind, he continued:

> For more details about the Ambrosian, Celtic, Gallican and Mozarabic Rites, I may, perhaps, be allowed to refer anyone who happens to be interested to four very long articles of my own in the New York *Catholic Encyclopaedia*.[18]

In his bibliography for this lecture, Jenner mentions the help he has received from Trinity College, Dublin, the Dean of Lichfield, the University Library at Cambridge, the Bodleian Library at Oxford, Lambeth Palace and the Royal Library at Stockholm about the Irish Gospel Books of Kells, Durrow, Dimma, Mulling and Armagh at Dublin, the probably Welsh St Chad Gospels at Lichfield, the Scottish Book of Deer at Cambridge, the Irish MacRegol Gospels at Oxford, the Book of MacDurnan at Lambeth, and the Stockholm Golden Gospels. This reads as an impressive and exhaustive list of sources.[19] Similarly, in an article on *Christian Worship in St Piran's Oratory in the Sixth and Seventh*

Centuries, Jenner wrote about the sort of services St Piran and his immediate successors held in the Oratory. This article started life as a paper read at the Oratory on 12 July 1911, during the Summer Excursion of the Royal Cornwall Polytechnic Society and was then printed in the Society's journal. There was considerable interest in St Piran's Oratory at the time, as it had recently been recovered from the sand and reclaimed. Jenner became the first chairman of the County Committee to deal with ancient monuments, under the 1913 Ancient Monument and Consolidation Amendment Act. The committee started by producing an inventory of ancient Cornish monuments, headed by St Piran's Oratory at Perranporth. Jenner concluded his remarks to the Royal Institution of Cornwall on the 1913 Act with these words:

> We have more prehistoric antiquities to the square mile in Cornwall than in any other county, except, perhaps, some parts of Wiltshire. We must set the best possible example to the county in our care of them.[20]

Jenner's part in founding and establishing the Cornish Gorsedd in 1928 is well known and recounted elsewhere. He had waited twenty-five years after becoming a Bard of the Breton Gorsedd for there to be a similar Celtic gathering in Cornwall. 'It soon became customary for a Cornish evensong to be sung on the Sunday after the Cornish Gorsedd in the parish church of the parish where the Gorsedd was held.'[21] This started in 1933, when the first church service of evensong in Cornish was held at Towednack, near St Ives, a tradition which continues to the present day. Jenner obviously inherited some musical ability from his father. In the year following the start of the Cornish Gorsedd he produced several hymns in Cornish for *The Cornish Song Book (Lyver Canow Kernewek)* by Ralph Dunstan. It was issued under the patronage of the Royal Institution of Cornwall, the London Cornish Association, the Federation of Old Cornwall Societies and the Cornish Gorsedd. In February 1929, in the introduction to one of his songs *The Story of Saint Just,* Jenner stated:

> I wrote this hymn in Latin and English for Canon Taylor of St Just. The tune is one I wrote down from a memory of nearly 70 years ago, and harmonized myself. It used to be sung at my old school, St Mary's College,

Harlow, where I was from 1858 to 1865. I have never been able to find out who composed it, but I am quite sure I did not. The Latin words are a humble imitation of Adam of St Victor.[22]

The songbook also contained The Cornish Fisherman's Hymn, *Can an Pescajor Kernewek*, which Henry Jenner used for his greetings card in 1905.

A Life 'hid with Christ in God'

Jenner became a Roman Catholic at the end of 1933. A few months later, on 8 May 1934, the feast day of the Apparition of St Michael at St Michael's Mount in A.D.495, he died. On his gravestone in the burial ground of St Uny, Lelant, near Hayle, is the following inscription:

PELYCAN TRUETHEK, ARLUTH JESU MAS, GLANHA VY, ANLANYTH, YN DHA WOS A RAS, GANS KEMMYS HA BANNA SYLWANS A-WRA RY DHE'N NORVYS YN TYEN OLL, A'Y VYLYNY.

[*Compassionate Pelican, good Lord Jesus, cleanse me, an unclean one, in the blood of Grace, just a drop of the salvation which gives forgiveness to the whole world for all its villainy.*][23]

This can be compared with a verse from a hymn of Thomas Aquinas, which is used as part of the service in honour of the Blessed Sacrament:

Pie pellicane Jesu Domine,
Me immundum munda tuo sanguine,
Cuius una stilla salvum facere
Totum mundum quit ab omni scelere.

The pelican was a well-understood symbol of Anglo-Catholic spirituality. For example, in London it adorns the interior of the Anglo-Catholic church of All Saints, Margaret Street, near Oxford Circus. The present guidebook to the church says, 'The ceiling is decorated with 'the Pelican in its Piety', the bird piercing its breast to feed her young. The motif is symbolic of the Fall and Redemption of man, for the pelican was supposed to slay her rebellious off-spring then revive them with her own blood.'[24] The words of the inscription on Jenner's gravestone come from the verse of a hymn, Adoro Te Devote, which is sometimes sung at the Jenner Foundation Mass at Hayle at the beginning of May. They combine Jenner's love of the Cornish language with his religious devotion to Jesus Christ in the Anglo-Catholic tradition. A final word comes from the Revd. John Pearce, formerly vicar of Sithney, Cornwall, who, in *Seeking a See*, a book about the visit that Jenner's father made to New Zealand, wrote the following:

> Those who knew Henry Jenner best saw that all these attributes stemmed from his deeply mystical spiritual life. He followed the Pauline injunction, his life was hid with Christ in God. This, perhaps, from a feeling of delicacy, has never been stated by those who have written of him. But it must not be forgotten. Those who in their earlier years were favoured by his friendship follow him to their reward. Before it is too late we must witness that we thank God upon every remembrance of him.[25]

Notes

1. Annual Report of the Royal Cornwall Polytechnic Society, 1914, pp.68–70.
2. Geoffrey Faber (1954) *Oxford Apostles* London: Penguin.
3. John Henry Newman, Apologia Pro Vita Sua London: Dent, pp.67–70
4. John Pearce (ed) (1984) *Seeking a See: a Journal of The Rt. Revd. Henry Lascelles Jenner D. D. of his visit to Dunedin, New Zealand in 1868–1869*, Dunedin: Standing Committee of the Diocese of Dunedin, p.20.
5. In a dispute over the erection of a stone altar and credence-table by the churchwardens of the Church of the Holy Sepulchre, Cambridge and the Cambridge Camden Society, Jenner-Fust ruled in 1845 in favour of the imcumbent, who opposed the 'restoration' work.
6. Ibid. p.81ff.
7. *The Harlovian* 1933, p. 659.
8. Ibid.
9. Ibid. p. 79.
10. Letter from the Archbishop of Canterbury to the British Museum 18 April 1870, in the archives of the British Museum
11. Minutes of the Society of Antiquaries.
12. Letter from G. K. Fortescue 17 July 1900 in the archives of the British Museum.
13. Joyce Coombs (1969) *Judgement on Hatcham,* London: The Faith Press.
14. Henry Jenner (1905) 'Cornwall: A Celtic Nation' in *The Celtic Review* 1, 1905, p. 239.

15. *Celtia* vol. 7 no. 8, Dec. 1907, p.127.

16. *Journal of the Royal Institution of Cornwall*, vol. xxi part 2, no.70, 1923, p.114f.

 7. Ibid. p. 115.

18. Ibid. p. 123.

19. Ibid. p. 145.

20. 'The Ancient Monuments Consolidation and Amendment Act 1913...' in *Journal of the Royal Institution of Cornwall*, vol. xix parts 58–61, 1912–14, p. 445.

21. H. Miles Brown (1976) *A Century for Cornwall – The Diocese of Truro 1877–1977*, Truro: Oscar Blackford, p. 35.

22. Ralph Dunstan (1929) *Cornish Song Book* London: Reid Bros. p. 34f.

23. I am indebted to the late Richard Jenkin for this translation.

24. *Guidebook to All Saints, Margaret Street* (1990) Hampshire: Pitkin Pictorials, p. 8.

25. Pearce (1984) p. 15.

Select Bibliography of the Writings of Henry and Katharine Lee Jenner

Derek R. Williams

Although he produced only one major work, *A Handbook of the Cornish Language*, the centenary of the publication of which this anthology celebrates, Henry Jenner wrote extensively over a sixty-five year period on a wide variety of themes. Essays on Cornish and Celtic subjects form the core of his output, of course, but there were, in addition, several pieces with a royalist flavour, some on liturgical matters and a number of historical and biographical studies, the latter for both *The Royalist* and the *Dictionary of National Biography*.

The Courtney Library at the Royal Institution of Cornwall is home to a veritable cornucopia of material about the Jenners and other luminaries of the Cornish Movement in the first few decades of the twentieth century. In addition to the Jenner Collection itself, it houses the Robert Morton Nance Bequest containing the manuscripts of many of Jenner's essays and lectures and some other relevant material. The British Library contains about 700 letters from Henry to Kitty Lee written mainly at the time of their engagement (Deposit 10053). There are also a few letters dated 1900 from Jenner to the then Bishop of Dover in the Canterbury Cathedral Archives (U58/3). Another important collection of Jennerana, including Kitty Lee's diaries for the period 1873–1880 and Henry's schoolboy notebooks, is in private hands (The Beazley Archive). Finally, the Penzance Library's Jenner Room, as well as being an international centre of

Gravestone of Henry and Katharine Jenner at Lelant

Derek R. Williams

study for the six Celtic languages, does contain copies of many of Jenner's pamphlets.

Of Henry Jenner's writings, only those that relate to Cornwall and the other Celtic countries are listed in this bibliography. Fuller lists can be found in '[Portrait Gallery] III: Henry Jenner, F.S.A., President 1916', *Royal Cornwall Polytechnic Society Annual Report*, new series, vol. 3, 1917, pp. 168–173 and '[Portrait Gallery]: Henry Jenner, M.A., F.S.A., *Royal Cornwall Polytechnic Society Annual Report*, new series, vol. 8, 1934, pp. 62–64. Many essays and letters that were published in newspapers such as the *Western Morning News* and the *Royal Cornwall Gazette* await cataloguing.

Henry Jenner

'The Dialogue of the Passion' [from the Breton]. Published in *Churchman's Shilling Magazine*, vol. 13, 1873

'The Cornish Language'. Published in *Transactions of the Philological Society, 1873–74*. [Read before the society 21 March 1873]. Also issued as a pamphlet by Asher & Co., London, [1873]

'The Manx Language: its grammar, literature and present state'. Published in *Transactions of the Philological Society, 1875–76*. [Read before the society 18 June 1875]. Also issued as a pamphlet by the Philological Society

'Traditional Relics of the Cornish Language in Mount's Bay in 1875'. Published in *Transactions of the Philological Society, 1875–76*. [Read before the society 4 February 1876]. Also issued as a pamphlet by Asher & Co., London, 1876

'The History and Literature of the Ancient Cornish Language'. Published in *Journal of the British Archaeological Association*, vol. 33, 1877. [Read before the society at Penzance 19 August 1876]. Also issued as a pamphlet by the British Archaeological Association, London, 1877

[Prospectus of the] Cornish MSS. Society [with W.C.Borlase], no printer's name, [2 October 1876]. Also published in *Journal of the Royal Institution of Cornwall*, 1877 and *Journal of the British Archaeological Association*, vol. 32, 1876

'An early Cornish fragment'. Published in *The Athenaeum*, 1 December 1877

'Cornwall in 1715'. Published in *The Royalist*, April 1890

'Flora Macdonald'. Published in *The Royalist*, July 1890

'Donald Cameron of Lochiel'. Published in *The Royalist*, August 1890

'Alaister MacMhaighstir Alaister' [Alexander Macdonald]. Published in *The Royalist*, November 1890

'MacMhurich Chlanaidh' [Ewan Macpherson of Cluny]. Published in *The Royalist*, December 1890

'The Clans of Culloden'. Published in *The Royalist*, September 1892–April 1894

Sequentia in honorem Sancti Iusti Filii Regis Gerontii… [Sequence in honour of St Just, son of King Geraint], c.1900. Reprinted in Dunstan, *Cornish Song Book*, 1929

'Notes aux textes inédits en Cornique moderne' [Notes in English on Professor Loth's Cornish edition of Genesis iii and St Matthew ii and iv]. Published in *Revue Celtique*, vol. 24, Avril 1902. Also issued as a pamphlet by the *Revue Celtique*, Paris, 1902

'Kan Nadelik; En Tavaz Kernuak an Sethdegvas Cans Vledhan' [A Christmas Song in the Cornish Language of the 17th century]. Published in *Celtia*, vol. 2, no. 6, June 1902. [Dated Nadelik 1901]

'Some rough Notes on the present Pronunciation of Cornish Names'. Published in *Revue Celtique*, vol. 24, Juillet 1902. Also issued as a pamphlet by the *Revue Celtique*, Paris, 1902

Offeren Crist [The Christ-Mass]. Privately printed, Christmas, 1903

A Handbook of the Cornish Language, chiefly in its latest stages with some Account of its History and Literature, London: D. Nutt, 1904. Reprinted by AMS Press, New York, 1982

Steren Bethlem [The Star of Bethlehem]. Privately printed, Christmas, 1904

'Cornwall: a Celtic Nation'. Published in *The Celtic Review*, vol. 1, 1905 [Read before the Pan-Celtic Congress at Caernarfon, August 1904]

'Bro Goth Agan Tassow'. Published in *Celtia*, vol 4, no.6 (Congress Number0, 1904. Reprinted in Dunstan, Cornish Song Book, 1929.

'The Trelawny Song'. Published in *The Royalist*, April 1905.

'Can Contellyans an Kernewon, en Mis Hedre en Vledhan 1715' [The Gathering Song of the Cornishmen in October 1715]. Published in *The Royalist*, April 1905

Can an Pescador Kernuak [Cornish Fisherman's Hymn]. Privately printed, Christmas, 1905. Reprinted in Dunstan, *Cornish Song Book*, 1929

'The Most Correct Versions [of The Lord's Prayer and The Apostle's Creed]'; 'Cornish Translation of the Trelawny Song…'; 'Bishop Trelawny v. Sir John Trelawny'; 'The Traditional Tune of the Trelawny Song'; 'Lhuyd's mss. have been utilized'; '[The Cornish Celtic Society]: Still in Existence'; 'Mr Jenner Corrects and Explains [concerning the Helston Furry Song]. Published in Peter Penn (ed), *Cornish Notes and Queries*, Cornish Telegraph, Penzance, 1906

Devedhyans an Matern, Can Nadelek [The Coming of the King, a Christmas Carol]. Privately printed, Christmas, 1906

'The Celtic Rite'. Published in *The Catholic Encyclopaedia*, New York, 1907

'The Cornish Drama pts. I and II'. Published in *The Celtic Review*, vol. 3, no. 12, April 1907 and vol. 4, no. 3, July, 1907. Also issued as a pamphlet by Norman Macleod, Edinburgh, 1907

'Benneth Gernûak/A Cornish Blessing'. Published in *Celtia*, vol. 7, no. 8, December 1907

'Who is the Heir of the Duchy of Cornwall?'. Published in *The Celtic Review*, July, 1909

'Cornish Place-names'. Published in *Journal of the Royal Institution of Cornwall*, vol. 18, pt. 1, 1910 [Read at the Annual Meeting 9 December 1909]

['The Psychological Nature and Origin of the Belief in Fairies in Celtic Countries']: 'Introduction…' [dated July 1910] to the Cornish section of W. G. Evans Wentz's *The Fairy Faith in Celtic Countries*, O.U.P., 1911

'Cornish Place-Names'. Published in the *Truro Diocesan Magazine* [1910] [Lecture given at Truro Church Institute 6 December 1910]. Also issued as a pamphlet

'Perran Round and the Cornish Drama'. Published in *Annual Report of the Royal Cornwall Polytechnic Society*, 1912. [Read at the summer excursion to Perran Round on 12 July 1911].

'Christian Worship in St Piran's Oratory in the Sixth and Seventh Centuries'. Published in *Annual Report of the Royal Cornwall Polytechnic Society*, 1912 [Read at the summer excursion to St Piran's Oratory on 12 July 1911]. Also a pamphlet printed by Blackford, Truro

'History in Cornish Place-names'. Published in *Annual Report of the Royal Cornwall Polytechnic Society*, 1913 [Lecture given at Falmouth 27 August 1912]. Also issued as a pamphlet by the RCPS, Falmouth, 1912

'The Royal House of Damnonia'. Published in *Annual Report of the Royal Cornwall Polytechnic Society*, 1919. [Presidential address at the summer meeting 30 July 1918]. Reissued as a pamphlet by Oakmagic Publications, Penzance, 2001

'Some Possible Arthurian Place-Names in West Penwith'. Published in *Journal of the Royal Institution of Cornwall*, vol. 19, pt. 1, 1912. [Read at the summer meeting 6 June 1911]. Reissued, together with 'Tintagel Castle in History and Romance', as *King Arthur in Cornwall* by Oakmagic Publications, Penzance, 1996

'Descriptions of Cornish Manuscripts I. The Borlase Manuscript'. Published in *Journal of the Royal Institution of Cornwall*, vol. 19, pt. 2, 1913. [Read at the annual meeting 1912]. Also issued as a pamphlet

'[Portrait Gallery]: Sir Richard Rawlinson Vyvyan, Bart; John Samuel Enys; Edward William Wynn Pendarves'. Published in *Annual Report of the Royal Cornwall Polytechnic Society*, 1913

'The Ancient Monuments Consolidation and Amendment Act 1913, with Provisional List of Ancient Cornish Monuments adopted by the County Committee – 23 July 1913'. Published in *Journal of the Royal Institution of Cornwall*, vol. 19, pt. 3, 1914. [Read at the annual meeting 16 December 1913]. Also issued as a pamphlet

'St Columb in 1715'. Published in *Royal Cornwall Gazette*, 12 February 1914. [Lecture given at the St Columb Institute 30 January 1914]. Also issued as a pamphlet

'Dingerein and the Geraints'. Published in *Annual Report of the Royal Cornwall Polytechnic Society*, 1914. [Read at the summer excursion to Dingerein in Gerrans 15 July 1913]. Also issued as a pamphlet

'The Alabaster Carvings in the Chapel of St Michael's Mount'. Published in *Annual Report of the Royal Cornwall Polytechnic Society*, 1914. [Read at the summer excursion to the Mount on 17 July 1913]. Also issued as a pamphlet

'The Hut-clusters of Chysauster'. Published in *Annual Report of the Royal Cornwall Polytechnic Society*, 1914 [Read at the summer excursion to Chysauster on 17 July 1913].

'Thomas Hodgkin, Historian'. Published in *Annual Report of the Royal Cornwall Polytechnic Society*, 1914. Also issued as a pamphlet

'[Portrait Gallery]: John St Aubyn, 1st Lord St Levan; John Townsend St Aubyn, 2nd Lord St Levan'. Published in *Annual Report of the Royal Cornwall Polytechnic Society*, 1914

'The Tristan Romance and its Cornish Provenance'. Published in *Journal of the Royal Institution of Cornwall*, vol. 19, pt. 3, 1914. [Lecture given to the Penzance Natural History & Antiquarian Society 28 November 1913 and to the Arts Club, St Ives 27 January 1914]. Issued as a pamphlet in 1914 by both societies. Reissued, together with Thurstan Peter's 'Tristan and Iseult', as *Tristan and Iseult: a Cornish romance* by Oakmagic Publications, Penzance, 1998

'[Portrait Gallery]: John Taylor, F.R.S.; John Williams, F.R.S.'. Published in *Annual Report of the Royal Cornwall Polytechnic Society*, 1915

'Descriptions of Cornish Manuscripts II. The Fourteenth Century Charter Endorsement'. Published in *Journal of the Royal Institution of Cornwall*, vol. 20, pt. 1, 1915. [Read at the annual meeting 1 December 1914]. Also issued as a pamphlet

'Piskies: a folk-lore study'. Published in *Annual Report of the Royal Cornwall Polytechnic Society*, 1916. [This address, read at the opening of the summer meeting exhibition 2 September 1915, is an extended version of 'The Psychological Nature and Origin of the Belief in Fairies in Celtic Countries']

Hymnus in honorem Sanctae Hyae et Sociorum [Hymn written for the opening of the
Chapel of St Ia and her Companions at Riviere, Phillack] Privately printed, 1916
'[Portrait Gallery]: Charles Fox; Sir Arthur Pendarves Vivian; Henry Jenner, F.S.A.'.
Published in *Annual Report of the Royal Cornwall Polytechnic Society*, 1916
'The Irish Immigrations into Cornwall in the late Fifth and Sixth Centuries'.
Published in *Annual Report of the Royal Cornwall Polytechnic Society*, 1917
[Presidential address 29 August 1916].
'The Present Position and Prospects of Celtic-Cornish Studies in Cornwall'.
Published in D. Rhys Phillips (ed.), *The Celtic Conference 1917...*, Perth: Milne,
Tannehill & Methuen, 1917.
'The Legend of the Church of the Holy Cross in Cornwall' [with Rev T. Taylor] –
Appendix I – Notes... contributed by Jenner. Published in *Journal of the Royal
Institution of Cornwall*, vol. 20, pts. 3/4, 1917–1918. Also issued as a pamphlet by
the RIC, Truro, 1918. Reissued, together with Sabine Baring-Gould's 'Curious
myths of the Middle Ages', as *The Legend of the Holy Cross in Cornwall* by
Oakmagic Publications, Penzance, 1998
'The Easter Sepulchre and its Uses, with Some Remarks on the Dramatic Element
in Church Services'. Published in *Journal of the Royal Institution of Cornwall*, vol.
20, pts. 3/4, 1917–1918
'Thurstan Collins Peter: A Biographical Notice'. Published in *Journal of the Royal
Institution of Cornwall*, vol. 20, pts. 3/4, 1917–18
'The Dedication of Churches'. Published in *Annual Report of the Royal Cornwall
Polytechnic Society*, 1918 [Presidential address at the summer meeting 21 August
1917]. Also issued as a pamphlet by Brendon, Plymouth, 1917
'The Progress of Celto-Cornish Studies in Cornwall since the Celtic Congress of
1918'. Published in *Transactions of the 3rd Celtic Congress*, Edinburgh, May 1920
'Roche Rock Hermitage'. Published in *Journal of the Royal Institution of Cornwall*,
vol. 20, pt. 7, 1921 [Read at the summer excursion, 1920]
'An Incident in Cornwall in 1715'. Published in *Journal of the Royal Institution of
Cornwall*, vol. 20, pt. 7, 1921 [Read at the annual meeting 9 December 1920].
Also issued as a pamphlet by Blackford, Truro, 1921
'The Dukes and Earls of Cornwall'. Published in *Annual Report of the Royal
Cornwall Polytechnic Society*, 1920 [Presidential address 16 July 1919].
'The Renaissance of Merry England'. Published in *Annual Report of the Royal
Cornwall Polytechnic Society*, 1921–22 [Presidential address read at the summer
meeting September 1920]. Also issued as a pamphlet
'The Preservation of Ancient Monuments'. Published in *Annual Report of the Royal
Cornwall Polytechnic Society*, 1921–22 [Presidential address read at the summer
meeting 6 July 1921]. Also issued as a pamphlet.

'Castle-an-Dinas and King Arthur'. Published in *Annual Report of the Royal Cornwall Polytechnic Society*, 1921–22 [Read at Castle-an-Dinas, St Columb 5 July 1921]. Also a pamphlet printed by Cornish Echo County Printers, Falmouth, 1921. See also 'The Men Scrifa'

'The Men Scrifa'. Published in *Journal of the Royal Institution of Cornwall*, vol. 21, pt. 1, 1922 [Presidential address read at the annual meeting 8 December 1921]. Reissued, together with 'Castle-an-Dinas and King Arthur' and 'A Roman Milestone at Breage', as *The Men Scryfa and other Cornish antiquities* by Oakmagic Publications, Penzance, 2001

'The Bodmin Gospels'. Published in *Journal of the Royal Institution of Cornwall*, vol. 21, pt. 2, 1923 [Presidential address read at the spring meeting 23 May 1922]. Also issued as a pamphlet by Blackford, Truro, 1923

'The Manumissions in the Bodmin Gospels'. Published in *Journal of the Royal Institution of Cornwall*, vol. 21, pt. 3, 1924 [Presidential address read at the spring meeting 1 June 1923]. Also issued as a pamphlet by Blackford, Truro, 1924

'A Roman Milestone at Breage'. Published in *Journal of the Royal Institution of Cornwall*, vol. 21, pt. 3, 1924 [Read at the autumn meeting at Penzance 23 October 1923]. See also 'The Men Scrifa'

'A Cornish Oration in Spain in the year 1600'. Published in *Annual Report of the Royal Cornwall Polytechnic Society*, 1923. Also issued as a pamphlet

'The Cornish Manuscript in the Provincial Library at Bilbao in Spain'. Published in *Journal of the Royal Institution of Cornwall*, vol. 21, pt. 4, 1925 [Read at the autumn meeting at St Austell 21 October 1924]. Also issued as a pamphlet

'The Preservation of Ancient Monuments in Cornwall'. Published in *Old Cornwall* no. 1, April 1925

'The Arthurian Sculptures on the Porta della Pescheria of Modena Cathedral'. Published in *Journal of the Royal Institution of Cornwall*, vol. 22, pt. 1, 1926 [Read at the autumn meeting at St Ives 30 October 1925]. Also issued as a pamphlet by Blackford, Truro, 1926

'Tintagel Castle in History and Romance'. Published in *Journal of the Royal Institution of Cornwall*, vol. 22, pt. 2, 1927 [Read at the summer excursion to Tintagel 22 June 1926]. Reissued, together with 'Some Possible Arthurian Place-Names in West Penwith', as *King Arthur in Cornwall* by Oakmagic Publications, Penzance, 1996. Reissued, together with J. Hambley Rowe's 'Tristram, King Rivalen and King Mark' as *Tintagel Castle: its history and romance* by Oakmagic Publications, Penzance, 1999

'The Gorsedd of Boscawen-Un'. Published in *Old Cornwall*, no. 7, April 1928 [Read at Boscawen-Un 25 June 1927]

'King Teudar'. Published in *Tre, Pol and Pen: Cornish Annual*, Dodsworth, London, 1928

Who are the Celts and what has Cornwall to do with them? Federation of Old Cornwall Societies, St Ives, [1928]

'Dew Saw'n Myghtern' [God Save the King]; 'Bro Goth Agan Tasow' [Land of our Fathers]; 'Trelawny: Can Tus an Houlsedhas' [3 versions]; 'Can an Pescajor Kernewek' [The Cornish Fisherman's Hymn]; 'The Story of Saint Just'; 'Carol' [an imitation of a Folk-Carol]. Published in Ralph Dunstan, *Cornish Song Book*, Reid, London, 1929

'A recently discovered inscribed stone at Lancarffe, Bodmin' [with C. Henderson]. Published in *Journal of the Royal Institution of Cornwall*, vol. 23, pt. 2, 1930

'Some Miscellaneous Scraps of Cornish'. Published in *Annual Report of the Royal Cornwall Polytechnic Society*, 1929 [Read at the summer meeting 1928]. Also issued as a pamphlet

'[Portrait Gallery]: Hon. Sir John Langdon Bonython, K.C.M.G.'. Published in *Annual Report of the Royal Cornwall Polytechnic Society*, 1931

'The Lannaled Mass of St Germanus in Bodleian ms. 572'. Published in *Journal of the Royal Institution of Cornwall*, vol. 23, pts. 3/4, 1931–1932

'Cornish Archaeology: two recent books'. Published in *Old Cornwall*, vol. 2, no. 5, Summer 1933

'A Dead Language'. Published in *Old Cornwall*, vol. 5, no. 4, Winter 1953

'Gwaynten in Kernow'. Published in *Old Cornwall*, vol. 5, no. 7, 1956

'Dew Saw'n Vyghternes' [God Save the Queen]. Published in *Journal of the Royal Institution of Cornwall*, new series vol. 7, pt. 4, 1977

A Cornish grace for use at the opening or close of a ceremony [music by Kenneth Pelmear, words by William Bullock with Cornish translation of Henry Jenner], Dyllansow Truran, Redruth, c. 1984

'Bro Goth Agan Tasow/Ancient Land of Our Fathers'; 'Devedhyans an Matern/The Coming of the King'; 'Dhô'm Gwrêg Gernuak/To My Cornish Wife'; 'An Pemthak Pell/The Fifteen Bezants'; Can Wlascar Agan Mamvro/Patriotic Song of our Motherland'. Published in Tim Saunders (ed), *The Wheel: An Anthology of Modern Poetry in Cornish 1850–1980*, Francis Boutle, London, 1999

Translations into Cornish, by way of comparisons with Welsh and Breton versions, of Latin and English prayers, hymns etc... Published in *Cennad Catholig Cymru* [*The Catholic Messenger of Wales*]

The Nation of Cornwall. Reprint from a Truro newspaper of an address to [Truro] Rotary Club, [n.d.]

Katharine Lee Jenner

'The Wooing of Gudrun in the Elf-world, a saga of Nordland'. Published in *The Monthly Packet*, Christmas number, 1879

A Western Wildflower, 3 vols, Bentley, London, 1882

In the Alsatian Mountains: a narrative of a tour in the Vosges, Bentley, London, 1883

In London Town, 3 vols, Bentley, London, 1884

Katharine Blythe, 3 vols, Bentley, London, 1886

An Imperfect Gentleman, 3 vols, Bentley, London, 1888

Love or Money, 3 vols, Bentley, London, 1891

When Fortune Frowns, being the Life and Adventures of Gilbert Cosworth, a Gentleman of Cornwall, Horace Cox, London, 1895

Christ in Art, Methuen, London, 1906; 2nd edition, Methuen, London, [1923]

Our Lady in Art, Methuen, London, 1907

Christian Symbolism, Methuen, London, 1910

Christmas Verses with Christmas Greetings and Best Wishes for the New Year from H. and K.L.J., Bospowes, Hayle, Cornwall, Beare & Son, Penzance, 1919

Songs of the Stars and the Sea, Erskine Macdonald, London, 1926

'A Grey Day'; 'The Boats of Sennen'. Reprinted in Dunstan, *Cornish Song Book*, 1929

Notes on Contributors

Brian Coombes, a native of Falmouth, was a town planner before being ordained in retirement as a non-stipendary Anglican priest. Having served Cornwall as Grand Bard of Gorseth Kernow (1994–97), Examinations Secretary of the Cornish Language Board and President of the Cornwall Amateur Fencing Union, he is currently President of the Federation of Old Cornwall Societies and Secretary of the Bishop's Advisory Group for Services in Cornish. He has contributed articles to *Old Cornwall* and *An Baner Kernewek*.

David Everett is completing a PhD at the Institute of Cornish Studies on the subject of Henry Jenner. He was parish priest of Treslothan, near Camborne, where he completed an MA in Celtic Christianity at the University of Wales, Lampeter. He is currently rector of five villages in the Diocese of Peterborough.

Dr Alan M. Kent was born in St Austell in 1967. He lectures in Literature for the Open University, as well as being a poet, novelist and dramatist. He has published extensively on Anglo-Cornish and Cornish literatures. He is the author of *The Literature of Cornwall: Continuity, Identity, Difference 1000–2000* (2000) and most recently has edited *The Dreamt Sea: An Anthology of Anglo-Cornish Poetry 1928–2004*.

Donald R. Rawe began his writing career in 1950 with a story in the first series of *The Cornish Review*. Since then he has written novels, short stories, plays and poetry in both Cornish and English, being made a Bard of Gorseth Kernow in 1970 for his services to Cornish drama. His plays include *Hawker of Morwenstow* and *The Last Voyage of Alfred Wallis*. *Petroc of Cornwall, The Trials of*

St Piran and a modern acting version of *Gwryans an Bys* have all been produced at Piran Round. His poetry collection *Eglosow Kernow* (Cornish Church Poems) is due out in 2004.

Tim Saunders was born in Northumberland and brought up in Cornwall. He is a broadcaster and author who has published extensively on the Cornish language and its literature. He is editor of *The Wheel: An Anthology of Modern Poetry in Cornish 1850–1980* (1999) and co-editor of *Looking at the Mermaid: A Reader in Cornish Literature 900–1900* (2000).

Derek R. Williams was born and brought up near Camborne and has retained very close links with his homeland, despite working trans-Tamar as a librarian for many years. He is the author of *Prying Into Every Hole and Corner: Edward Lhuyd in Cornwall in 1700* (1993) and has contributed to *Old Cornwall, An Baner Kernewek, Cornish Scene* and *Country Quest*.